THE COWBRIDGE RAILWAY

COLIN CHAPMAN

Oxford Publishing Company

ISBN 0-86093-284-2

Typesetting by:
Aquarius Typesetting Services, New Milton, Hants.

Printed in Great Britain by:
Netherwood Dalton & Co. Ltd., Huddersfield, Yorks.

Published by:
Oxford Publishing Co.
Link House
West Street
POOLE, Dorset

Acknowledgements

Railway historical research tends to thrive in an atmosphere of mutual co-operation and ready exchange of information. I have been very fortunate to have been able to write this history in such a climate. Of the many who have given valuable assistance over the years, special mention must go to Eric Mountford, for information relating to locomotives and general Taff Vale Railway history, to C. J. Taylor for unlocking the mysteries of bus service development in the 1920s and 1930s, and to Iorworth Prothero for his work on the railway development of the Vale of Glamorgan. Others who have helped, in various ways, include Cliff Harris, Ian Wright, the late Trefor Jones, D. S. Barrie, Harold Morgan, John Dore-Dennis, Dr. Stuart Owen-Jones, D. Chaplin, John Lewis, Mike Lloyd and other members of the Welsh Railways Research Circle, and all those who were kind enough to share their memories with me.

Bibliography

The existing railway literature contains few references to the history of the Cowbridge Railway. However, it was from choice, as much as necessity, that this history has been compiled, almost entirely, from primary source material.
Works which have been consulted include:

The Chronicles of Boulton's Siding by *A. R. Bennett*
A Certaine School: a History of the Grammar School at Cowbridge by *I. Davies*
The Border Vale of Glamorgan by *D. J. Francis*
Cowbridge and Llanblethian Past and Present by *B. L. James and D. J. Francis*
Locomotives of the Great Western Railway by *The Railway Correspondence & Travel Society*
Glamorgan Historian (various volumes) by *S. Williams (Ed)*

Contemporary newspapers consulted include: *The Cambrian, The Cardiff & Merthyr Guardian, The Cardiff Times, The Western Mail, The Barry Dock News and The Glamorgan Gazette.*

In a work of this nature it is not possible to provide detailed notes and sources. I have, therefore, deposited a copy of my research notes and source material with the Central Reference Library, Cardiff.

Contents

Preface

My first contact with the Cowbridge Railway was as a small boy in the early 1950s. My parents were in the habit of making frequent day trips from our home in Llantwit Major to my grandparents in the Rhondda Fach, about twenty miles away. This outing involved a long and tedious bus journey, requiring no less than five changes of bus en route. One redeeming feature of this mobile purgatory was the change from the Western Welsh to the Rhondda bus at Cowbridge. In order to minimize the chances of a missed connection (the two companies hardly seemed to be on speaking terms), it was our practice to get off the bus from Llantwit at the Eastgate end of the town, whilst the bus continued to its terminus at Cowbridge Town Hall. The Rhondda bus came up from the town hall past Eastgate, before continuing to Talbot Green near Llantrisant. The five minute interlude between buses at Eastgate provided a welcome opportunity to take advantage of the excellent vantage point available from the old railway bridge on the Llantrisant Road. From here, I was able to gaze out over the former passenger station and, with any luck, watch the branch goods shunting the yard. It was a constant source of regret that we were unable to continue our journey by this infinitely more civilized form of transport.

My next encounter with the Cowbridge Railway came when I was a pupil at Cowbridge Grammar School in the early 1960s. By this time the line was in the late evening of its existence, with signs of impending closure not hard to discern. Despite the fact that the old station was 'out of bounds', it was a continuing source of interest, especially as there appeared to have been not one, but two passenger stations in the town. It was from these early contacts that my interest in the Cowbridge Railway grew. At first this was in a random and uncoordinated fashion, but in later years it developed into a more concerted approach, which resulted in the preparation of this book.

The Cowbridge Railway was, at first sight, something of an oddity in South Wales; a truly rural branch line. However, this impression was somewhat superficial as its history was closely interwoven with the industrial development and intense railway competition that characterized South Wales in the nineteenth century. Indeed, one of the original reasons for its promotion was the prospect of coal and iron-ore traffic from the Llanharry district, situated between Cowbridge and Llantrisant. Having said that, it was still essentially a rural enterprise and, as such, its life story had the familiar ring of excessive local optimism, inadequate traffic and a generally impecunious existence which has characterized the history of such lines throughout the country.

The story of the Cowbridge Railway is very much a study in local history. It was a product of its local social and economic circumstances and, in its turn, it played a part in the development of Cowbridge, at least for the first half-century of its life. What has become clear its that railway history cannot be viewed in isolation from its environment, be it social, economic or physical.

Whilst putting together the first draft of this history, I learned, with sadness, of the passing of the last surviving ex-Taff Vale railwaymen at Cowbridge, all within the space of about six months. These were Porter Mr Bishop, Driver Frank Williams and Platelayer Walter Carswell. It is to the memory of their honest labours that this book is dedicated.

C. Chapman
Braunston
1984

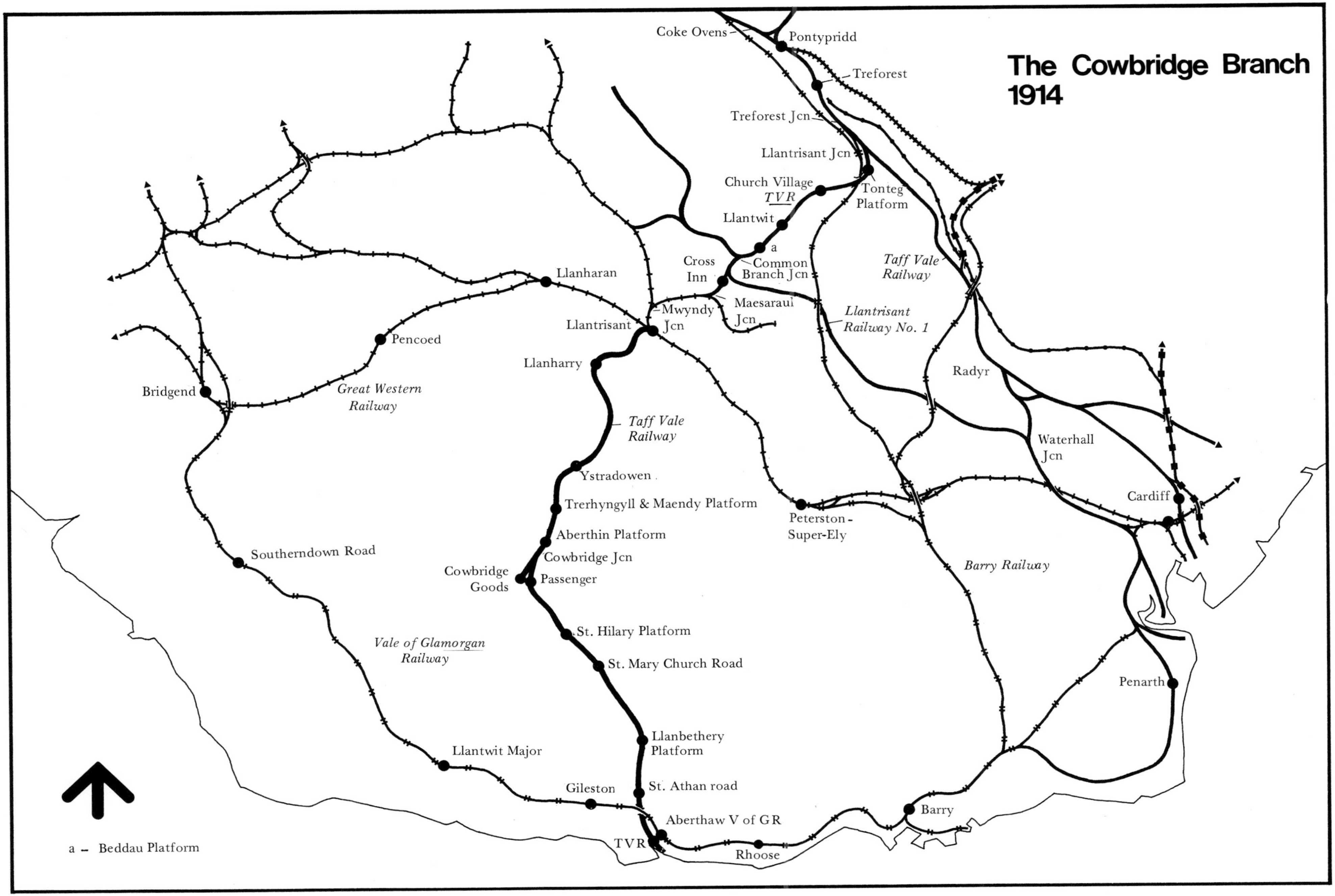

The Cowbridge Branch
1914

Coke Ovens

Pontypridd

Treforest

Treforest Jcn

Llantrisant Jcn

Tonteg Platform

Church Village *TVR*

Llantwit

a

Common Branch Jcn

Cross Inn

Maesaraul Jcn

Mwyndy Jcn

Taff Vale Railway

Llantrisant Railway No. 1

Radyr

Waterhall Jcn

Cardiff

Penarth

Barry Railway

Barry

Peterston-Super-Ely

Llantrisant

Llanharan

Llanharry

Taff Vale Railway

Ystradowen

Trehyngyll & Maendy Platform

Aberthin Platform

Cowbridge Jcn

Passenger

Cowbridge Goods

St. Hilary Platform

St. Mary Church Road

Llanbethery Platform

St. Athan road

Aberthaw V of GR

Rhoose

TVR

Gileston

Pencoed

Great Western Railway

Bridgend

Southerndown Road

Llantwit Major

Vale of Glamorgan Railway

a – Beddau Platform

The seal of the Cowbridge Railway Company.

Welsh Industrial & Maritime Museum

Chapter One
The Greatest Improvement of the Age

'Cowbridge is an old-fashioned town, consisting of one long street which is likely to bear a crop of grass as soon as the South Wales Railway is in operation'. In these pessimistic terms, C. F. Cliffe summed up the prospects for Cowbridge in *The Book of South Wales* of 1847. His subject was a small market town at the heart of the Vale of Glamorgan, situated at the point at which the Cardiff to Bridgend road left the high central ridge of the 'Vale' to cross the valley of the River Thaw. The South Wales Railway, upon which work had commenced the previous year, was to take a broad sweep to the north, avoiding Cowbridge by about five miles, as it followed the course of the River Ely to Pontyclun, before turning for Bridgend and the west.

Although a Roman settlement, thought by some to have been the lost fort of Bovium, is known to have existed at the crossing of the River Thaw by the Roman road from Isca (Caerleon) to Moridunum (Carmarthen), the modern town of Cowbridge dates from the middle of the thirteenth century, when Richard de Clare, Earl of Gloucester, founded a borough at this crossing point. This action proved to be a wise one, given the favourable location enjoyed by the new borough, and Cowbridge prospered as the market, social and administrative centre for the Vale of Glamorgan.

This prosperity was greatly enhanced by the development of road transport in the eighteenth century. In 1764, an Act was obtained for the creation of a Turnpike Trust for the Cardiff to Swansea road through Cowbridge, and in 1786 a mail coach began operating between London and Swansea, which later extended to Milford Haven, calling at Cowbridge en route. Thus at the time our story opens, Cowbridge was at the peak of its prosperity, a prosperity which was based, to a significant extent, on a system of transport which was soon to be eclipsed.

Cowbridge experienced a brief, but stillborn, involvement in the pre-history of railways in the early years of the nineteenth century. By 1816, a tramroad had been proposed from Llanharry Colliery, on the common to the north of that village, to Cowbridge, which had been supplied with coal from this source since at least 1775. In 1825 an attempt was made to promote a railway or tramroad from Trecastle Colliery, near Pontyclun, to Cowbridge. On 30th November 1825 a meeting of 'proprietors of lands and other interested parties' at the Bear Hotel, Cowbridge resolved that such a tramroad would be of 'great public utility and benefit'. However, in spite of this enthusiastic reception and talk, early in 1826, of an extension to Aberthaw, where the natural harbour at the mouth of the River Thaw still handled much of the external trade of the Vale of Glamorgan, nothing came of this early scheme.

The dawn of the 'Railway Age', as far as the County of Glamorgan was concerned, could be said to have occurred in 1836, when the Taff Vale Railway was incorporated to build a railway from Cardiff to Merthyr, together with a number of short mineral branches. In the same year, a committee 'of some of the best people' in South Wales was formed, to promote the construction of a railway from South Wales to London. Although a survey of a route from Gloucester to Swansea was undertaken by Brunel, the concept of a trunk railway from South Wales to the metropolis was not to materialize for another fourteen years.

The Taff Vale Railway, opened between Cardiff and Navigation House (Abercynon) on 9th October 1840 and on to Merthyr on 12th April 1841, proved an immediate success, and provided a local illustration of the benefits which could accrue from railway development. On 25th April 1844, a private branch railway, built by Thomas Powell to serve his Dihewyd Colliery near Llantwit Fardre, was connected to the TVR at Maesmawr about 2¼ miles below Treforest. Leaving the TVR main line, this branch, variously known as Dihewyd Railway, the Lantwit Vadre (sic) Railway or the Llantwit Branch, curved sharply to the west, before climbing out of the Taff Vale by means of a self-acting 1 in 6.6 inclined plane worked on the balanced load principle. From Incline Top, the railway followed a winding, but perfectly level, course to its terminus at Dihewyd Colliery. The line was later extended about ½ mile to Ystradbarwig Colliery. This obscure mineral line was later to form an important key in the provision of a rail link between Cowbridge and the TVR.

Towards the end of 1843, a proposal for a South Wales Railway was accepted by the Great Western Railway, and Brunel embarked on a survey for a trunk railway from Gloucester to Fishguard. It appeared to many that the shortest route for the railway across the Vale of Glamorgan would be via Cowbridge, a prospect which did not meet with the approval of the corporation or the inhabitants of the town. Whether or not this antipathy influenced the eventual choice of route for the SWR is not known, but in the summer of 1844 the prospectus of the SWR appeared, giving the route through the Vale of Glamorgan as follows:

'From Cardiff the railway passes by the Valley of Ely through the rich agricultural district adjacent to Llantrissant (sic), Cowbridge, Bridgend, Porthcawl and Pyle, the produce of which would thus be rendered available towards the supply of the surrounding manufacturing population.'

As for Cowbridge itself, its position in relation to the question of the route of the SWR was summed up in September 1844, by a director of the Bristol & Gloucester Railway, who commented that 'it has been reported that the proposed railroad will run through the coal works about five miles to the north of Cowbridge, and the good people of that ancient borough are well pleased to be left undisturbed, as no symptom of any wish to have the railway nearer has yet been evinced.'

Not all the inhabitants of Cowbridge were hostile to the SWR. For in 1845, the Reverend Edmondes, Vicar of Cowbridge (one of only two people from the town to have attended the public meeting held in Cardiff the previous year to discuss the proposal for the SWR) wrote to Dr J. Nichol MP. He requested that provision for a railway to Cowbridge be inserted in the SWR Bill, then before Parliament. Reverend Edmondes subsequently received a reply from Mr Hunt of the solicitors to the SWR Bill, pointing out that 'having due regard to the main features of the undertaking, and to considerations of an engineering

character, it would be impossible that every town throughout a line of this length should be equally accommodated.' Hunt did offer the assistance of the SWR, however, if a self-financed branch line was promoted locally.

This letter was referred to by Reverend Edmondes in 1855. He refuted the suggestion that it had been intended to route the SWR via Cowbridge, but that this had been prevented by the mistaken opposition of its inhabitants. This version of events has since become part of the folk-history of the Vale of Glamorgan, but the clear implication of Hunt's letter is that the route via Pontyclun was chosen for engineering reasons. Although a route via Cowbridge would have been more direct, it would have involved significant gradients and earthworks, compared with the easier route provided by the valleys of the Ely and the Ewenny, between Cardiff and Bridgend. Perhaps the best idea of the relationship between Cowbridge and the route of the SWR can be gained from the contemporary writings of David Jones of Wallington, the local historian who was born in Llanblethian, who said:

'No one had ever believed the action of the Corporation to have compelled the SWR to pass by Cowbridge. The point of the accusation against them was that, under the force of apathy, they were hostile to the railway when as guardians of the welfare of the town, they should have taken active steps in getting the railway to enter their neighbourhood'.

The first section of the SWR, from Chepstow to Swansea, opened to traffic on 18th June 1850, with a station for Llantrisant at Pontyclun, about five miles to the north of Cowbridge. The impact of the opening of the SWR on Cowbridge was immediate and catasrophic; the mail coach service was withdrawn on 5th July 1850, and with it went much of its associated trade. That year also saw the last occasion on which the Quarter Sessions were held in the town. Whilst its function as a market centre continued largely unimpaired, the loss of the coaching trade, coupled with the decline in its role as a social and administrative centre, undermined the prosperity of Cowbridge and led to its stagnation.

The effect of the SWR on Cowbridge was soon realized, however. A correspondent to the *Cardiff & Merthyr Guardian* in 1853, reporting on that year's Glamorgan Show, remarked that 'the want of railway accommodation reduces Cowbridge, and its delightful environs, to a state of hopeless isolation, and cuts them off from the rest of the world . . . The absence of the greatest improvement of the age confines Cowbridge to the humble position of a small country market town, and there is not, at present, any hope of its advancement'.

Within Cowbridge, people began to advocate the construction of a branch railway as a means of restoring at least part of the town's lost fortunes. Two competing schemes for a railway to Cowbridge emerged: one involved the building of a broad gauge branch from Llantrisant Station to Cowbridge, and on to Aberthaw where the creation of a port was advocated; the other, an altogether more ambitious scheme, involved the construction of a loop line from the SWR at Peterston-super-Ely through Cowbridge to rejoin the SWR at Bridgend. It was hoped that the SWR would find it advantageous to transfer the passenger service from the main line to the loop line, as a more direct route between Cardiff and Bridgend.

A general view of Cowbridge Station, photographed between 1906 and 1908, and showing one of the locomotive and coaches workings which survived for a time in the railcar era. The train consists of a four-wheeled brake van, which was one of six built by the Oldbury Carriage & Wagon Company and the Metropolitan Carriage & Wagon Company in 1883, 2 six-wheeled thirds, eleven of which were built by the Metropolitan Carriage & Wagon Co. in 1890, and a first/second class composite coach, one of three built by Ashburys in 1891. The black structure to the left of the station building is the loco coal shed.

Lens of Sutton

The passenger station staff at Cowbridge, circa 1920.

C. Chapman

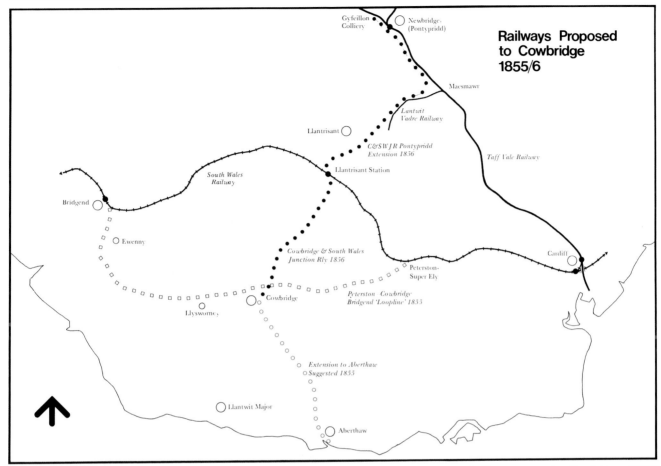

Railways proposed to Cowbridge : 1855/6

The 'five long years of agitation' for a railway to Cowbridge, as the *Cardiff & Merthyr Guardian* described the period following the opening of the SWR, culminated in the holding of a public meeting at Cowbridge Town Hall, on 6th December 1855. A provisional committee was formed to promote the construction of a broad gauge railway from Llantrisant to Cowbridge. The two schemes for a railway to Cowbridge were put to the meeting, but the loop line was considered over-optimistic, in terms of the traffic it could be expected to attract. The possibility of an extension to Aberthaw was set aside, until after a railway had been provided from Llantrisant Station to Cowbridge.

An attempt to get the SWR to provide financial support for a railway to Cowbridge was rejected by the directors of that company, on 21st December 1855. Despite this setback, the promoters of the Cowbridge & South Wales Junction Railway, as it had become known, pressed on with their scheme. In fact, it was enlarged to include an extension from Llantrisant Station to Pontypridd, in order to tap the developing coalfield around that town.

A survey was prepared by Mr J. T. Williams, the engineer engaged by the Provisional Committee of the C&SWJR, for a railway from Cowbridge to Gyfeillon Colliery, just above Pontypridd. This would provide a junction with the SWR at Llantrisant Station. The route between Cowbridge and Llantrisant Station was somewhat shorter than that

followed by the later Cowbridge Railway. This fact, coupled with certain engineering parameters quoted by Williams, suggests that the C&SWJR may have been routed via Talygarn rather than via Llanharry as was later followed by the Cowbridge Railway. It would, therefore, have approached Llantrisant Station from the east. The C&SWJR would have been well laid out and easily graded throughout, but with a cost to match of £125,801 12s. 10d. which was about twice the cost per mile as that of the later Cowbridge Railway. Despite an attempt later in 1856 to enlist support for the proposed railway in Pontypridd, the C&SWJR failed to attract sufficient financial backing to allow Parliamentary proceedings to take place.

The failure of the C&SWJR to attract the necessary support was accompanied by the emergence nearby of another scheme, which proved somewhat more successful. The Ely Valley Railway was incorporated on 13th July 1857, to build a broad gauge mineral line from Llantrisant Station through the upper reaches of the Ely Valley to Penrhiwfer. The following year, a further Act was obtained for the construction of a branch from this line, to serve a number of hematite iron ore workings near Mwyndy, about a mile to the south of the town of Llantrisant. Although this branch provided an outlet for the Mwyndy ore, it proved to be inadequate as the main markets for the ore, North Glamorgan and South Staffordshire, were on the narrow gauge, so that transport

9

necessarily involved either circuitous routes via the limited broad gauge network, or costly transhipment. The EVR was leased to the GWR in February 1861, this being confirmed by the Great Western Railway's Act of 1st June 1861.

The continuing isolation of Cowbridge from the growing railway network of South Wales was reflected by the decision of Cowbridge Corporation, on 5th January 1860, to make a grant of £10 towards the expenses of obtaining an omnibus link between Cowbridge and Llantrisant Station. This service, when introduced, operated twice daily in connection with the SWR trains. At the time of the passing of the Cowbridge Railway Act in 1862, it was said to be carrying the greatest number of people travelling between Cardiff and Cowbridge. An omnibus also ran twice weekly between Llantwit Major and Cardiff, via Cowbridge, taking four or five hours for the eighteen mile journey. Apart from these services, public transport was provided by various carriers to Bridgend, Cardiff and Llantwit Major.

Goods traffic, to and from Cowbridge, consisted mainly of the inward movement of coal and other domestic and agricultural supplies, and the outward transport of agricultural produce and livestock. Coal was brought from Llandaff on the TVR, or from Bridgend on the SWR, or direct from the collieries of the Llantwit Fardre district.

Shop goods were brought in by cart from Cardiff. Agricultural produce, for the industrial areas around Merthyr and Aberdare, was taken either to Llandaff Station for transfer to the TVR, or to Bridgend Station for the broad gauge route via the SWR and the Vale of Neath Railway. Livestock was taken via one of these routes, or driven all the way by road to the industrial areas.

Although the attempt to promote the C&SWJR had, in 1856, ended in failure, the need remained for a railway connecting Cowbridge with the industrial and commercial centres of South Wales. After another four years of isolation and stagnation for the 'Ancient Borough', the next development in the story of the provision of such a link came from a distant and unexpected source: the speculative initiation of a Merthyr solicitor, named Simons.

Mr Simons had conceived a scheme for providing an improved outlet for the iron ore of the Llantrisant area. On 12th September 1860, he appeared before the Board of the TVR and announced that he had acquired the Lantwit Vadre Railway from Thomas Powell. He was prepared to transfer this asset to the TVR, on appointment as a solicitor to a company to be formed, to convert and extend the LVR to the Mwyndy iron workings, providing he was granted a premium on his purchase. There followed a satisfactory report on the engineering and traffic prospects of

Eastgate Street, Cowbridge, in the early years of this century, showing part of the station frontage of the old passenger station.

D. Brown & Sons

Cowbridge Station, circa 1904. The passenger train has pulled forward so that the Class M1, 0-6-2T locomotive can be watered at the rather primitive tank situated just beyond the end of the platform. The carriages date from the 1870s and 1880s.

Pamlin Prints

this proposal from their engineer, George Fisher. The TVR Directors then agreed to recommend to their shareholders that the TVR subscribe £10,000 towards a new undertaking, to be known as the 'Llantrissant & Taff Vale Junction Railway'. The prospectus for this railway was published on 16th October 1860.

As well as placing this proposal before the TVR Directors, Simons also approached the Mayor of Cowbridge, R. C. Nichol-Carne, and suggested that an independent railway, with himself as solicitor, be promoted to link Cowbridge with the proposed L&TVJR. After the disappointment of the C&SWJR scheme, Nichol-Carne welcomed this idea enthusiastically, and a public meeting was arranged to discuss the proposal.

This meeting took place at Cowbridge Town Hall, on Thursday 27th September 1860, with Nichol-Carne in the chair. After outlining the main points of Simons' scheme, Nichol-Carne went on to suggest that the proposed railway could be extended from Cowbridge to Aberthaw, where a floating harbour could be constructed. This notion appears to have enjoyed some support in Cowbridge, but Simons seemed to have been sceptical, and to have advised that efforts be concentrated on the Llantrisant Station to Cowbridge section. He advised that the question of an extension be left until later. It was estimated that the cost of a narrow gauge, single track railway from Cowbridge to the L&TVJR would be £25,000, inclusive of land acquisition.

One voice raised against Simons' scheme was that of Richard Bassett, Managing Director of the EVR. He pointed out to the meeting that any proposal for a railway to Cowbridge should be related to the SWR, as the principal rail route of the district, and that a narrow gauge railway, from Cowbridge to the TVR, would not be welcomed by the EVR or the SWR. Accordingly, it was agreed that the meeting would be adjourned while Richard Bassett approached the Directors of the SWR, in order to establish their views regarding the proposed railway. At the same time, Alex Bassett, Engineer, was instructed to prepare plans for the Cowbridge Railway for presentation to the adjourned meeting.

The SWR Directors were non-committal, when Bassett approached them with details of the Cowbridge meeting, but were prepared to give favourable consideration to any suggestion for a junction between the Cowbridge Railway and the SWR at Llantrisant Station.

The adjourned public meeting took place at Cowbridge, on Tuesday 23rd October 1860. Alex Bassett had prepared a plan and section of the proposed railway, and outlined his scheme to the meeting. It involved the construction of a railway from Cowbridge to join the L&TVJR at Maesaraul. It crossed the SWR between Llantrisant Station and the turnpike bridge just west of that station, in a convenient place for an interchange between the two railways. A short branch would run from the main line of the Cowbridge Railway to a point opposite the SWR goods shed, this line allowing goods to be exchanged between the two railways.

After Simons had reported on the progress of the L&TVJR, R. C. Nichol-Carne, to the evident surprise of Simons, put forward a proposition that the entire railway from Cowbridge to the TVR should be built by one company. This, in effect, meant the TVR. Despite protestations by Simons, that such a suggestion was not only impossible, but absurd, this proposition, seconded significantly by Richard Bassett, was adopted by the meeting.

This surprising outcome suggests some intervention by Richard Bassett on behalf of the broad gauge interests, a view shared by a 'Cowbridge tradesman.' In an indignant letter to the editor of the *Cardiff & Merthyr Guardian*, the tradesman asked 'as the public meeting was brought to an unforeseen end, mainly through the instrumentality and address of the supporters of the broad gauge scheme, may I be allowed to ask Mr Richard Bassett and others, who . . . merely attended the meeting for the purpose of putting a drag on the wheel . . . is he or any of his friends prepared to bring forward a better or cheaper plan'.

As Simons had warned, Nichol-Carne's proposition turned out to be both impossible and absurd, as no amount of resolution-passing could persuade the TVR to extend the L&TVJR to Cowbridge against its wishes. Nichol-Carne appears to have been a victim of an attempt by Richard Bassett, on behalf of the broad gauge parties, to delay or stop the progress of the Cowbridge Railway, as a narrow gauge extension from the L&TVJR. Hopes were raised that the L&TVJR would itself be extended to Cowbridge, when early in 1861, Dr J. W. Nichol-Carne, R. C. Nichol-Carne's brother, became a director of that company, but this was not to be the result of his appointment. As for Simons, his grand scheme ended in failure, at least as far as his own ambitions were concerned. This was because the TVR eventually came to a fresh agreement with Thomas Powell, for the purchase of the LVR. Simons was excluded, and was then replaced as solicitor to the L&TVJR Bill.

Chapter Two
Our Little Line: 1861-1865

The realization that the construction of a railway to Cowbridge was dependent upon the actions of its supporters in Cowbridge and the surrounding district, rather than on the benevolence of some larger company, led to the formation, in 1861, of a Provisional Committee, to promote the Cowbridge Railway. The Corporation and tradespeople of Cowbridge, and the Vale gentry were well represented on this committee, which included two TVR Directors and a Director of the Llanharry Iron Ore Company.

The seal of the Llantrissant & Taff Vale Junction Railway.
Welsh Industrial & Maritime Museum

The L&TVJR was incorporated on 7th June 1861, to build a railway from the TVR main line, about a mile below Treforest Station. This would join the Mwyndy branch of the EVR at Maesaraul. Running powers were granted to the L&TVJR, from Maesaraul Junction to the south-east terminus of the Mwyndy branch, but not from Maesaraul Junction to Llantrisant Station, as has often been stated.

The passing of this Act gave a renewed impetus to the quest for a railway to Cowbridge. It was quickly followed, on 1st July 1861, by the publication of the Prospectus for the Cowbridge Railway, with a capital requirement of £30,000. The Provisional Committee confidently expected that the proposed railway would 'meet with the general and liberal approval of all parties residing in and connected with the Cowbridge District, as there can be no doubt that a direct railway communication between the extensive agricultural district of Cowbridge and the various ironworks in this and adjacent counties will be productive and of great advantage to all classes of the community'.

It was anticipated that the construction of the Cowbridge Railway would enable the farmers of the Vale of Glamorgan to transport their produce to the industrial areas more cheaply. They could, therefore, compete more effectively with imports from Somerset, which had benefited from the improved inland communications from Cardiff Docks provided by the TVR. It was also hoped that the new railway would bring about a reduction in the cost of coal in Cowbridge, which, at 20/- per ton, was twice the price of that in Cardiff. Further potential traffic was provided by the iron ore reserves of the Llanharry area, which were about to be exploited. As this ore would be carried over three miles of the Cowbridge Railway, it was expected that it would bring in a useful revenue to the Company. Finally, the works involved in the construction of the proposed railway were expected to be very light, and capable of being executed at a cost 'far below the average costs of railways in the district'.

An auto-train at Cowbridge, circa 1908.

C. Chapman (Courtesy of Mrs Jones)

Cowbridge Passenger Station and staff, circa 1920.

C. Chapman

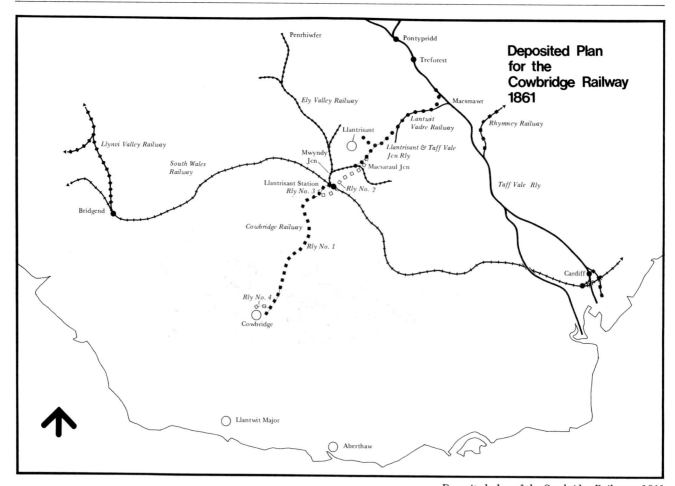

Deposited plan of the Cowbridge Railway : 1861

Following the publication of this Prospectus, a retired farmer of Merthyr Dyfan, near Barry, Mr John Thomas put forward an ambitious proposal for a Glamorgan Coast Branch Railroad. It involved the construction of a railway from the SWR at Pencoed, to Cowbridge, Aberthaw, Barry, where he advocated the creation of a port, and Penarth. If the Cowbridge Railway was constructed, it could act as a branch to this system. Although nothing further was heard of this proposal, it is of interest in that, with the exception of the Pencoed to Cowbridge section, railways were built, in later years, by one company or another along this route. A major port at Barry was later developed as originally proposed.

A great boost to the prospects of the Cowbridge Railway came in November 1861 when, in response to a request from its promoters, the TVR agreed to subscribe up to £5,000 towards the undertaking. It was also agreed that powers would be inserted in the Cowbridge Bill to enable the TVR to make this subscription.

Although this was very good news for the Cowbridge Company, it could not disguise the fact that great difficulty was being experienced in attracting the necessary funds to the undertaking. The tradespeople of Cowbridge had come forward to support the railway with many modest subscriptions, but the wealthy landowners of the surrounding district remained reluctant to contribute towards the railway.

The Cowbridge promoters were anxious to reduce the anticipated cost of constructing their railway, especially in the light of this continuing shortfall of subscriptions, so they approached the SWR with a suggestion that the direct link from the proposed Cowbridge Railway to the L&TVJR be abandoned in favour of the provision of a third rail over the broad gauge Mwyndy branch of the EVR. This would join the L&TVJR at Maesaraul Junction. It was also suggested that the Cowbridge Railway be granted running powers over this section. However, the prospect of such a narrow gauge incursion into what it regarded as broad gauge territory was not welcomed by the SWR, and the Cowbridge Railway Company's suggestion was rejected outright. The SWR stated that 'it would not be for the interest of this company to give any assistance or support to a narrow gauge railway in the direction you propose.'

The Cowbridge promoters, therefore, were forced to proceed on the assumption that the expense of the direct line to Maesaraul Junction would be necessary in order to bypass the opposition of the SWR.

The Notice of the Cowbridge Railway Bill was published on 13th November 1861, giving details of the proposed railway, and stating that it was intended to apply to Parliament in the next Session, for an Act of Incorporation. At the same time, plans and sections of the route of the proposed railway, together with a Book of Reference of properties affected along the line, were deposited with the Clerks of the Peace of the County of Glamorgan. Four lines of railway were proposed:-

Railway No. 1: The main line, commencing in the Parish of Cowbridge at or near the East Turnpike Gate, to a point near the Turnpike bridge over the SWR at Llantrisant Station.

Railway No. 2: Commencing at the termination of Railway No. 1, and continuing roughly parallel to the Mwyndy branch of the EVR, before crossing that line and making a junction with the authorized L&TVJR at Maesaraul.

Railway No. 3: A branch from Railway No. 1, from a point near Velin Mawr Mill, near Pontyclun, to a point opposite the SWR goods shed at Llantrisant Station.

Railway No. 4: A branch from Railway No. 1, 20 chains north of its Cowbridge terminus, to a point at, or near, the West Turnpike Gate of the town.

Railways Nos. 1 and 2 were to form the main line of the Cowbridge Railway, the end-on junction between the two being the site of the intended Cowbridge Railway Station at Llantrisant. This was conveniently situated for passengers wishing to transfer to the SWR. Railway No. 3 would enable goods to be exchanged between the two railways. The terminus at Cowbridge was to be in a field, to the north of Eastgate Street, near the East Turnpike Gate, although the Limits of Deviation shown on the Deposited Plan extended right up to the line of Eastgate Street.

Railway No. 4, the branch to the West Turnpike Gate, Cowbridge, did not survive long, however. It was deleted before the Cowbridge Railway Bill was examined before th Committees of the House, in order to reduce the estimates of the cost of the proposed railway. Alex Bassett, in his later evidence to the House of Lords Committee, stated that this branch had been proposed because it

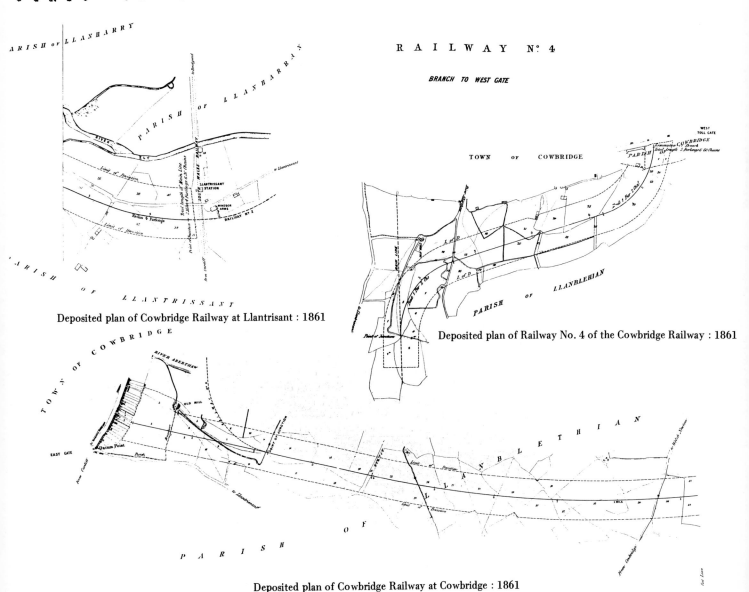

Deposited plan of Cowbridge Railway at Llantrisant : 1861

Deposited plan of Railway No. 4 of the Cowbridge Railway : 1861

Deposited plan of Cowbridge Railway at Cowbridge : 1861

might be a convenience to that end of the town and that in all probability, the principal station would have been on the No. 4 Railway, one station for goods on the branch line and the other for passengers.

A somewhat different perspective on the origin of this branch was given in October 1962, by Dr J. W. Nichol-Carne, in response to criticism that the terminus of the Cowbridge Railway, at East Gate, was unsuitable for a future extension of the railway to the south. Railway No. 4 had, he said, been inserted into the Bill on his suggestion, in order to give the company a choice of routes for such an extension. Although Dr Nichol-Carne had favoured a route via this line, the engineer had argued that an extension would have to be taken from the Eastgate Terminus by means of a tunnel under the road from Cowbridge to Llanblethian, known as the Broadway.

The idea of an extension to the south of Cowbridge was as old as that of a railway from Llantrisant to Cowbridge. Below Cowbridge, the valley of the River Thaw provided an obvious and relatively easy route to Aberthaw. Here, the natural harbour still handled a significant trade, even though its relative importance had declined considerably by the 1860s, and where the creation of a port was advocated by certain people. It is clear that an extension to Aberthaw figured prominently in the long-term plans of the promoters of the Cowbridge Railway, although by 1862, this seems to have been connected more with a desire to exploit the agricultural resources of the lower Vale of Glamorgan, than with the development of a port at Aberthaw, which was never to be a practical proposition. An undated sketch map, attributed to Dr Nichol-Carne, has survived which, in addition to an extension to Aberthaw, also shows two routes for a line from Cowbridge to Llantwit Major, a small town about five miles south of Cowbridge. One route branched off the Aberthaw extension at Flemingston,

whilst the other continued from Railway No. 4 to Llantwit Major, via Llysworney. The use made of Railway No. 4 suggests that this proposal may have been contemporary with the Cowbridge Railway Bill.

Although its plans had been deposited, the prospects for the Cowbridge Railway remained uncertain, as there was still a substantial shortfall on the capital requirement of £30,000. Of this sum, only about half had been subscribed or promised, £5,000 being from the TVR. The impecunious state of the Cowbridge Company, a condition which was to remain chronic throughout its independent existence, even cast doubt on the question of an application to Parliament for its Act of Incorporation. It was only after the TVR had agreed to lend the company £500, from the promised subscription, that it was able to forward the Parliamentary deposit of £2,800, which had to be paid into the Court of Chancery, before the Bill could proceed.

The Cowbridge Railway Bill was examined before the Committees of the House in June 1862. The main opposition to the Bill came from the SWR and the EVR (both companies being satellites of the GWR) on the grounds that the proposed Railway No. 2, the direct line to Maesaraul, would duplicate facilities already provided by the Mwyndy branch of the EVR. It was also stressed that the arrangements proposed at Llantrisant Station would result in difficulties for the exchange of passengers and goods. In a complete reversal of its previous hostility towards a railway to Cowbridge, which must have come as something of a surprise to the promoters of the Bill, the SWR suggested that the Cowbridge Railway should be a broad gauge line, and approach Llantrisant Station from the east. Through running would therefore be possible, via the SWR station directly on to the EVR. Mixed gauge track could be provided as far as Llanharry Iron Ore Mine, if this was thought desirable.

Ex-GWR 0-6-0PT, No. 6425 stands at Cowbridge Passenger Station with an auto-car on 20th May 1950.

Ian L. Wright

Cowbridge Station, photographed from the air in 1929. By this date, the locomotive depot was disused, although the sidings remained intact for many years. A passenger train has just arrived from Aberthaw, bringing a solitary passenger to Cowbridge. The vast extent of the railwaymen's allotments at Cowbridge is apparent.

Aerofilms

An important contribution to the Cowbridge Railway case was made by Mr John Bethell, who had recently acquired the Llanharry Iron & Coal Works. Bethell wished to send his iron ore to North Glamorgan and South Staffordshire, via the Cowbridge Railway and the narrow gauge system. A broad gauge branch would not be suitable, as it would involve a break of gauge en route. If the Cowbridge Railway was not built, then he would be forced to construct a line of his own. He also wished to transport coal from Llanharry to Cowbridge.

Following this significant intervention, the SWR opposition was overruled and the Cowbridge Railway Bill was passed by the Committee of the House of Lords. On 29th July 1862, an Act for making Railways from Cowbridge in the County of Glamorgan to join the L&TVJR and the SWR, and for other purposes, received the Royal Assent.

As incorporated under this Act (25 & 26 Vict cap 179), the Cowbridge Railway Company had an authorized capital of £35,000, comprising 3,500 shares of £10 each. The company was now empowered to build a narrow gauge railway from Cowbridge to Maesaraul, with a branch to a point adjoining the SWR at Llantrisant Station. It could borrow on mortgage up to £11,600, but this right could only be exercised when the whole of the authorized capital had been subscribed, and half actually taken up. The TVR was empowered to contribute up to £5,000 towards the undertaking, to work the authorized railways and to appoint one director to the Board of the Cowbridge Company, who could vote on its behalf.

The news that Parliament had passed the Cowbridge Railway Bill was greeted as a famous victory over the SWR, and was a cause of great celebration in Cowbridge. However, in spite of the continued exhortations of the Directors and others, the landowners of the Vale remained reluctant to contribute towards the undertaking. By October 1862, with work under way on the L&TVJR, it was becoming imperative that a start be made on the construction of the Cowbridge line.

In an attempt to raise additional capital, John Stockwood, Secretary of the Cowbridge Railway Company, contacted John Bethell with a request for assistance for what he termed 'our little line'. Stockwood pointed out that some £12,000 had been subscribed towards the undertaking, together with the promise of £5,000 from the TVR, and assured Bethell that the Cowbridge Directors were unwilling to purchase land or commence work until a much larger number of shares had been taken up. Although Bethell did not respond to this particular request, he was later to take shares in the undertaking under rather contentious circumstances.

At the same time, a request for further help was made to the TVR. However, the TVR refused to alter its previous arrangement and, in an ominous foretaste of future relations between the two companies, a resolution was made, but was later deleted from the minute book by the Chairman, James Poole, to the effect that the Cowbridge Railway should instead ally itself with the GWR.

This continuing financial problem was the main concern at a meeting of the shareholders of the Cowbridge Railway Company, on 29th October 1862. A deputation was formed to seek an arrangement with the GWR for the use of the Mwyndy branch between Llantrisant Station and Maesaraul Junction. This would obviate the need for the construction of the direct line between the Cowbridge Railway and Maesaraul Junction, and would result in a significant reduction in the costs of making the railway.

The deputation, consisting of Dr J. W. Nichol-Carne, Alex Bassett and John Stockwood, travelled up to London, on Tuesday 4th November 1862. Having some time in hand the next day, before their appointment with the GWR representatives, they called on Mr Bethell at 38 King William Street. Bethell advised them to seek an arrangement with the GWR, for the use of the Mwyndy branch; although this would entail a reversal at Llantrisant, he did not feel that this would hinder his iron ore traffic. He also advised that the Cowbridge Directors should borrow the necessary money, purchase materials themselves and employ local contractors, rather than engage a major contractor, who would require a high price as an encouragement to take a large number of shares in part payment for his services. Bethell also agreed to take one hundred shares in the Cowbridge Railway. He later claimed that he had been misled by the deputation who, he said, had assured him that construction would not commence until a much greater subscription had been achieved. When he discovered that construction had commenced under somewhat less favourable circumstances, Bethell accused the deputation of deception.

Following this meeting, the deputation, now joined by John Homfray, another Director of the Cowbridge Company, met Richard Bassett of the EVR and Frederick Saunders of the SWR at 10 Eastbourne Terrace, Paddington. After some preliminary discussion, Saunders proposed that the GWR would provide a third rail over the EVR from Llantrisant Station to Maesaraul Junction, and would grant running powers over this section to the Cowbridge Railway, at a fixed rent of £400 per annum. A rateable sum would be payable for any traffic above that required to produce the fixed rent. The deputation considered this fixed rent to be excessive, as it was likely to be greater than the interest payments required for the capital to construct the direct Railway No. 2. Nevertheless, they asked that the GWR present written terms for their proposal to the Cowbridge Railway Board of Directors; Richard Bassett and Saunders were unwilling to do this, however, without first consulting the Board of the GWR.

Before returning to South Wales, the deputation met Mr Savin, the famous railway contractor. Savin was involved with a number of Welsh railways, including the Brecon & Merthyr Railway and the Cambrian Railways. Savin strongly advised against any arrangement with the GWR, and urged the deputation to proceed with their independent line, as authorized by Parliament. He also promised to consider the deputation's suggestion that he act as contractor for their railway.

Following the meeting with Richard Bassett and Frederick Saunders, John Stockwood informed James Poole, Chairman of the TVR, of the details of the GWR's proposition. Poole was extremely sceptical of the motives of the broad gauge parties, as past experience had shown him that they tended to look with a 'single selfish' eye on any arrangement which they might put forward. However, he was prepared to concede that there might be certain advantages for the Cowbridge Company in the suggested arrangement, provided the fixed rent could be reduced to a reasonable level.

Cowbridge Railway ~ Alternative Schemes at Llantrisant

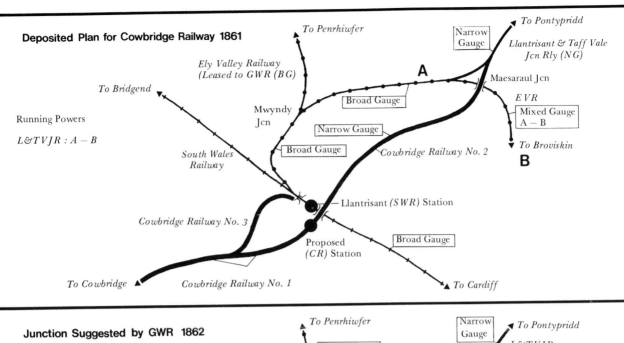

Deposited Plan for Cowbridge Railway 1861

To Penrhiwfer

Ely Valley Railway
(Leased to GWR (BG)

Narrow Gauge

To Pontypridd

Llantrisant & Taff Vale
Jcn Rly (NG)

A

Maesaraul Jcn

EVR

Broad Gauge

Mwyndy Jcn

Mixed Gauge
A – B

To Bridgend

Narrow Gauge

Broad Gauge

Cowbridge Railway No. 2

To Broviskin

B

Running Powers

L&TVJR : A – B

South Wales Railway

Llantrisant (SWR) Station

Cowbridge Railway No. 3

Proposed (CR) Station

Broad Gauge

To Cowbridge

Cowbridge Railway No. 1

To Cardiff

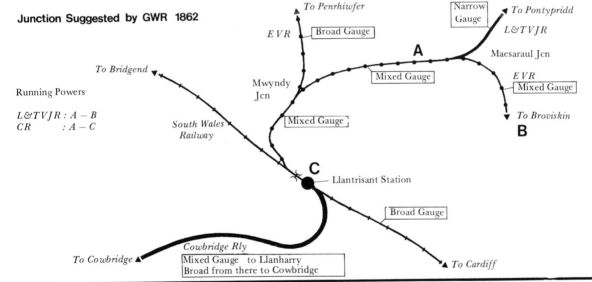

Junction Suggested by GWR 1862

To Penrhiwfer

EVR

Broad Gauge

Narrow Gauge

To Pontypridd

L&TVJR

A

Maesaraul Jcn

Mwyndy Jcn

Mixed Gauge

EVR

Mixed Gauge

To Bridgend

To Broviskin

B

Running Powers

L&TVJR : A – B
CR : A – C

South Wales Railway

Mixed Gauge

C

Llantrisant Station

Broad Gauge

To Cowbridge

Cowbridge Rly

Mixed Gauge to Llanharry
Broad from there to Cowbridge

To Cardiff

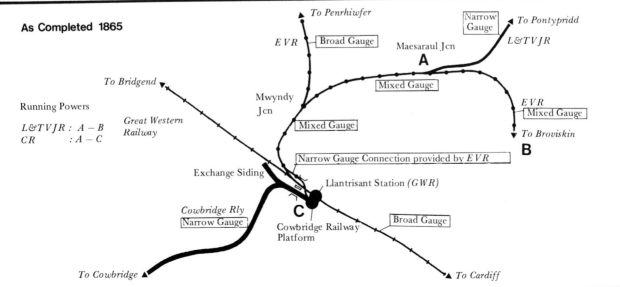

As Completed 1865

To Penrhiwfer

EVR

Broad Gauge

Narrow Gauge

To Pontypridd

L&TVJR

Maesaraul Jcn

A

Mwyndy Jcn

Mixed Gauge

EVR

Mixed Gauge

To Bridgend

Great Western Railway

Mixed Gauge

To Broviskin

B

Running Powers

L&TVJR : A – B
CR : A – C

Narrow Gauge Connection provided by EVR

Exchange Siding

Llantrisant Station (GWR)

Cowbridge Rly

Narrow Gauge

C

Cowbridge Railway Platform

Broad Gauge

To Cowbridge

To Cardiff

Alternative proposals for the Cowbridge Railway at Llantrisant : 1861-5

Cowbridge Passenger Station, circa 1905.

Lens of Sutton

In his report to his Directors, on 11th November 1862, Alex Bassett was able to state that although Savin had declined to act as contractor for the railway, Bethell had offered to supply the permanent way materials and to take half the cost in shares. In addition, Bassett had been approached by Messrs Griffiths & Thomas, contractors, of Newport, who were prepared to build the line at prices quoted. He had also given serious consideration to the GWR's proposition, but had concluded that such an arrangement would not be in the interests of the Cowbridge Railway, partly because the rent was too high, and also because to make use of the SWR station at Llantrisant, it would be necessary to obtain Parliamentary sanction for a deviation from the Deposited Plans of the Cowbridge Railway.

However valid Bassett's reservations may have been, one factor outweighed them in the minds of his Directors. If a satisfactory arrangement could be reached with the GWR, then the capital required for the construction of the Cowbridge Railway would be reduced by the £10,000 estimated as the cost of Railway No. 2. Although the rent suggested by the GWR for use of the Mwyndy branch was too high, it at least offered some hope of reduction through negotiation. In addition, such a rent would represent a charge on revenue rather than on precious capital. Therefore, negotiations were to continue with the GWR in the hope that the suggested rent would be moderated.

With the prospect of an agreement with the GWR, the progress of the Cowbridge Railway accelerated markedly. In January 1863, tenders were invited for the construction of the railway, and for the provision of the necessary materials and in March 1863, Messrs Griffiths & Thomas

were employed as contractors for the building of the railway. In addition, Board of Trade sanction was obtained for a deviation from the Deposited Plans of the Cowbridge Railway, whereby the branch to the SWR at Llantrisant, known as Railway No. 3, would be extended across the River Ely to terminate alongside the SWR passenger station.

A major step forward was made in May 1863, when the Cowbridge Railway Directors, R. C. Nichol-Carne, John Homfrey and Rowland Fothergill, entered into a Bond to the Crown for the sum of £5,600, for the completion of the railway. Following this action, and with every prospect of an agreement with the GWR, the TVR decided to apply for the 500 shares it had promised to take up.

Further negotiations with the GWR led to the reduction in the suggested rent from the £400 originally put forward, to a more acceptable £200 per annum, a figure below the interest payments required for the construction of Railway No. 2. In June 1863, a meeting took place in London between Alex Bassett, John Stockwood and J. C. Nichol-Carne for the Cowbridge Railway, and officers of the GWR. At this meeting, the Heads of Agreement, for the laying of the third rail between Llantrisant and Maesaraul Junction, and the granting of running powers over this section to the Cowbridge Railway, were provisionally agreed. Under this agreement, the Cowbridge Railway would abandon Railway No. 2, and extend Railway No. 3 into the SWR station at Llantrisant. Cowbridge trains would then have to reverse at Llantrisant Station, before continuing over the EVR to Maesaraul Junction and the L&TVJR.

A view of the former train shed at Cowbridge in 1920. The shed was then in use as a carriage shed. Little had changed since the transfer of the passenger service to the new station on the Aberthaw line in 1892.
Locomotive Publishing Co.

With these developments, construction of the Cowbridge Railway could begin at last, and a ceremony of the cutting of the first sod of the railway was arranged for Tuesday 9th June 1863.

After the prolonged interval since the passing of the Cowbridge Railway Act, the prospect of a start on the building of the railway was welcomed with considerable enthusiasm in Cowbridge and, on the day of the cermony, the town was thronged with people from Cowbridge and the surrounding district. At 3.30 p.m. the procession, led by the Band of the 18th Company Volunteer Corps, left the Town Hall. It included the Corporation of the Borough, officers and Directors of the Cowbridge Railway Company the contractors and tradesmen of the town, and shareholders in the company. It then proceeded slowly through the cheering crowds towards the site of the terminus in Eastgate Street.

At the site of the terminus, the Mayor of Cowbridge, R. C. Nichol-Carne, addressed the assembled multitude and announced that they were there that day to celebrate a very important day in the history of the ancient borough. A day from which, he predicted, its future greatness would be dated. After prayers had been said for the success of the undertaking, Dr J. W. Nichol-Carne, Chairman of the Company, who was dressed as a 'navvy', announced that he was about to start the construction of the railway. As the Cowbridge Railway Company was not wealthy, they could not afford the customary handsome barrow and fine spade which would have been necessary had a lady been performing the ceremony, and instead they had to be content with a common barrow and shovel. To the deafening cheers of the crowd, Dr Nichol-Carne proceeded to cut and turn the first sods of the Cowbridge Railway. With the ceremony satisfactorily concluded, the procession reformed and marched back to the Bear Hotel, where a public dinner was held to mark the occasion.

Construction of the Cowbridge Railway now began in earnest. However, the pace of work was hindered, repeatedly, by the slowness with which possession was obtained for land on the route of the railway. By the end of

June 1863, about one mile of fencing was complete, and ditches had been dug for a distance of over two miles and work had begun on the first cutting.

The third Half-Yearly Meeting of the shareholders of the Cowbridge Railway Company took place at the Town Hall, Cowbridge, on Monday 30th June 1863, and was an occasion of self-congratulation and hope for the future. The shareholders were told that the provisional agreement with the GWR had been entered into, and that contracts had been agreed for the construction of their railway, and for the supply of materials at prices which were generally below the estimates of the engineer. Finally, they were told that construction was proceeding apace.

On a sadder note, the death of a Director, Mr D. Williams, of Miskin Manor, was reported. A number of changes in the composition of the Board of Directors were also announced, which reflected the closer relationship which was developing between the Cowbridge Company and the TVR. James Poole, Chairman of the TVR, had joined the Cowbridge Board as its Chairman, in place of Dr Nichol-Carne, who had stepped down to become Deputy Chairman. R. C. Nichol-Carne had retired from the Board, his place being taken by the Resident Director, i.e. Managing Director, of the TVR, W. Done Bushell. With such a strong TVR representation, it was generally assumed that it was only a matter of time before the Cowbridge Railway was leased to the TVR,

By the end of August 1863, the abutments and piers of the Cowbridge line bridge, over the Ely at Llantrisant, were nearing completion. This enabled a temporary road to be put across between the piers, so as to provide access for the excavation of ground to the south of the SWR station. The earth removed from this area was then used to form an embankment alongside the SWR, on which transfer sidings were laid. Although the GWR had constructed the piers for the widening of its bridge over the Ely, no arrangements had been made for the provision of the third rail to Maesaraul Junction. The overbridges at Ty Draw and Llanharry Road had been started, but apart from this, construction continued to be hindered by delays in obtaining land.

Llantrisant Station, circa 1910, showing the Cowbridge bay on the left. The station building on the island platform was erected as part of the rebuilding of the station, which was completed in 1890, and was jointly occupied by the GWR and the TVR.

Lens of Sutton

A particular problem at this stage was the tendency for men working on the railway to leave that employment in order to assist in the harvest. This took place in spite of what Alex Bassett regarded as the high wages paid by the contractors. Problems also arose as a result of the failure of suppliers to deliver essential permanent way materials, so that Bassett was forced to seek alternative sources of supply, in order to continue work on the line.

By October 1863, the railway was beginning to take shape. The line had been formed from just outside Llantrisant Station to the Llanharry Road bridge. Work had also started at the Cowbridge end of the line. Girders had been laid across the Ely Bridge at Llantrisant Station, and the bridges at Ty Draw and Llanharry Road were nearly ready for their girders. Work faltered somewhat in October as a result of unfavourable weather, which prevented work in the Ystradowen cutting. Even so, about one fifth of a mile of formation had been constructed between Ystradowen and Cowbridge, and the permanent way had been laid between Llantrisant Station and Llanharry Road bridge.

By the end of 1863, the situation had improved somewhat as more land had been obtained and the weather had been kinder. The formation was complete from Llantrisant to the middle of the moor, between Llanharry Road and Ystradowen, a distance of two miles. The Welsh St. Donats Road bridge was nearing completion, and work had started on the Newton Road bridge.

The Heads of Agreement, between the GWR and the Cowbridge Railway Company, for the provision and use of the third rail to Maesaraul Junction, were signed on 9th January 1864. Despite this, there appeared to be no immediate prospect of the GWR actually providing the third rail, a matter which began to cause some concern to the Cowbridge Company.

However, work on the Cowbridge Railway was progressing well, with some forty two chains of permanent way laid from Llantrisant Station to Llanharry, and a further 1½ miles ready for the permanent way. With construction well in hand, Alex Bassett requested instructions regarding the preparation of plans and specifications for the stations at Cowbridge, Ystradowen and Llantrisant. Later that month, tenders were received for the provision of a turntable at Llantrisant Station, of which that of Messrs Cochrane & Co. of Dudley was accepted.

In his report of 18th March 1864, Alex Bassett was able to announce, with evident relief, that at last the GWR had given instructions for the laying of the third rail over the EVR line to Maesaraul Junction. Work had continued satisfactorily on the Cowbridge line, with the cutting at Ystradowen well under way, and with a considerable length of permanent way laid. April saw the erection of the turntable at Llantrisant, and the completion of the drawings and specifications for that station.

With work about to start on the formation for the station at Cowbridge, Bassett sought instructions for the design of the station. He pointed out that as the line might be extended to the south, a temporary wooden station should suffice. However, although Bassett presented plans for such a station in May 1864, the issue remained unresolved and he was instructed to prepare additional plans for a permanent station. Following further consideration of the matter, a meeting took place at the site of the intended station, on 4th July 1864, involving Alex Bassett, Dr Nichol-Carne, Captain Gould, George Fisher and John Stockwood. It was agreed that a permanent station would be erected, with the station building in the line of Eastgate Street.

By this date, the permanent way had been laid over almost the entire length of the line. However, as the third rail section had yet to be provided, the contractors had been unable to get an engine on to the railway, which had been constructed using horses as motive power.

On 5th July 1864, Bassett met the Traffic Manager of the GWR at Llantrisant, and agreed the positions of the signals at the junction. Following this meeting, Bassett wrote to Messrs Stevens, the signalling contractors, requesting that they send a man to estimate the cost of signalling the line. Points and crossings were ordered from Messrs Parfitt & Jenkins of Cardiff. So encouraging was the progress of the construction that, in July 1864, the Secretary forwarded a notice to the Board of Trade, requesting sanction for the opening of the line to passengers. However, this move proved to be premature, and Stockwood was forced to withdraw the notice on the grounds that the railway was still not complete.

The progress of the line was reported with some pleasure to the shareholders of the Cowbridge Railway at their fifth Half-Yearly Meeting in August 1864. The railway was nearing completion, and could be opened as soon as the GWR had laid the third rail over the EVR, a deficiency which had prevented the TVR from working an engine and carriages on to the Cowbridge Railway. Turning to the ever present problem of finance, the Directors announced that as a large part of the capital remained unsubscribed, and because the company was unable to exercise its borrowing powers owing to the restriction contained in its Act, they had considered it expedient to issue Lloyds Bonds to the contractors, suppliers and others who were owed money, to be payable within two or three years from the date of issue. Although this action was understandable at the time, it was based on an optimistic view of the railway's prospects which, if not fulfilled, was sure to rebound on the company, when the time came for the bonds to be realized.

A number of minor works remained to be completed on the railway, however: the contractors had postponed the final ballasting until an engine was available; the turntable and carriage shed at Cowbridge had yet to be delivered; a siding was required for exchange purposes with the GWR at Llantrisant; and the branch to Bethell's mines at Llanharry had still to be constructed.

In his last report of 1864, Bassett was able to inform his Directors that their railway was complete, apart from various minor items, and that it was intended to forward a notice to the Board of Trade at once. However, he had also received news that although the notice for the third rail section of the EVR would be submitted by the GWR at the same time, the L&TVJR did not intend to install their signals at Maesaraul Junction until after the Board of Trade inspection. Bassett feared that this could lead to a considerable delay in the opening of the Cowbridge Railway. He also suggested that additional land, in the form of a strip some thirty yards wide, should be acquired on the west side of the Cowbridge goods yard, in order to provide additional siding accommodation. Finally, an application had been received from Mr Bethell for his siding connection at Llanharry, and this was being attended to.

Thus at the end of 1864, with its railway complete, the Cowbridge Railway Company was ready to commence operations. The TVR had agreed to work the line for twelve months at cost price, and all that remained was to obtain Board of Trade sanction for the passenger service over the line. On 12th December 1864, John Stockwood wrote to the Board of Trade, informing them that the Cowbridge Railway intended to commence its passenger service, and requested an inspection of the railway. However, the obtaining of this sanction was to prove a more formidable obstacle than the Directors, or their Engineer, had anticipated.

The original Cowbridge Railway Station building, pictured in 1951 in use as a warehouse. Conversion to this use involved the blocking up of the original central doorway and the creation of a new loading bay in place of the left-hand window. The gentleman who is inspecting the car (origin and owner unknown) is Mr Billy Lewis, the former station master at St. Mary Church Road Station and later Ystradowen Station.

C. Chapman

Llantrisant Station, circa 1910, with a GWR stopping train in the 'down' platform. The lack of a connecting service in the Cowbridge bay is not unexpected as the greater priority was given, by the TVR, to connections at Pontypridd. A bookstall, owned by Messrs Wymans, was housed in the 'down' side station buildings. No doubt this would have provided some relief to the tedium of a long wait for a connection to Cowbridge.

Lens of Sutton

Chapter Three
Getting fearfully out of Repair

The railway which awaited Colonel Yolland, the Inspector appointed by the Board of Trade, was a single track line, 5 miles and 60 chains long. It followed an undulating and, in places, sharply curved route between the valleys of the Ely and the Thaw. Although complete, it had yet to see an engine or train as the third rail section over the Mwyndy branch of the EVR was still not ready. Its track consisted of double-headed rails weighing 65 lb. per linear yard in lengths of 21 ft., which was affixed by cast-iron chairs to 9 ft. sleepers and ballasted with gravel. The gravel, in accordance with contemporary practice, covered the tops of the sleepers. The line avoided level crossings, with turnpike and public roads being carried over the railway by means of a total of eight overbridges. Gradients were steep, with a maximum of 1 in 45 near Ystradowen, and there were some sharp reverse curves near Llantrisant Station.

The Cowbridge Railway Station, at Llantrisant, was situated alongside that of the SWR, which had opened in 1850. The town of Llantrisant was about 1½ miles to the north-east, on a hill overlooking the Ely Valley. At the time of the opening of the SWR, there was little in the way of a settlement at the station itself. The station was situated at the point at which the Cowbridge to Llantrisant turnpike road crossed the River Clun, a tributary of the River Ely, by a bridge known as the Pont Clun, which gave its name to the small settlement which grew up around Llantrisant Station. Opened in 1850, Llantrisant Station was a small wayside station, with 'up' and 'down' platforms, a single

goods siding serving a loading bank, and a goods shed on the 'up' side. The buildings were of standard SWR design, similar to those at nearby Bridgend. The opening of the EVR in 1860 brought with it a junction at the west end of the station, together with a complex of sidings and a locomotive depot.

The building of the Cowbridge Railway involved the reconstruction of the 'down' platform as an island platform, serving both the SWR 'down' line and the terminating line from Cowbridge. In the process, the 'down' side waiting-room of the SWR was removed, and a new one provided by the Cowbridge Company at the Cardiff end of the platform. The Cowbridge line terminated immediately to the west of the turnpike road bridge, over the SWR lines, its layout consisting of a run-round loop with both lines ending at a turntable, at the end of the platform. At the opposite end, a single narrow gauge line, provided by and the property of the GWR, left the Cowbridge Railway, crossed both lines of the SWR and, after running parallel with that railway for a short distance, joined the EVR just beyond its junction with the SWR. The Cowbridge Railway itself crossed the Ely by means of a double track girder bridge, close to the SWR bridge over the Ely, before making a sharp turn to the south through almost 90 degrees. Immediately to the west of the Ely bridge, a siding left the Cowbridge line, and then divided to serve the weighing machine siding and the exchange siding with the SWR.

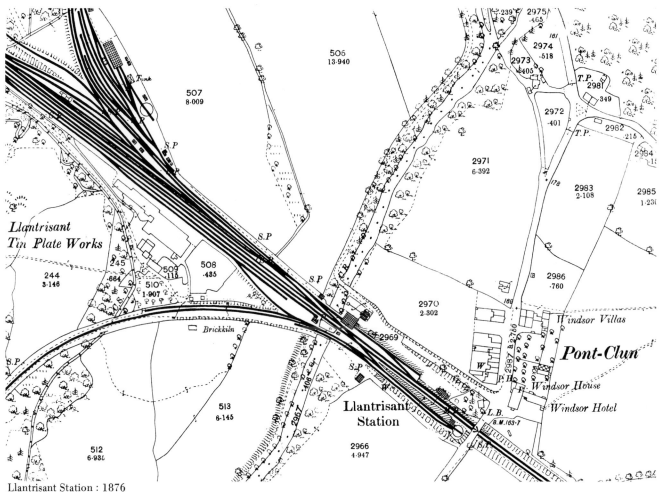

Llantrisant Station : 1876

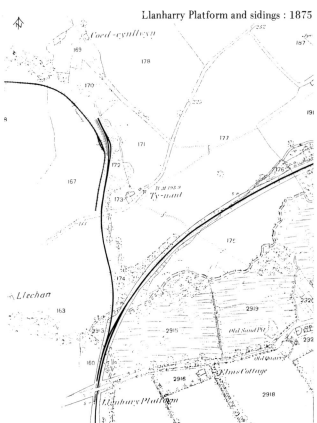

Llanharry Platform and sidings : 1875

At the first overbridge at Ty Draw, about half a mile from Llantrisant Station, the Cowbridge Railway turned through 90 degrees to the west, and ran alongside the Nant Felinfach, a small stream which fed the River Ely, towards the Llanharry Road bridge. Up to this point, gradients had been relatively easy, with a maximum of 1 in 185, but the gradient now steepened to 1 in 66 as the line climbed to the summit of the Llanharry Road bridge. Here, it left the headwaters of the Nant Felinfach for those of the Nant Rhydhalog, another tributary of the Ely, which ran in a south-westerly direction before turning north past Talygarn to join the River Ely near Llantrisant Station.

The summit at the Llanharry Road bridge was also the point at which the branch serving Bethell's iron and coal mines at Llanharry joined the Cowbridge Railway. This line made an indirect connection with the main line of the Cowbridge Railway, by means of a short siding which was facing for 'down' trains, and ran due north for about a quarter of a mile before terminating at a transhipment wharf, on the site of the 20th century iron ore mine. From this wharf, a tramway served both the coal mine at Gwaun Llanharry, and the iron ore mine at 'the Patch', near the village of Llanharry. However, the subsequent history of these early mines remains somewhat obscure, with official returns only listing J. Bethell & Co. for the years 1863–1865, with the Trimsaran Coal & Iron Co. being listed for 1872 and 1874.

Ystradowen Station, circa 1905, looking towards the summit of the Cowbridge Railway at the overbridge carrying the road to Cowbridge. The station was some distance from the village as a result of its relocation in 1865.

Lens of Sutton

Cowbridge Railway
Cowbridge Station 1877

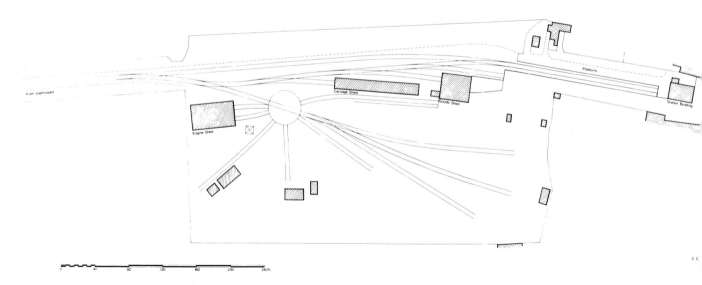

Cowbridge Station : 1877

From the Llanharry Road bridge, the Cowbridge line descended at a gradient of 1 in 84, before crossing under the Llantrisant to Cowbridge turnpike at Rhydhalog. The overbridges on the Cowbridge Railway were all of similar design, being single track only with either cast-iron girders, or timbers, carrying the roadway between stone piers and abutments. South of the Rhydhalog bridge, the railway left the course of the Nant Rhydhalog to cross the Morfa Ystradowen, the moor between Llanharry and Ystradowen, before climbing out of the catchment of the River Ely at Ystradowen.

Ystradowen was a small village, consisting of St. Owains Church, the White Lion public house and a number of farms and other dwellings spread out along the turnpike road. The railway climbed at a gradient of 1 in 45 to the summit in the Ystradowen cutting, at 15ft. deep, the heaviest earthwork on the line, before descending through Ystradowen Station. As completed in 1864, Ystradowen was the only intermediate station on the railway, and consisted of a passing loop with a platform on the 'up' line, and a single short siding serving a stone built goods shed to the rear of the platform. The goods shed was of the dead end type, with the roadway set diagonally opposite the rail approach. This arrangement required the reversal of carts up to the loading platform, a somewhat difficult manoeuvre with horse transport. The shed was without windows in any of its walls but, in later years at least, a roof light was fitted. No details of the original passenger accommodation have, however, been traced.

From Ystradowen Station, the railway descended into the catchment of the Thaw, past the small hamlets of Trerhyngyll, Maendy and Prisk. The last two miles to the terminus at Cowbridge were relatively straight and easily graded, as the line crossed the broad flood plain of the Thaw to the north of the town.

Cowbridge Station was situated on the north side of the long main street of the town, not far from the East Turnpike Gate. The station layout was a rather odd and restricted affair, which proved to be a serious handicap in the operation of the station in later years. It comprised a short run-round loop, from which a number of sidings ran off. The first of these went to an engine turntable, from which sidings emerged at all angles to all parts of the rectangular site. Two short lines ran back to the engine shed, with a number of other sidings serving various facilities around the yard. The main siding, having crossed the turntable, branched into three goods sidings. Three other short spurs ran from the loop, serving respectively the carriage shed, a corrugated ironclad structure with an arc roof, the goods shed, a stone building of similar design to that at Ystradowen, and the cattle pens and end loading bay.

The running line continued past the goods yard, to terminate at a single platform which occupied a strip of land between properties in Eastgate Street, which was initially without any form of shelter. The station building was a single storey red brick building of modest, yet classical, proportions, fronting on to Eastgate Street and set at a slightly higher level than the platform to which it was linked by a short ramp.

The terminus of the Cowbridge branch, on 15th August 1957, showing the old passenger station, end loading bay, and part of the goods shed. The crossover which once existed at this point was removed in the early 1950s.

Ian L. Wright

Colonel Yolland completed his report on 17th December 1864. As an engine had not been available, he had been forced to make his inspection of the railway in a horse-drawn wagon. He was not over-impressed with the Cowbridge Railway, however, and identified a number of significant defects in its design and construction. As Cowbridge trains would need to cross both lines of the SWR at Llantrisant, it was essential that the signalling arrangements at the junction should be centralized. One signalman would control these, in a cabin equipped with proper interlocking, to prevent any collisions arising from human error. Not having been able to run an engine over the underbridges, Yolland did not feel able to pass any comments regarding their strength. The waiting-room at Llantrisant caused particular concern, in view of its proximity to the running lines of the SWR and the Cowbridge Railway. He pointed out that the requirements of the Board of Trade, which had been circulated to all railway companies, stipulated that no pillars or other fixed obstructions should be placed within 6 ft. of the edge of the platforms, so as to avoid accidents to passengers who might collide with such obstacles. If the waiting-room was to be retained, it would have to be reduced in width and detached from the platform. A further cause of concern was the position of the Ystradowen Station on a very steep gradient, particularly as it would have been possible either to ease out the gradient or relocate the station on a level section just to the north. In addition, if Ystradowen was to be used as a passing place, another platform would be required on the loop line. Finally, the line had had no chance to become consolidated, and there had been a number of slips in the cuttings.

Yolland was sufficiently concerned by these defects to report that by reason of the incomplete state of the railway, he could not recommend that sanction be granted for the opening of the line to passengers, without danger to the public using it.

The Board of Trade informed the Cowbridge Railway of its decision on 19th December 1864, and directed the company to postpone the opening of the line to passengers for one month, whilst the various defects were corrected. A further set-back came with the news that the L&TVJR had been forced to withdraw its request for Board of Trade sanction, because the junction at Maesaraul was still incomplete. The delay which was to result from the failure to complete the arrangements at Maesaraul was to prove more troublesome to the Cowbridge Railway, than the alterations required to its own line.

Reporting the unfavourable news from the Board of Trade to his Directors on 29th December 1864, Alex Bassett sought to deflect any criticism of his engineering competence by suggesting that although the waiting-room at Llantrisant was satisfactory for ordinary purposes, the GWR might run wider carriages over the SWR. This appears to have been a rather free interpretation of Yolland's report, which was clearly related to general requirements and not to the sort of specific reference made by Bassett. Whilst the contractors had been instructed to carry out the required alterations at Llantrisant, the problem at Ystradowen proved to be of a more difficult and costly nature. It was considered necessary to remove the platform to the level stretch of line in the cutting to the north of the original station. Even so, Bassett managed to extract some benefit from this embarrassing situation, by suggesting that the original platform would provide a convenient coal yard for Mr Bethell, thereby admitting that the goods facilities intended at Ystradowen were likely to be inadequate. It had been intimated to Bassett that the Board of Trade would not object to the opening of the railway when the alterations at Llantrisant Station were complete, provided that Ystradowen Station was not opened to passengers until it had been relocated.

In the event, the necessary alterations were not completed within the time specified by the Board of Trade, and the notice for the opening of the Cowbridge Railway was withdrawn until such time as the railway was ready for re-inspection. The modifications at Llantrisant were undertaken during January 1865, at a cost of £20. Those at Ystradowen proved rather more costly, however, and involved the removal of some 5,000 cubic yards of earth, at a total cost of £500.

Ystradowen Station in 1965, after the closure of the Llanharry to Cowbridge section. The loading platform was the original station platform which was rejected by the Board of Trade in 1865. The building to the right of the goods shed is the station master's house.

Lens of Sutton

Despite these set-backs, it was essential that some revenue be attracted to the railway as quickly as possible. Although sanction had been refused for the passenger service, there was no reason why goods traffic should not commence as soon as the junction at Maesaraul was ready. On 16th January 1865, the TVR was able to work an engine over the junction and the mixed gauge section of the EVR on to the Cowbridge Railway. This engine then worked back and forth throughout the day. This trial working was reported to have given general satisfaction to those engaged in the undertaking.

However, this satisfaction does not appear to have extended to the TVR Engineer, George Fisher, who, when reporting the results of the trial working to his Directors on 20th January 1865, commented that the works on the Cowbridge Railway were remarkably light, and had been executed in the cheapest possible manner. He was not optimistic about the consequences of such economy, as the effect would be felt in costly maintenance, excessive wear and tear and, in all probability, compensation payments for accidents. Considerable alterations would be required before TVR engines could work safely over the railway, and the line would require constant attention and repair during its first year of operation.

With regard to the traffic prospects of the railway, Fisher felt that the best way of encouraging its use and ensuring its proper operation was for the TVR to appoint a traffic manager, who would be responsible for supervising its working, canvassing traffic and the keeping of accounts of the cost of train working. The TVR would hire an engine and rolling stock to the Cowbridge Company and supply the train crew. These recommendations were accepted by the TVR Directors.

In the premature euphoria which had preceded the Board of Trade inspection, the Corporation of Cowbridge had resolved 'that a public breakfast be given . . . on the occasion of the opening of the Cowbridge Railway to passenger traffic', and had conferred the Freedom of the Borough upon Dr Nichol-Carne as 'a slight acknowledgement of his indefatigable exertions in obtaining the Cowbridge Railway.' Having decided on a celebration, the Corporation was not going to be deflected by the inconvenient fact that the Board of Trade sanction had not been forthcoming. Accordingly, it was agreed to go ahead with the full panoply of an opening ceremony, but as it would be for goods traffic only, it was an oddly incomplete occasion, with the most important guest, the passenger train, absent from the proceedings.

Thus, on Monday 30th January 1865, a train of nine wagons arrived at Cowbridge Station to the accompaniment of great rejoicing in the town. The inaugural train contained some fifty tons of Llantwit coal, of which ten tons each had been given by Thomas Powell, jun., the proprietor of the Llantwit Collieries, and Alex Bassett, the Engineer. Thirty tons, costing £10, had been subscribed by the Corporation of Cowbridge. The coal was distributed to the poor of the town and the adjoining Parish of Llanbethian.

However, the regular goods service itself did not commence until over a week after the opening ceremony. On Wednesday, 8th February 1865, a train of nine wagons, some empty, some loaded, arrived at Cowbridge; the former were to convey hay to Aberdare, whilst the latter brought in timber and slates for the town. Reporting on this event to his Directors, Alex Bassett advised that as payment to the TVR would be on the basis of a charge per train mile

worked, it was essential that only the minimum mileage required for the needs of the traffic should be worked and, for this, two trains per day would suffice. He also reported that the TVR had appointed Mr Edwards as their traffic manager at Cowbridge, and that a tender had been received from Messrs Griffiths & Thomas for the maintenance of the railway for a period of twelve months, at a cost of £500 to be paid quarterly in cash.

Although sanction for passenger trains had been withheld by the Board of Trade, at least one appears to have worked over the line at some date prior to 30th June 1865, as the half-yearly accounts to that date include a sum of £10 0s 9d attributed to passenger revenue.

In their sixth Half-Yearly Report to their shareholders, in February 1865, the Cowbridge Directors attempted to gloss over the debacle of the Board of Trade inspection, by invoking the convenient image of bureaucratic red tape blocking the opening of the railway, but they neglected to mention any of the points raised by Colonel Yolland, with the exception of the need for the track to consolidate before the passenger service could begin. On a more positive note, the Directors were able to report that an arrangement had been made with the TVR, for working the railway at cost price for a year, after which both companies would be in a better position to consider the question of a permanent agreement.

Work on the alterations required by the Board of Trade, with the exception of the rebuilding of Ystradowen Station, was complete by early March 1865, when John Stockwood invited the Board of Trade to reinspect the Cowbridge Railway. Captain Rich was appointed as Inspecting Officer, and examined the railway on 22nd March 1865. He found that the waiting-room at Llantrisant Station had been reduced in width, and that Ystradowen had been abolished as a passenger station pending the completion of the relocated platform. Rich was informed that it was intended to work the railway on the one engine in steam system, and he recommended that, subject to an undertaking to this effect being provided by the Cowbridge Railway, the line could be opened to passengers without danger to the public using it.

This welcome result for the Cowbridge Company was accompanied by further news of a set-back for the L&TVJR. On the same day that Rich had inspected the Cowbridge Railway, he had also examined the L&TVJR and the third rail section of the EVR. Although satisfied with the standard of the L&TVJR itself, he was less happy about the junctions at each end of the new railway. That, with the TVR main line, took the form of a trailing connection to the 'up' line, with a crossover between the 'up' and 'down' lines. Rich felt that this junction should be replaced by a conventional double junction, which the TVR agreed to do. With regard to the junction with the EVR at Maesaraul, Rich was concerned that this was situated at the foot of a 1 in 40 incline from the L&TVJR, and recommended that it should be moved about 300 yards to the west, and placed under the control of a raised cabin. These considerations, coupled with the fact that the third rail over the EVR was still incomplete, led Rich to recommend the refusal of sanction for the introduction of the passenger services over these lines.

Although it would have been possible to have worked a passenger service between Cowbridge and Llantrisant only, the opening of the Cowbridge Railway to passengers was deferred until trains could run right through to Pontypridd.

The Cowbridge branch auto-train at Cowbridge in 1947. The train consists of 'Metro' tank No. 3586 and auto-car No. 35. Auto-car No. 35 had been built as a corridor third for the 'Cornishman' in 1894, being converted for auto-working in 1905. It was withdrawn in October 1949. The railway staff are (from left to right) Fireman Howard Adams, Driver Dick Killick, the guard, and Booking Clerk Miss Davies.

Ian L. Wright

Unfortunately, this was delayed as a result of a dispute between the TVR and the GWR, over who was responsible for the cost of the alterations at Maesaraul Junction required by the Board of Trade.

Board of Trade approval for the L&TVJR and the Llantrisant to Maesaraul Junction section of the EVR was finally granted on 29th August 1865. After the prolonged delay in commencing the passenger service, the Cowbridge Directors determined on a low key opening in comparison with that of the previous January, with the inaugural train, on 18th September 1865, conveying the officials of the company, its engine decked out in evergreens. However, the Directors did hold a celebratory dinner that evening at the Bear Hotel in Cowbridge. Even without passenger trains, the railway appears to have had some impact on the fortunes of Cowbridge; the price of coal had fallen, and business activity had been stimulated in the town, with a number of new houses under construction.

The initial passenger service over the Cowbridge Railway consisted of three Cowbridge to Llantrisant round trips each day, with two of these continuing to and from Pontypridd. A Sunday service of two Cowbridge to Pontypridd round trips was also provided. With the exception of these Sunday trains, all trains ran 'mixed'. The first train on weekdays left Cowbridge at 8.50 a.m. and connected with 'up' and 'down' GWR trains at Llantrisant,

and arrived at Pontypridd in time to connect with departures for Merthyr, Aberdare and the Rhondda, before returning to Cowbridge at 10.06 a.m. The second 'up' train departed from Cowbridge at 11.28 a.m. for Llantrisant, where the carriages were left, whilst the train continued as a goods working to Maesaraul Junction. It was here that traffic was exchanged with the L&TVJR, before returning as a 'down' goods to Cowbridge. After sorting in the yard at Cowbridge, the goods returned to Maesaraul Junction to exchange 'up' traffic. It then ran back to Llantrisant Station, picked up the carriages which it had left earlier in the day, and formed the 2.39 p.m. mixed train to Cowbridge. The last working of the day left Cowbridge at 5.55 p.m., connected with 'up' and 'down' GWR trains at Llantrisant, and with the 'up' and 'down' evening trains of the TVR at Pontypridd, before returning to Cowbridge at 7.29 p.m.

Reporting on the inauguration of the Cowbridge passenger service, to his Directors on 22nd September 1865, was George Fisher, the TVR Engineer. He commented that whilst the service might be considered satisfactory, there was a pressing need for intermediate station accommodation 'attended with convenience to the public and advantage to the company.' This would consist of Ystradowen, when eventually opened, and new stations on the L&TVJR to serve Llantrisant and Llantwit Fardre. Fisher also recommended that an interchange station be provided at the junction of the L&TVJR with the TVR main line, so that Cowbridge trains could be kept clear of the TVR main line, and running costs reduced accordingly. The station at Llantwit Fardre was opened in 1867, but that serving Llantrisant did not open until 1869. However, no evidence has been found to suggest that the proposed interchange station at Llantrisant Junction was ever provided.

The introduction of the passenger service brought a welcome additional source of revenue to the Cowbridge Company. The initial results were encouraging, with over 1,000 passengers per week in the first three weeks, although by the fourth week the novelty appears to have begun to wane, with the total down to 850. Total receipts for the first month of passenger operations amounted to £212, and it was confidently predicted that if receipts continued at this level, a surplus would be available from which a dividend could be paid. Despite a seasonal decline in the number of passengers, receipts increased steadily to the end of 1865.

In spite of these encouraging results, concern was growing with regard to the quality of the engineering advice and practice, which had been supplied by Alex Bassett, as Engineer to the Cowbridge Railway. The new TVR Directors on the Cowbridge Board appear to have been particularly vocal in this respect, having the benefit of the experience of their Engineer, George Fisher, to draw upon. Accordingly, Consulting Engineer Charles Gregory was appointed to examine the works of the railway and report to the Cowbridge Board whether they had been constructed and finished according to the terms and conditions of the contract, and generally to express views as to the design and execution of the works.

Gregory visited the railway on 18th January 1866, and walked its entire length in order to complete his inspection. He was strongly critical of various features of its design and construction, especially the almost complete disregard which had been paid to the question of the drainage of the railway. As an example of false economy, which had been the rule, he noted that the culverts had been constructed with tree trunks, in place of the required masonry! This penny-pinching approach was also evident in the inferior quality of the ballast, the flimsy standard of fencing and the unfinished appearance of the earthworks.

In spite of these defects, Gregory was reluctant to condemn outright the work of Alex Bassett, and concluded his report by stating that in other respects, the works had been properly executed in accordance with the specification laid down. With regard to the design of the work, he was diplomatically circumspect, merely noting that 'engineers are not always agreed to the design of stations and sidings.' However, it does not take a great deal of reading between the lines to come to the conclusion that Gregory would not have undertaken the design and construction of the Cowbridge Railway in the same manner as Bassett had done.

In their eighth Half-Yearly Report to their shareholders, on 22nd February 1866, the Cowbridge Directors were able to point, with evident satisfaction, to the fact that the passenger traffic on the railway had exceeded even their expectations. They predicted that it would increase further during the summer months. Coal and goods traffic had been very good considering the nature of the district. They were also able to announce that the station at Ystradowen had been opened for passenger traffic earlier in the month. The resited platform was some way from the village, in the cutting beyond the original ill-fated passenger station. The latter had been converted into a goods wharf, served by a short siding which represented the truncated remains of the former passing loop.

The first anniversary of the opening of the railway to goods traffic found the Cowbridge Company still without a permanent agreement with the TVR for either working or leasing the railway. The temporary expedient of hiring the rolling stock from the TVR did not provide a satisfactory long-term basis for the operation of the line, particularly as maintenance of the permanent way remained the responsibility of the Cowbridge Company. It was in order to find a more secure arrangement, that Dr Nichol-Carne, Rowland Fothergill and John Stockwood appeared before the TVR Board on 6th April 1866, with a proposition that the TVR enter into an agreement for leasing the Cowbridge Railway. The TVR responded by instructing George Fisher to investigate the traffic on the Cowbridge Railway, with particular reference to the proportion which found its way to, or from, the TVR, and also to examine the working expenses of the line.

Station staff at Cowbridge in the early years of this century, with no less than 38 employees on parade. The gentlemen in bowler hats are believed to be from the locomotive department.

C. Chapman

(Courtesy of G. Punter)

George Fisher reported to his Directors on 18th May 1866. He stated that during the last six months of 1865, the gross receipts of the Cowbridge Railway had been £951 16s 8d, with working expenses of £703 5s 11d, leaving a balance of £248 10s 9d. For the first three months of 1866, receipts had amounted to £656 11s 11d. If this level of receipts was to continue for the rest of the first half of 1866, it would represent nearly a 30 per cent increase over the preceding six months. However, these accounts did not include any allowance for maintenance and the renewal of the permanent way. On the basis of these returns George Fisher felt that 'with considerable increase in traffic, freedom from accidents and rigid economy, some time must elapse before the Cowbridge Railway Company can have a disposable balance of £1,000 per annum.'

Turning to the proportion of gross receipts represented by traffic to and from stations on the TVR system, Fisher found that two thirds of the total receipts of the Cowbridge Railway were represented by such traffic. However, whilst this was a very significant figure as far as the Cowbridge Company was concerned, it represented a minute proportion of the total traffic of the TVR, a consideration which led George Fisher to conclude that he did not regard the Cowbridge Railway as an important feeder to the TVR.

Although no immediate action followed the receipt of the report, it marked a fundamental turning point in the relations between the two companies. Thereafter, any question of the TVR leasing the Cowbridge Railway was very definitely in abeyance. After the doubts about the construction of the line raised by Charles Gregory, Fisher's report appears to have seriously undermined any remaining confidence the TVR Directors may have had in the Cowbridge Railway, as a paying proposition. This change of attitude was reflected in the subsequent departure of James Poole and Done Bushell, from the Board of the Cowbridge Company.

The TVR eventually responded to the request for a permanent arrangement for leasing the Cowbridge Railway by inviting its Directors to bring forward their own detailed terms. These were presented to the TVR Board, at its meeting on 13th August 1866. The Cowbridge Company was prepared to lease its railway to the TVR on the following terms: at 3 per cent per annum on £52,000 until 1st January 1870; at 4 per cent per annum on the same sum from then until 1st January 1875, and 5 per cent from then until the end of the term. The Traffic Account for the Cowbridge Railway, for the first six months of 1866, was also submitted to the directors of the TVR; this showed receipts of £1,436 0s 2d against working expenses of £973 15s 10d. However, this was not as encouraging as it seemed, as the accounts did not include any allowance for the annual rent of £200 paid to the GWR for the use of the third rail section of the EVR, nor did they include any provision for the maintenance of the permanent way which, in the first year of operation of the line, had been entrusted to the care of the contractors, Messrs Griffiths & Thomas, for a sum of £500. Taking these items into consideration, it is apparent that the Cowbridge Railway was only just breaking even at this date.

Faced with this situation, there was little the Cowbridge Company could do to improve matters. The attraction of new traffic to the railway was very much a long-term task, given the nature of the district served, and the difficult national economic circumstances which attended its opening. Costs could hardly be reduced by cutting services, as these were probably at the minimum which could reasonably be offered in the first place and, in any case, such a move was not likely to assist in the generation of additional traffic. Two means of reducing costs were open to the Cowbridge Directors. They could try to persuade the TVR to reduce its charges for working the railway, or they could cut those costs for which they themselves were responsible. The former approach was advocated by Alex

Diesel railcar No. 18 is seen at Cowbridge Passenger Station on 5th May 1951. At the end of the platform, on the line to the goods yard, can be seen the original Cowbridge signal cabin, which was abolished in 1897. It survived as a permanent way hut until closure of the line. Immediately to the right of the station building is the stone wall which may be the remains of the original Cowbridge Railway engine shed, which was closed in 1886.

R. C. Riley

Bassett, who tried, unsuccessfully, to get the TVR to grant a rebate on traffic passing to the TVR from the Cowbridge Railway. The latter course, in effect, meant reducing the amount of money spent on the maintenance of the railway. Although this occured more by default than intention, it proved to be an extremely false economy which was bound to harm the company in the long run.

The TVR Board considered the Cowbridge terms on 14th August 1866. After some discussion, it was agreed that a permanent arrangement for leasing or working the Cowbridge Railway was not in the TVR's interest, but that the Cowbridge Company would be offered every assistance in coming to an alternative arrangement with the GWR. With such an outright rebuff, the Cowbridge Railway was condemned to continue its hand-to-mouth existence in the hope that something might turn up. A further attempt was made, in 1867, to persuade the TVR to lease the Cowbridge line, this time for a term of ten years at a guaranteed annual payment to be agreed upon, but the TVR was not interested in this suggestion either. As for the possibility of an alternative arrangement with the GWR, the idea that this company would wish to involve itself with an impoverished narrow gauge concern was hardly realistic, especially whilst the South Wales main line remained broad gauge. Despite the direct intervention of the TVR, nothing came of this suggestion.

A further damaging blow to the prestige of the Cowbridge Railway, and to its relations with the TVR, came in April 1867, when Messrs Guest & Co. issued writs against the Cowbridge Railway, for the non-payment of a sum of £817 owed for the supply of rails. Although Lloyds Bonds, which the company had issued to the contractors and suppliers in lieu of cash, were becoming due for redemption, its continuing impoverishment meant that the Cowbridge Company was in no position to honour its Bonds. As a result, a number of writs were issued against it, for the recovery of outstanding debts, and in April 1867, the bailiffs took possession of the railway and its receipts. The news of this event did little to enhance the TVR's increasingly jaundiced view of the undertaking, particularly as it regarded a large proportion of the receipts as its own property.

An auction of movable assets was held at Cowbridge, Ystradowen and Llantrisant stations on 29th April 1867, on the instructions of the Under Sheriff, in order to raise cash to satisfy certain creditors. It was only thanks to the public-spirited intervention of the Chairman of the Cowbridge Railway, R. C. Nichol-Carne, that this sale did not result in the cessation of traffic over the line. Nichol-Carne stepped in to purchase the engine turntables, carriage shed, weighbridges, water tank and pump, which he then leased back to the company. This humiliating blow was compounded later that year when, as a result of an action against the Cowbridge Company, the National Provincial Bank of England was granted possession of the Cowbridge Railway.

The lack of adequate maintenance, on top of the inferior standard of construction, had a cumulative effect, which began to cause increasing concern to the TVR as the provider of the engine and rolling stock. The decrepitude of the Cowbridge Railway was the subject of a report by George Fisher to his Directors in October 1868. Little appeared to have been done to remedy the defects identified by Charles Gregory nearly three years before, with the result that the track was deteriorating rapidly. This state of affairs did not improve, however, and at the end of 1868 Mr Kineath, the TVR station master at Cowbridge, wrote to John Stockwood pointing out that the railway was getting 'fearfully out of repair,' and requesting that Stockwood take the necessary steps to rectify the situation.

However, the standard of maintenance did not improve, and in January 1869 the issue finally came to a head when the TVR Directors resolved that 'notice be given to the Cowbridge Railway Company that if their line is not placed in good working condition previously to the 1st of March next, this company will feel obliged to withdraw its rolling stock and plant.'

This ultimatum was conveyed to the Cowbridge Railway shareholders at their Half-Yearly Meeting at Cowbridge, on 26th February 1869. Their reaction was one of acceptance of the inevitability of the TVR's withdrawal, coupled with a determination to work the railway themselves, should this prove necessary. Foremost amongst those urging this last course was Daniel Ithiel Edwards, a Cowbridge surgeon, who had been actively involved with the promotion of a railway to Cowbridge since the days of the unsuccessful C&SWJR scheme of 1855. Mr Edwards announced that he had heard a rumour that morning that the TVR intended to continue to work as far as Llantrisant, after it had withdrawn from working the Cowbridge trains. If this was the

An 0-4-2T, No. 1471 is pictured in Cowbridge yard on 13th July 1957. The waste ground to the right of the engine is the site of the second engine shed which was opened in 1886 and demolished in 1927.

H. Davies

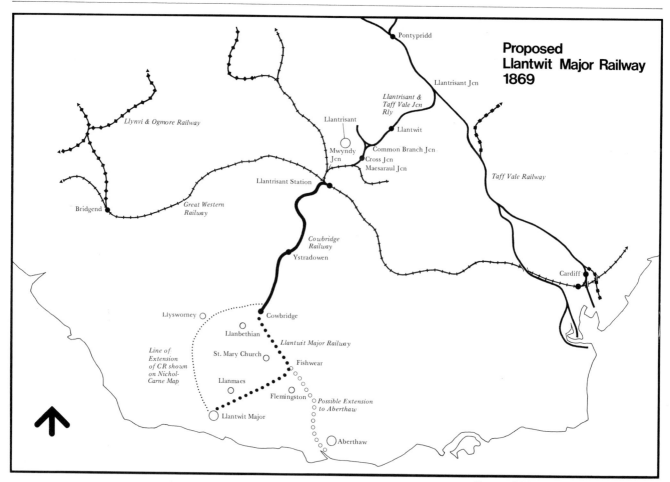

Proposed
Llantwit Major Railway
1869

Proposed Llantwit Major Railway : 1869

case, then he felt that it would not prove too difficult for the Cowbridge Company to work its own traffic between Cowbridge and Llantrisant. Although this suggestion met with unanimous approval from those present, it was decided to make a final attempt to persuade the TVR to withdraw its threat, and a deputation of freighters from the town and neighbourhood was formed to approach the TVR.

The deputation met Mr Done Bushell and George Fisher the following day, and pressed their case to such effect that the TVR representatives agreed to continue to work the line if it was repaired immediately. But the TVR would withdraw as soon as an alternative agreement could be arrived at for working the railway. It was agreed that the TVR would supply ten wagon loads of ballast, if the freighters arranged for men to carry out the repairs to the track. This was done, and the TVR continued to work the line.

Even at this desperate time for the Cowbridge Railway, a move was afoot to promote its extension to the south. On 15th February 1869, Dr Nichol-Carne chaired a meeting at Llantwit Major at which a Provisional Committee was formed to promote a railway from that town to join the Cowbridge Railway. This proposal originated amongst the inhabitants of Llantwit Major, who were anxious to

improve communications between their somewhat isolated community and the outside world.

A further meeting took place at Cowbridge Town Hall, on 2nd March 1869, chaired by R. C. Nichol-Carne. Although he had not been involved in the first meeting, he had agreed to take the chair in response to a request from John Thomas, the Secretary of the Provisional Committee of the Llantwit Major Railway. Nichol-Carne's nephew, Mr Blandy, an engineer by profession, who as Mr Blandy Jenkins was later to become the first Chairman of the Glamorgan County Council, had prepared a plan for the railway. It would extend from the Cowbridge terminus across Eastgate Street, by means of a level crossing, then via a tunnel under the Broadway, before rejoining the valley of the River Thaw just south of the town. Mr Blandy's proposed route then followed the west side of the Thaw through Llandough, before turning off for Llantwit Major at a place called Fishwear, just above Flemingston. Provision was included in the plans for a branch from this line at Fishwear, down the valley of the Thaw to Aberthaw, should this be thought desirable. Blandy estimated that the cost of the Llantwit Major Railway would amount to £30,000, exlcusive of land acquisition, which he hoped would be achieved by landowners along the route contributing land in lieu of cash for shares.

This proposal was welcomed by the limited attendance in the town hall, and a Working Committee was formed to further the scheme and to establish what subscriptions could be obtained towards Parliamentary and other preliminary expenses.

The publicity given to the Llantwit scheme aroused some controversy in the local press over the best destination for an extension of the railway from Cowbridge, be it Llantwit Major or Aberthaw. The former could offer some passenger potential, but limited freight prospects, while the latter, with its harbour and limestone, offered the possibility of maritime and industrial development, but with negligible passenger traffic.

The difficulties being experienced by the Cowbridge Railway did not auger well for the promotion of the Llantwit Major Railway, and as the necessary support was not forthcoming, nothing more was heard of this scheme. Interestingly, one of the correspondents on the subject of the most suitable destination for an extension of the Cowbridge line, speculated that it was more likely that Llantwit Major would eventually be served by a railway from Bridgend to Barry, rather than by an extension from Cowbridge. The following March, Mr Tolme, Engineer to the abortive Barry Railway proposal of 1865, and Mr Price-Williams, later the Engineer of the unsuccessful Ogmore Docks & Railway, failed to persuade the TVR to back their proposal for a line from Bridgend to Barry. In the event, the luckless inhabitants of Llantwit Major had to wait nearly thirty years for their railway, until the opening of the Vale of Glamorgan Railway in 1897. With the demise of the Llantwit Major Railway scheme, and the continuing difficulties of the Cowbridge Railway, any remaining prospect of an extension to the south of Cowbridge faded away.

In an attempt to find an alternative agreement for working the Cowbridge line, Alex Bassett met Messrs A. & J. Brogden of the Llynvi Iron Co. and the Llynvi & Ogmore Railway, in March 1869, to discuss the possibility of the Brogdens working the railway. Although no longer acting as Engineer to the Cowbridge Railway, Bassett nevertheless retained a significant interest in the affairs of the company, as both a shareholder and bondholder. Although terms were put forward by the Brogdens, these did not prove acceptable to the Cowbridge Directors and, as a result, nothing came of this initiative. It is intriguing to speculate whether this interest on the part of the Brogdens was in any way connected with their desire to break out of the encirclement of the L&OR by broad gauge lines. Between 1864 and 1871 a number of grandiose schemes were promoted by the Brogdens, for railways connecting the L&OR to Cardiff and Penarth docks, and other destinations.

September 1869 saw the improvement of the passenger service between Cowbridge and Pontypridd, with the opening of Cross Inn Station, about half-way between Maesaraul Junction and Common Branch Junction. It catered for the town of Llantrisant on the hill about half a mile to the west, and an additional train between Cowbridge and Pontypridd was introduced. This provided a mid-morning train from Cowbridge returning, at noon, from Pontypridd. The Sunday service remained unchanged.

Alex Bassett was involved in another intervention on behalf of the Cowbridge Company in September 1869. Having walked the line, he wrote to George Fisher drawing his attention to what he considered to be the dangerous state of the permanent way. In a somewhat tart reply, Fisher pointed out that maintenance was the responsibility of the Cowbridge Railway, and that the TVR was not in the remotest degree responsible. However, he was prepared to concede some involvement in that the rolling stock used on the line was provided by the TVR, and agreed to place the matter before his Directors. A further letter from Bassett to Fisher brought forth the retort that the Cowbridge Railway was cheaply and indifferently constructed and had not been efficiently maintained.

Having reported the contents of this correspondence to his Directors, George Fisher was instructed to examine the state of the track on the Cowbridge Railway. He concluded that although the permanent way was not dangerous, it would soon become so unless money was spent on its improvement and maintenance.

The Directors of the Cowbridge Railway were saddened later that year by the news of the death of R. C. Nichol-Carne at his home at Nash Manor, outside Cowbridge, on 24th November 1869. His health had been in decline for some time, but the deepening problems of the Cowbridge Railway can have contributed little to his peace of mind.

The state of the Cowbridge Railway did not, however, improve, and in December 1869 Mr Kineath, the station master at Cowbridge, was forced to complain to the TVR Board about the condition of fences along the railway. The TVR Directors ordered a copy of this complaint to be forwarded to Stockwood, accompanied by the intimation that if the fences were not placed in a complete state of repair forthwith, the company would be compelled to withdraw their rolling stock.

This renewed threat finally appears to have convinced the Directors of the Cowbridge Company that they would have to take matters into their own hands. Having decided on their course of action at a meeting at the Cardiff office of Alex Bassett, on 3rd February 1870, a deputation of Directors, together with John Stockwood appeared before the TVR Board on 11th February 1870. They put forward four options for the future of the Cowbridge Railway: they asked if the TVR would be prepared to either purchase, lease or work the line at a fixed percentage of the receipts; if none of these avenues was acceptable to the TVR, the deputation wished to know if the TVR would be prepared to enter into fair arrangements for the working of through traffic, if the Cowbridge Company worked its own railway. This approach was considered the next day by the TVR Directors; they rejected the first three options, but requested further details of the proposal for the Cowbridge Company to work its own traffic.

Having exhausted all other possibilities, the Cowbridge Company went ahead with arrangements for working the railway itself. A Traffic Manager, George Howell, late of the L&OR, was appointed, and on 28th February 1870, John Stockwood informed the TVR of his company's intention to take over the working of their railway, from the morning of Monday, 5th April 1870.

					Sundays	
Cowbridge	dep. 7.33 a.m.	10.37 a.m.	1.33 p.m.	6.00 p.m.	8.29 a.m.	3.39 p.m.
Llantrisant	dep. 7.56 a.m.	11.00 a.m.	1.52 arr.	6.23 p.m.	8.51 a.m.	4.01 p.m.
Pontypridd	arr. 8.32 a.m.	11.36 a.m.		7.00 p.m.	9.27 a.m.	4.37 p.m.
Pontypridd	dep. 8.46 a.m.	12.00 noon		7.36 p.m.	9.48 a.m.	4.58 p.m.
Llantrisant	dep. 9.30 a.m.	12.39 p.m.	2.35 p.m.	8.19 p.m.	10.27 a.m.	5.37 p.m.
Cowbridge	arr. 9.49 a.m.	12.58 p.m.	3.00 p.m.	8.38 p.m.	10.46 a.m.	5.56 p.m.

Although the TVR accepted this general arrangement, dispute arose over who was to be responsible for working the traffic between Maesaraul Junction and Llantrisant Station, and for the payment to the GWR of the annual rent of £200 for the use of this section. The TVR had originally considered terminating its passenger trains at Maesaraul, but had rejected this idea, partly because it did not own land or have powers for siting a station at the junction. After much argument the TVR agreed, in December 1870, to pay the rent for the use of this section. However, a further dispute arose between the two companies in 1871, concerning the question of the apportionment of station expenses at Llantrisant Station. The Cowbridge Company argued that a proportion of these expenses were attributable to the TVR, for the use of the station by its trains from Pontypridd. This dispute was eventually resolved when the TVR agreed to pay £70 per annum to the Cowbridge Company for the use of its facilities at Llantrisant Station.

On taking over the working of its railway, the Cowbridge Company inaugurated what, by previous standards, can only be described as an intensive shuttle service between Cowbridge and Llantrisant stations, with seven return workings on weekdays and no less than four round trips on Sundays.

								Sundays		*Sundays*		
Cowbridge	dep. 7.20	8.30	11.15	1.15	4.25	5.55	7.30	8.20	10.00	2.25	5.40
Llantrisant	arr. 7.45	8.50	11.40	1.40	4.50	6.18	8.00	8.40	10.25	2.50	6.05
Llantrisant	dep. 7.55	9.30	12.36	2.20	5.22	6.40	8.20	8.50	11.15	3.30	6.20
Cowbridge	arr. 8.25	10.00	1.00	2.45	5.47	7.10	8.45	9.15	11.40	3.40	6.45

The traffic potential of the Cowbridge Railway did not justify this level of service, however, and the number of round trips was gradually reduced to five each day, with the Sunday service being withdrawn completely from 1871. The TVR continued to work its service of only three trains each way between Pontypridd and Llantrisant, where connections were made with certain Cowbridge trains.

An additional passenger facility was provided in August 1871, when Llanharry Platform opened. This was of a very modest nature, without any form of shelter and was situated just south of the Llanharry Road bridge, about ¾ of a mile to the east of the village it was intended to serve.

After years of criticism, the GWR finally decided to abandon the broad gauge in South Wales, and in April and

Llanharry Station on 15th July 1960. The engine and brake van have just arrived from Cowbridge. Whilst engine No. 9780 makes its way into the iron-ore mine sidings, the brake van rolls gently forward to a point just beyond the siding connection. It will then be at the front of the train when it is propelled to Llantrisant.

H. C. Casserley

May 1872, the South Wales main line between Gloucester and Milford Haven was converted to narrow gauge. The last broad gauge train worked through from Milford Haven on Saturday, 11th May 1872. The end of the broad gauge removed the need for the transhipment of goods between the GWR and the CR at Llantrisant, and the former transhipment siding was connected to the 'down' sidings of the GWR, to enable the direct exchange of traffic between the two railways. A further improvement came in 1874, when the GWR doubled the Ely Valley line between Llantrisant Station and Mwyndy Junction.

In addition to providing its own rolling stock, the Cowbridge Company now had to employ a full complement of staff to work its railway. An income tax return, for May 1872, gives the following details of the staff and their remuneration:

George Howell of Llantrisant	Manager	£200 0s 0d per annum
Henry Williams of Cowbridge	Driver	£93 13s 0d per annum
William Thomas of Brynsadler	Station Master	£62 8s 0d per annum
Benjamin Gronwr of Cowbridge	Fireman	£59 10s 4d per annum
Aaron England of Cowbridge	Station Master	£57 4s 0d per annum
H. Besant of Brynsadler	Ganger	£57 4s 0d per annum
Richard Hughes of Aberthin	Porter	£46 9s 6d per annum
Ivor Arnott of Cowbridge	Porter	£44 4s 0d per annum
E. Howell of Penylan	Platelayer	£41 14s 8d per annum
E. Breast of Penylan	Platelayer	£41 14s 8d per annum
E. John of Penylan	Platelayer	£41 14s 8d per annum
Thomas Thomas of Penylan	Platelayer	£41 14s 8d per annum
Phillip Griffiths of Cowbridge	Guard	£52 0s 0d per annum
Mr Lacke of Llantrisant	Porter	£41 12s 0d per annum
W. Miford of Ystradowen	Porter	£33 16s 0d per annum
B. Howell of Llantrisant	Clerk	£31 4s 0d per annum
Joseph Rufus of Cowbridge	Cleaner	£28 12s 0d per annum

However, the takeover of the working of the railway did not prove to be the panacea the Cowbridge Directors had hoped for. The revenue attracted to the line remained insufficient to enable the standard of maintenance to be improved, or to pay off the debts which had been incurred in building the railway. As well as the contractors and suppliers, most of the landowners along the route had not received payment from the company. Out of a total of twenty three landowners, only three had received any cash. This unsatisfactory situation came to a head in January 1874, when a number of aggrieved landowners successfully sued the company for non-payment for land acquired for the railway. As the landowners concerned threatened to repossess their land, which now formed part of the route of the line, the very survival of the Cowbridge Railway was at risk.

This action provides the background to a fresh approach which the Cowbridge Directors made to the TVR in March 1875. With its railway threatened with breakup by the actions of certain landowners, and with its debts weighing increasingly heavily on its finances, the Cowbridge Company was anxious to come to an agreement with the TVR for the leasing of its railway. The terms put forward by the Cowbridge Directors involved the leasing in perpetuity of the Cowbridge Railway to the TVR, at a rent of £3,000 per annum for the first five years, this would then increase by £100 per annum to a maximum of £4,000 per annum in the fifteenth year. The TVR responded by offering to take a lease of the railway, but at half the initial and ultimate sums put forward by the Cowbridge Directors. A request that they reconsider this offer was rejected by the TVR, leaving the Cowbridge Company with no alternative but to accept the TVR's terms. This had to be, as the sale of the part of its railway involved in the suit of Lord Dynevor, was threatened for 25th August 1875. After this, it was expected that other landowners would take similar action.

The Cowbridge Directors finally and reluctantly agreed to recommend the TVR's terms to their shareholders in April 1875. This recommendation was accepted by an Extraordinary General Meeting of the shareholders at the Cowbridge Town Hall, on 4th May 1875. Their terms having been accepted by the Cowbridge Company, the TVR offered to work the railway at cost price from 1st July 1875.

The draft Heads of Agreement, for the lease of the Cowbridge Railway and its working by the TVR, were approved by a special meeting of the TVR shareholders on 24th August 1875. In addition to this agreement, a scheme of arrangement was agreed for satisfying the claims of the various landowners, contractors, suppliers and other creditors. This scheme involved the creation of new Cowbridge Railway Company Debenture Stock, in three categories: 'A', 'B' and 'C', for transfer to the creditors concerned.

After years of poor maintenance, the Cowbridge Railway was in a very sorry state when the TVR took over its working. So much so, that the passenger service between Cowbridge and Llantrisant was withdrawn on 30th November 1875, so that the railway could be put in good order. It had been intended to close the railway entirely during this period, but in the event an 'up' and 'down' goods train ran over the railway each day. Passengers between Cowbridge and Llantrisant were catered for by an omnibus service, provided by Mr Thomas, the proprietor of the Bear Hotel in Cowbridge. However, a special passenger train did run on the occasion of the Cowbridge Fatstock Show, on 7th December 1875. The railway was reopened to passenger traffic on Monday, 13th December 1875. The Cowbridge Railway was leased to the TVR from 1st January 1876.

TVR 2-4-0, No. 22 was one of the engines which gravitated to branch line work, on the introduction of more modern 2-4-0 engines between 1875 and 1878. As such, it may have appeared on the Cowbridge Railway between 1875 and its withdrawal in 1886.

C. Chapman

Chapter Four
A Lease in Perpetuity: 1876-1889

After the years of poverty and uncertainty, the leasing of the Cowbridge Railway by the TVR brought with it the prospect of a safe and secure future for the railway to Cowbridge. From 1876, the line was effectively an outpost, albeit a remote one, of the TVR system, and its continued existence as an independent company came to have only a nominal signficance. Its Board meetings ceased to have anything other than token importance, with the preparation of separate accounts for the Cowbridge Railway being discontinued in 1881. Although part of a larger and more complex system, this rural backwater was a world away from the vast and increasing cavalcade of coal from the valleys to the docks, which was the life-blood of the TVR.

The takeover of the working of the line by the TVR allowed the restoration of through trains between Cowbridge and Pontypridd. However, as this involved a reduction in the number of trains between Cowbridge and Llantrisant, from five to three each way, this change did not prove entirely popular with the residents of Cowbridge, and in February 1876, a petition or 'memorial' from the inhabitants of the town was placed before the TVR Directors, with a request for additional trains on their line. In contrast to later occasions, the TVR responded positively to this request, and added two 'up' and three 'down' trains between Cowbridge and Llantrisant. This made use of an additional set of carriages, and spare engine time. Thus the September 1876 service comprised a total of five departures from Cowbridge, and six arrivals.

Cowbridge	dep. 7.30 a.m.	10.15 a.m.	1.35 p.m.	5.00 p.m.	7.15 p.m.	
Llantrisant	arr. 7.50	10.35	2.00	5.20	7.35	
Llantrisant	dep. 8.00	10.45		6.20		
Pontypridd	arr. 8.32	11.21		6.57		
Pontypridd	dep. 8.44 a.m.	11.42 a.m.				7.34 p.m.
Llantrisant	arr. 9.15	12.16 p.m.				8.11
Llantrisant	dep. 9.25	12.23	2.30	6.25	7.40	8.15
Cowbridge	arr. 9.46	12.45	2.55	6.47	8.02	8.38

'Metro' class 2-4-0T, No. 3586 waits at Cowbridge in 1949. This locomotive was built in June 1899 and was auto-fitted in 1934. It was withdrawn in November 1949.

C. Chapman

A further improvement came in June 1876, when agreement was reached between the Post Office and the TVR for the working of the night mail from Cowbridge, a source of much complaint up until then. Under this new arrangement, the mail was taken by the 7.15 p.m. 'up' train from Cowbridge, for transfer to the GWR at Llantrisant Station.

A welcome addition to freight traffic came later in 1876, with the opening of a siding to serve the Trecastle Iron Ore Mine, near Llanharry. The siding left the Cowbridge line about 400 yards from Llantrisant Station, by a facing connection fully signalled and controlled by a four lever ground frame. It then ran for about ½ a mile, roughly parallel to the Cowbridge line, to serve the iron ore mine which was situated at Ty-du, about a ¼ of a mile to the north-east of Llanharry Platform. The mine was the property of the Mwyndy Iron Ore Company, and started production in 1878. Although the Mwyndy Company went into liquidation in 1884, mining continued at Trecastle, and in November 1888 the mine was transferred to the newly-formed Trecastle Iron Ore Company Limited. However, in spite of this development, the mine closed in 1891 as a result of competition from Spanish ore.

The passenger service was again revised in October 1878, when an additional round trip was introduced between Cowbridge and Pontypridd, replacing one of the short workings between Cowbridge and Llantrisant. At the same time, the 7.15 p.m. train from Cowbridge to Llantrisant was withdrawn, although the evening mail continued to be worked independently to Llantrisant at its usual time.

Cowbridge	dep. 7.30 a.m.	10.10 a.m.	1.55 p.m.	5.00 p.m.	6.00 p.m.	
Llantrisant	arr. 7.47	10.27	2.20	5.20	6.20	
Llantrisant	dep. 7.52	10.32	3.40		6.32	
Pontypridd	arr. 8.23	11.03	4.11		7.10	
Pontypridd	dep. 8.38 a.m.	11.16 a.m.		4.25 p.m.		7.34 p.m.
Llantrisant	arr. 9.10	11.48		5.02		8.11
Llantrisant	dep. 9.14	11.54	4.10 p.m.	5.25	6.50 p.m.	8.15
Cowbridge	arr. 9.35	12.15	4.40	5.46	7.12	8.38

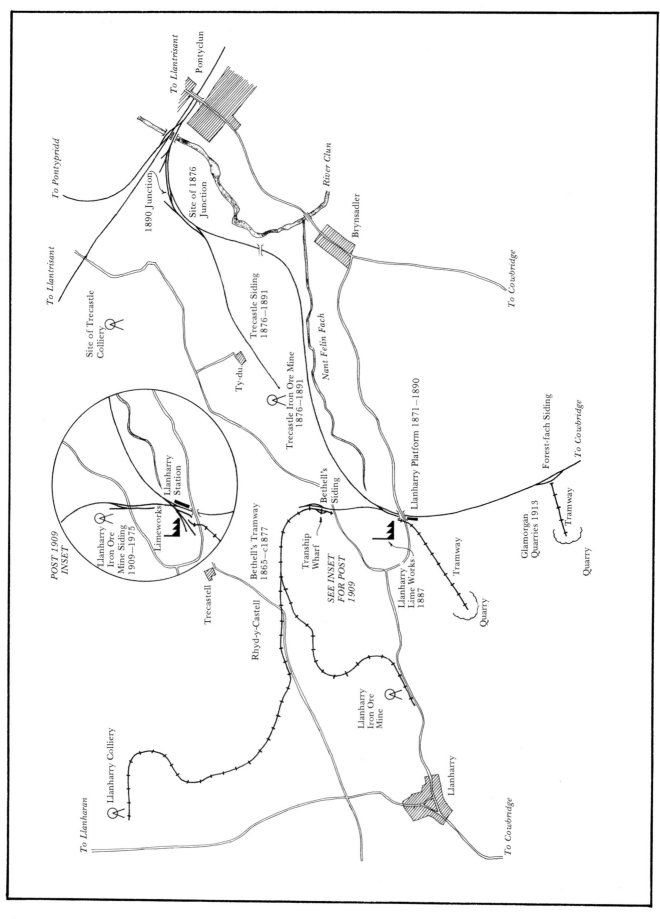

Private sidings, tramways and industries of the Llanharry area : 1865–1922

Map labels:

To Llantrisant
Pontyclun
To Pontypridd
To Llantrisant
1890 Junction
Site of 1876 Junction
River Clun
Brynsadler
To Cowbridge
Site of Trecastle Colliery
Trecastle Siding 1876–1891
Ty-du..
Trecastle Iron Ore Mine 1876–1891
Nant Felin Fach
Llanharry Platform 1871–1890
Forest-fach Siding
To Cowbridge
POST 1909 INSET
Llanharry Station
Llanharry Iron Ore Mine Siding 1909–c1975
Limeworks
Glamorgan Quarries 1913
Tramway
Quarry
Trecastell
Bethell's Tramway 1865–c1877
Bethell's Siding
Tranship Wharf
SEE INSET FOR POST 1909
Llanharry Lime Works 1887
Tramway
Quarry
Rhyd-y-Castell
Llanharry Colliery
Llanharry Iron Ore Mine
Llanharry
To Llanharan
To Cowbridge
To Cowbridge

This revised pattern of working formed the basis of the timetable, with certain modifications and additions, until introduction of steam railcars in 1905.

The first in a sequence of unrelated accidents involving Cowbridge trains took place at Pontypridd, on 19th October 1878. In September 1875 the TVR had introduced a new procedure for reversing Llantrisant branch trains after their arrival at Pontypridd, in order to ease the chronic congestion which was already being experienced at that station. From that date, the Llantrisant branch train, having unloaded at the 'up' platform at Pontypridd, continued up the Merthyr line to a point above the Northern Junction. The train was then reversed, wrong line, over the North Curve, (forming the third side of the triangular junction, between the Merthyr line and the Rhondda branch above Pontypridd), to Rhondda Cutting Junction, where it then ran forward on the 'down' Rhondda line, into the 'down' platform at Pontypridd, ready to depart for Cowbridge.

On the day of the accident, the third 'up' Cowbridge passenger train had arrived at Pontypridd at 4.11 p.m., and had proceeded to Northern Junction in the usual manner. However, thanks to an error on the part of the signalman at Northern Junction cabin, the train was reversed over the North Curve, straight into the path of a 'down' Rhondda branch passenger train. Whilst the guard of the Cowbridge train had a miraculous escape, casualties on the Rhondda train were severe, with twelve passengers killed and one hundred and three injured. Although the direct cause of the accident was attributed to the error of the signalman at Northern Junction, who had thought that the line was clear for the Cowbridge train, the TVR was criticized for the practice of working the empty stock of the Cowbridge trains, wrong line, over the North Curve.

As a result of this accident, and the recommendation of the Board of Trade Inspector, crossovers were installed at each end of the North Curve, so that reversing Cowbridge trains could run 'right line' from Northern Junction to Rhondda Cutting Junction. In later years, following track alterations at Northern Junction, the procedure was reversed so that Cowbridge line trains, having deposited their passengers at Pontypridd, continued up the Rhondda branch to a point just beyond Rhondda Cutting Junction, then reversed over the North Curve to Northern Junction before running forward on the 'down' Merthyr line into Pontypridd Station.

In addition, in the aftermath of this disaster, George Fisher was able to press for the installation of improved signalling and proper interlocking throughout those parts of the TVR which had not then been so equipped. In his report of 31st October 1878, he made particular reference to the need to carry out this work on the Cowbridge Railway, in view of its single track nature, at an estimated cost of £1,000. At that date, Cowbridge, Ystradowen and Llanharry were still signalled on the outdated station signalling principle; signalling also protected the junction at Llantrisant Station. It seems likely that the original Cowbridge signal cabin dated from the time of the signalling improvements, carried out as a result of Fisher's recommendation in 1878. It was a single storey timber structure, situated at the station 'throat' and survived after its demise as a signal cabin in the form of a permanent way hut, until the final closure of the line.

On 16th August 1879, the 4.10 p.m. 'down' mixed passenger and goods train from Llantrisant to Cowbridge was derailed at the junction of the Trecastle siding, just outside Llantrisant Station. The train, consisting of two carriages, seven goods wagons and a mineral brake van was travelling at about 12 m.p.h. when the engine left the tracks

TVR 'Standard Goods' 0-6-0, No. 262 was built in 1861 as No. 11, transferred to surplus stock and renumbered in 1881. It was one of 44 such engines built by the TVR between 1859 and 1872. Engines of this type handled goods traffic on the Cowbridge Railway until the arrival of the mixed traffic 0-6-2T engines in the early 1890s.

Locomotive Publishing Co.

and dropped down the embankment into the 'V' between the main line and Trecastle siding. Its tender was also derailed, and was spread across the tracks, whilst the first carriage fell on to its side. The second carriage and an empty goods wagon were also derailed. Of the twelve passengers on the train, seven were injured, although none seriously. The Board of Trade investigation suggested that the points to Trecastle siding, which were not equipped with a facing point lock, had not been properly closed, after an earlier shunting operation at the siding and this had led to the derailment. The Board of Trade recommended that a facing point lock to the points be installed immediately.

Christmas Eve 1880 brought yet another accident to a Cowbridge train, albeit of a relatively minor nature. The 7.30a.m. 'up' passenger train from Cowbridge overshot the platform at Llantrisant Station, and collided with the wall at the end of the line. Damage was slight and the accident was attributed to an error on the part of the driver, Mr Henry Heke, who was a very careful, steady and efficient driver, and who, until this one incident, had an unblemished record for his 26 years driving. However, in spite of this unfortuate abberation, Heke remained with the company until his retirement in 1902, when he was granted a gratuity of £40 in acknowledgement of his long service.

The last in this chapter of accidents occured on 18th February 1881 when, during a severe blizzard, a young doctor of Cowbridge, named Stanistreet, was killed by a passenger train near Llanharry Platform. Stanistreet had attended an inquest at Llanharry, and on mistakenly being informed that the train had left, he had decided to walk along the track to his Llantrisant surgery. In the fury of the storm, he did not hear the approach of the train, and was run down and killed.

In June 1880, in a relatively rare act of generosity towards the town of Cowbridge, the TVR agreed to donate £5 towards the cost of enlarging Cowbridge Sunday School.

An improvement to the passenger accommodation at Cowbridge Station was initiated in September 1881, when the TVR decided to erect a train shed, covering most of the station platform, at an estimated cost of £250. This had a corrugated iron roof, supported on iron columns. However, as no roof lights were fitted, and the west wall was sheeted in, the interior could be very dismal in the afternoons and evenings. The provision of the train shed appears to have been motivated as much by a desire to provide additional covered accommodation for the branch carriages, as by any concern for the welfare of intending passengers.

A further improvement to the facilities at Cowbridge was set in motion in March 1886, when the attention of the TVR Directors was drawn to the inadequate and awkward layout at Cowbridge. This layout, designed by Alex Bassett over twenty years earlier, had become an increasing handicap with the growth of traffic on the line. The limited siding space meant that additional train mileage was often required, and that delay to consignments was difficult to avoid. The position of the engine turntable, at the entrance to the goods sidings, was a particular problem. Shunting operations, of necessity, involved crossing and recrossing this turntable, with the result that a great amount of wear and tear to the turntable was unavoidable. In addition, when shunting was in progress, access to the engine shed was not possible, and if the turntable was out of action for any reason, then the locomotive depot and most of the goods station would also be immobilized.

These problems were highlighted in a report by the TVR Traffic Manager, Mr Hurman, in April 1886. He noted the considerable difficulty consequent upon the peculiar formation of the sidings and the fact that the turntable was in a very dilapidated condition. However, if the engine shed was to be retained, an improved layout and extended sidings would require the acquisition of additional land. This was prevented by the unwillingness of the adjoining landowner to sell. Fortunately, there was a narrow strip of land to the east of the running line, which could be used to provide a new engine shed and its associated facilities. This proposal was accepted, and the work was ordered to be carried out at an estimated cost of £800.

The new layout did away with the turntable, and allowed the extension of the goods sidings, which considerably

On 13th July 1957, ex-GWR 0-4-2T, No. 1471 edges its way out of the former passenger station at Cowbridge. The rather dismal interior of the former train shed is apparent in this view.
C. Chapman

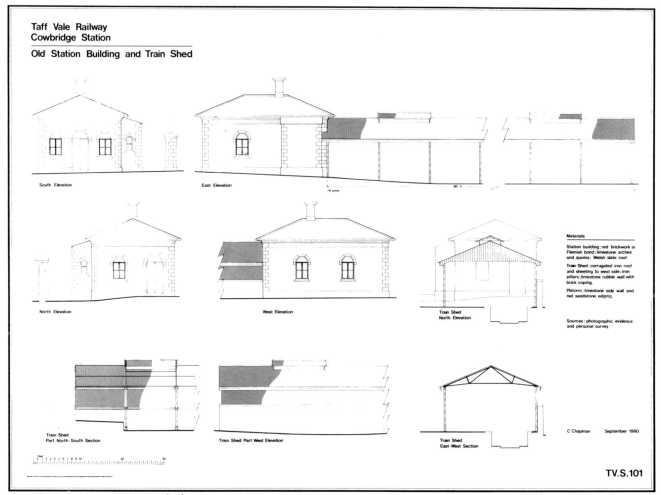

Cowbridge old station building and train shed

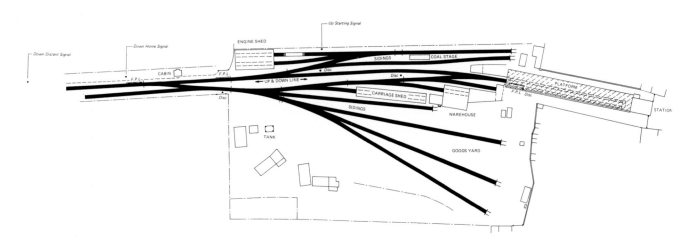

TVR plan of Cowbridge Station : 1886

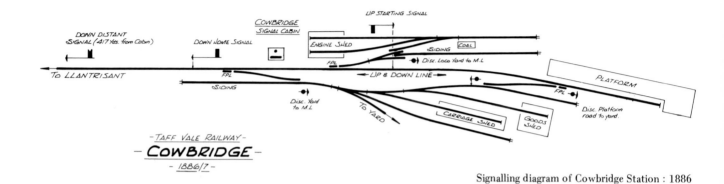

-TAFF VALE RAILWAY-
- COWBRIDGE -
- 1886/7 -

Signalling diagram of Cowbridge Station : 1886

eased the working of goods traffic. It also provided a far more efficient arrangement for the locomotive department, which considerably simplified the working of the station. The alterations were completed in time for inspection and approval by Colonel Rich of the Board of Trade, on 4th March 1887.

The TVR was involved in an incident which caused some interest in Cowbridge in September 1886. It objected to the transfer of the licence of the 'Ancient Druid' public house, to new and more commodious premises adjoining the entrance to the goods station, on the grounds that this would be against its interests, and would provide a temptation for its employees at the station. However, the Cowbridge Bench were not receptive to this argument, and overruled the TVR's objection, a decision which was met with applause from members of the public who were present! The new 'Ancient Druid' was a three storey brick building, which, together with the nearby Commercial Hotel, which opened on 26th July 1867, provided accommodation for commercial travellers and others arriving in the town by train.

The early 1880s was a period of relative stability, as far as traffic on the line was concerned. Although the numbers of passengers and tonnage of goods fluctuated over the years, no obvious trends were apparent. The number of passengers handled at Cowbridge was relatively modest, with a daily average of about 100, evenly divided between arrivals and departures. However, this average does not give a true picture of the daily passenger business at Cowbridge, as a considerable proportion of the passengers were accounted for by people travelling to and from Cowbridge Market on Tuesdays, and Pontypridd Market on Wednesdays. Allowing for this factor, the passenger traffic on the remaining days must have been very limited.

Passengers dealt with at Cowbridge Station
1880–1885

1880	32,644½
1881	33,673½
1882	27,594
1883	29,544
1884	34,618
1885	36,876

To handle this traffic, the passenger staff at Cowbridge, at this time, consisted of the station master, Oscar Hurford, who was later to be station master at Pontypridd, two clerks and three porters.

Passenger totals have survived for the stations on the Cowbridge line for the first six months of 1886, which show the limited passenger traffic of the intermediate stations at this period:

Llantrisant TVR	22,979
Llanharry Platform	410
Ystradowen	3,151
Cowbridge	14,554

The pattern of passenger train working had, by 1883, settled down to four round trips between Cowbridge and Pontypridd, with an additional short working between Cowbridge and Llantrisant in the early evening. Two sets of carriages were used, one covering the four through trains and the other the short working. The 8.30 a.m. train from Pontypridd, which arrived at Cowbridge at 9.26 a.m., and the 5.00 p.m. departure from Cowbridge, enabled pupils from the north of the town to travel by rail to Cowbridge Grammar School. A report to the Charity Commissioners in May 1887, noted that at that date, two or three boys came to school from Llantrisant by train. This traffic grew considerably over the years, although it was not until the service was reorganized in the early 1920s that the 'train boys', and, by then, girls as well, ceased to have to suffer a late arrival at school.

Cowbridge Station acted as a railhead for a large part of the Vale of Glamorgan, in particular the relatively isolated area to the south of the town. A long standing feature of the transport arrangements of the area was the conveyance which ran between Cowbridge Station and Llantwit Major in connection with certain trains. This service appears to have operated from the earliest days of the railway, as indicated by a report of a fatal accident to a pedestrian in May 1867 involving the Llantwit Major bus from Cowbridge Station. For many years this service was provided by Mr Christopher Punter of Cowbridge, although other operators also appeared at various times.

TVR coach No. 038 was a rather odd beast, having one second class compartment, one first class compartment and a luggage compartment. This illustrates the general style of TVR carriages which were built in the 1870s and used on the Cowbridge branch for many years.

C. H. W. Clifford (Courtesy of C. C. Green)

TVR Class J 0-4-4T, No. 4 was the first of the type to be produced, being converted from an 0-6-0 tender engine in 1876. She was painted in the old red-brown livery which the TVR retained for its passenger engines until the late 1890s. It would have been seen on the Cowbridge Railway in this style throughout the 1880s.

M. E. M. Lloyd

The former passenger station and the goods shed at Cowbridge, on 1st August 1958. The goods shed was originally served by a short siding which ran into the shed, the entrance having a sliding wooden door. This door was replaced by corrugated iron sheeting. The goods office, in front of the shed, was a red brick building and was erected by the TVR.

M. Hale

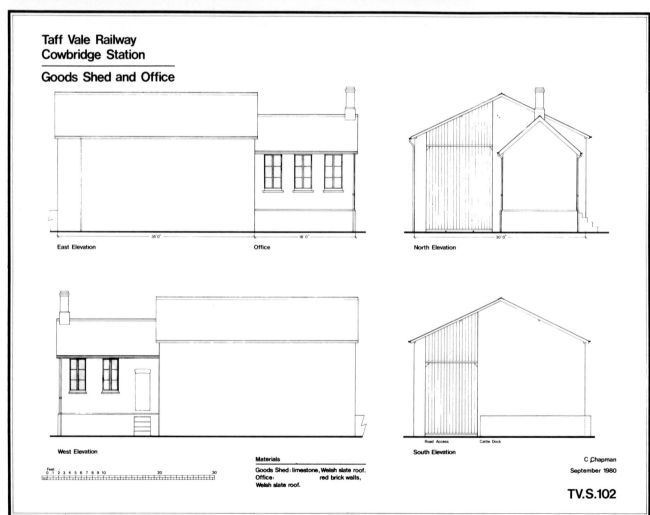

**Taff Vale Railway
Cowbridge Station**

Goods Shed and Office

East Elevation   35'0"   Office   18'0"

North Elevation   30'0"

West Elevation

Feet: 0.1 2 3 4 5 6 7 8 9 10   20   30

Materials
Goods Shed: limestone, Welsh slate roof.
Office: red brick walls, Welsh slate roof.

Road Access   Cattle Dock
South Elevation

C Chapman

September 1980

TV.S.102

Cowbridge goods shed

An interesting feature of train working over the branch at this time was the many excursions which ran to Cowbridge, on the occasion of the Cowbridge Races, which took place in March or April. These trains originated from places throughout South Wales, but one of particular note was the one which ran regularly from Cardiff to Cowbridge. This train, composed of GWR carriages, ran through from Cardiff to Cowbridge at 10.20 a.m., arriving at Cowbridge at 11.15 a.m. and returning to Cardiff after the races at 6.30 p.m. Horse-boxes were also conveyed by this train. In addition to these excursions, the TVR also issued reduced rate tickets to Cowbridge, for the races, from stations throughout its system.

Goods traffic at Cowbridge, during this period, was much as might be expected for a small market town, with agricultural produce and livestock forming the main outward flows. Agricultural and domestic supplies formed the bulk of incoming freight. Although the pattern of goods train working varied over the years, it always required at least two round trips per day, between Cowbridge and Maesaraul Junction. The working timetable for 1887 provides an illustration of goods train workings over the Cowbridge line, with three 'down' and two 'up' goods trains each day, the imbalance being corrected by the engine off the last 'down' goods returning to Llantrisant with the 7.15 p.m. 'up' mail.

During the period the railway was leased to the TVR, freight traffic was bolstered by the opening of a number of private sidings. The Trecastle Iron Ore Mine had provided useful traffic and, in the 1880s, was despatching nearly 300 tons of ore per week. In April 1887, a Private Siding Agreement was signed for a siding to serve the tinplate works at Llantrisant. The Llantrissant Tinplate Works had opened in 1872, and occupied a triangle of land between the GWR main line and the Cowbridge Railway. Following its lease of the Cowbridge Railway in 1876, the TVR became aware that a strip of land between the tin works and the GWR had been acquired by the Cowbridge Company, but that rights of ownership had never been exercised. The TVR threatened to take possession of this strip and fence it off, an action which, as it would have blocked access to the works, would have endangered its survival. However, the TVR did not carry out this threat and in May 1880, the tin company suggested that the disputed strip of land should be exchanged for a triangular piece of land in the 'V' between the GWR main line and the Cowbridge branch. The TVR eventually agreed to this proposition, and the exchange took place in 1882.

The tin company went bankrupt in 1880, and became the Ely Tinplate Works in 1885. Although a siding had been provided from the GWR at the time of the opening of the works, a connection to the TVR was not made until 1887.

Lime wagon No. 33 was one of five 10 ton covered lime wagons which were built for the Llanharry Lime, Stone & Gravel Company in 1905 by R. Y. Pickering & Co., and numbered 33 to 37. The wagons were painted light cream, with black lettering shaded in vermilion.
R. Y. Pickering & Company, Wishaw Collection (Courtesy of the Historical Model Railway Society)

Five 10 ton open lime wagons were also built for the Llanharry Lime, Stone & Gravel Company in 1905 by R. Y. Pickering & Co. These were numbered 28 to 32.

R. Y. Pickering & Company, Wishaw Collection (Courtesy of the Historical Model Railway Society)

The siding left the machine siding, and made use of the piece of land exchanged in 1882. A bridge carrying the access road to the tin works was constructed across the Ely around 1875; half the bridge was owned by the Cowbridge Railway, and half by the tin company. In addition to providing road access to the tin works, this bridge also served that part of the mileage siding, which was to the west of the River Ely.

Further down the line at Llanharry, a new siding was agreed, in February 1887, to serve the Llanharry Limeworks, which was constructed on a piece of land adjoining the old siding which had connected Bethell's branch to the Cowbridge line.

The service of four trains each way between Cowbridge and Pontypridd was not exactly intensive, and in 1887 a committee, representing the residents of Llantwit Fardre, Llantrisant and Cowbridge, was formed to press for an improvement. A deputation of this committee attended the TVR Board on 24th March 1887, and asked the TVR to provide additional trains between Cowbridge and Pontypridd, and to open a new station to serve Church Village, near Llantwit Fardre.

Reporting on this request to his Board on 13th April 1887, Mr Hurman stated that he considered the passenger traffic on the line was not sufficient to justify the running of additional trains, besides which, the operational difficulties involved in working such trains over the long single line sections would make it most detrimental to the traffic and a consequent loss to the company, it being with the greatest difficulty that the service could be worked. Long stopping times were necessary for goods and mineral trains,

in order to avoid the danger of 'wild runs' on the severe gradients. An additional train at midday would have disorganized the pattern of working considerably. With regard to the request for a new station at Church Village, Hurman was more encouraging, and recommended that one be provided, a conclusion which was accepted by the Directors. Church Village Station opened, to passengers only, on 1st October 1887.

Another plea for an additional station was placed before the TVR Directors in October 1887, when Mr Hurman reported a request from the Reverend Hill for a new station at Maendy Bridge. It would serve the villages of Prisk, Welsh St. Donats, Trerhyngyll and Maendy. However, Hurman did not feel that an additional station so close to Ystradowen would materially benefit the public, or bring additional traffic to the railway.

Although the old layout at Cowbridge Station had been superseded, another legacy of Alex Bassett's ideas of station design persisted at Llantrisant. Despite the constraints which it imposed on train working, the TVR did nothing to improve matters until forced to do so by an initiative on the part of the GWR.

The GWR station had grown piecemeal from the small wayside station which had opened in 1850, and by 1887 it had become adequate for the needs of the traffic. In May 1887, Mr Hurman drew the attention of his Directors to a letter from Mr Grierson of the GWR, containing proposals for the reconstruction of Llantrisant Station. The alterations proposed by the GWR would also require the TVR to modify its layout and facilities at a cost of £2,700. The GWR also demanded to take over the station work for

The branch auto-train storms up the bank from Cowbridge Junction, towards the passenger station, in 1949.

H. T. Hobbs

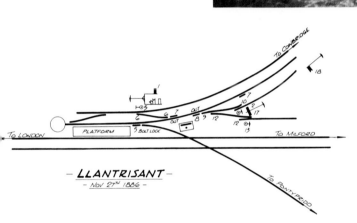

– LLANTRISANT –
– Nov 27th 1886 –

Nº	RELEASED BY	LOCKS	Nº	RELEASED BY	LOCKS
1	5 8	6	10	11	
2	8		11		
3			12	9	10
4			13	5 7 12	
5			14		
6		17	15	5 7 10	
7		6	16		
8		9	17	5 7	9
9		8 17	18	17	

Signalling diagram of Llantrisant Station : 1886

– TRECASTLE –
– Nov 27th 1886 –

Nº	RELEASED BY	LOCKS
1	2	
2		3,4
3		2,5
4	3	2,5
5		3,4
6	5	

– LLANHARRY –
– Nov 27th 1886 –

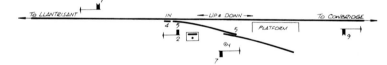

Nº	RELEASED BY	LOCKS	Nº	RELEASED BY	LOCKS
1	2		6		
2		4,5	7		4,5
3			8		
4		2,7	9	7	
5		2,7			

Signalling diagram of Llanharry and Trecastle sidings : 1886

– YSTRADOWEN –
– Nov 27th 1886 –

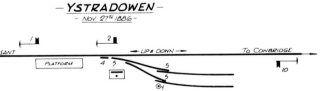

Nº	RELEASED BY	LOCKS	Nº	RELEASED BY	LOCKS
1	2		6		
2	4	5 9	7		
3			8		
4		5	9		2,5
5		2,4,9	10	9	

Signalling diagram of Ystradowen Station : 1886

– COWBRIDGE –
– Nov 27th 1886 –

Nº	RELEASED BY	LOCKS	Nº	RELEASED BY	LOCKS
1		2,3,4,5,7,8	7	8	1,9
2		1,9	8		1,9
3	2	1,9	9		2,3,4,5,7,8
4	5	1,9	10	9	
5		1,9			
6					

Signalling diagram of Cowbridge Station : 1886

the TVR. However, as the TVR would still have had to retain a goods agent and porter for its traffic, it would only have been able to dispense with the services of one booking clerk.

The TVR responded to this move of the GWR by preparing plans for a direct railway between the Cowbridge branch and Maesaraul Junction. Although the general intention of this proposal echoed that of the abandoned Railway No. 2, which had been authorized under the Cowbridge Railway's Act of 1862, it would have followed an entirely different route between the Cowbridge line and Maesaraul Junction. The connection with the Cowbridge line would have been just to the west of Llantrisant Station, from where it would have climbed to cross the GWR main line, to the east of the turnpike bridge. It would then have followed a more circuitous route than the old Railway No. 2., to the south of Cefn yr Hendy to join the L&TVJR just north of Maesaraul Junction.

Further discussions with the GWR did not prove satisfactory to the TVR, and in November 1887 plans were deposited, as part of the TVR's Additional Powers Bill, for the direct line from the Cowbridge Railway to Maesaraul Junction. In addition to seeking powers for the construction of this line, known as Railway No. 1 in the Additional Powers Bill, the TVR also sought powers to permit the amendment or cancellation of the agreement between the Cowbridge Railway and the GWR of 9th January 1864, with respect to any alterations required for the construction of Railway No. 1.

The Additional Powers Bill was withdrawn after its first reading, however, on agreement being reached between the TVR and the GWR on a wide range of contentious issues, including the apportionment of the costs which would be incurred in the rebuilding of Llantrisant Station. This agreement, dated 14th March 1888, provided for the improvement of the facilities at Llantrisant Station for the benefit of the traffic of both companies; the TVR would pay 7 per cent per annum on a sum of £900 out of the total expended by the GWR on the improvements at the station. On completion of these works, the TVR would continue to use the station under the terms of the 1864 Agreement. The rebuilding of Llantrisant Station was completed during 1890.

The opening of a new cattle market at Cowbridge, on 5th February 1889, brought with it the prospect of increased livestock traffic for Cowbridge Station. Special arrangements were made with the TVR, for the conveyance of cattle from Cowbridge to Pontypridd early in the afternoon on market and fair days.

Over the years, the TVR had accumulated, on lease, a number of subsidiary railway companies, including the Cowbridge Railway and the Llantrissant & Taff Vale Junction Railway. It was in order to rationalize this situation and to reorganize its capital structure that the TVR promoted its Amalgamations and Capital Bill of 1889. This Bill sought powers (inter alia) for the amalgamation of the Cowbridge Railway Company with the TVR, a proposal which was agreed by the Cowbridge Board, on 9th

Llantrisant Station, looking towards Bridgend, circa 1905. The TVR goods shed can be seen on the left, with an 0-6-2T locomotive shunting in the yard. The close relationship between the GWR and TVR signal cabins can clearly be seen.

Lens of Sutton

February 1889. The Amalgamations and Capital Act received Royal Assent on 26th August 1889. In addition to the powers it contained for the amalgamation of the Cowbridge Railway with the TVR, the Act also authorized the creation of new TVR stocks, in exchange for Cowbridge Railway Company Stocks as set out in the following schedule:

Description of Cowbridge Railway Capital	Amount issued	TVR Stocks to be created in exchange for Cowbridge Railway Stocks issued	
		3% Debenture Stock	4% Debenture Stock
£10 Shares	£18,850	–	£8,310
'A' Debenture Stock	£11,350	£17,025	–
'B' Debenture Stock	£28,600	£28,600	–
'C' Debenture Stock	£10,101	£8,414	–

Thus, after 27 years of existence as a separate concern, the Cowbridge Railway was finally absorbed by the TVR. Although the line had not brought the riches that some of its promoters had hoped for, or led to a great increase in the prosperity and development of Cowbridge, it had provided a vital link between the town and the outside world. This had helped mitigate the worst effects of the stagnation which had followed the opening of the South Wales Railway, in 1850. Evidence of improved fortunes of the town is provided by the growth of its population between the years 1871, 1881 and 1891, when it reached a peak of 1,377 persons. This growth, however, must be placed in the context of the phenomenal increases which occured throughout South Wales during this period. Although the railway had proved to be of undoubted benefit to the town as a whole, and to the farmers who relied on its market, it had been something of a mixed blessing to certain shopkeepers and traders of the town. These people had previously prospered, as a result of its relative isolation, but the railway now allowed people to go outside the town for their shopping requirements, and also enabled finished goods to be imported to the disadvantage of local producers.

'Metro' class 2-4-0T, No. 3586 with an auto-car is seen at Cowbridge in 1949. The auto-car was formerly GWR No. 106 which had been converted from one of the original straight-sided steam railcars, No. 2, in 1903.

C. Chapman

Chapter Five
This otherwise comparitively useless piece of Railway
The Cowbridge & Aberthaw Railway: 1888-1895

Although the promoters of the Cowbridge Railway, and many of the inhabitants of the southern part of the Vale of Glamorgan, had favoured the extension of the railway to the south of Cowbridge, the TVR does not appear to have been attracted to this idea until events of the late 1880s forced it to take an interest in such an extension. After the demise of earlier schemes, the abortive Llantwit Major Railway proposal of 1869 represented the last serious attempt to promote an extension of the railway to the south of Cowbridge, for almost twenty years. During this period, various requests were made to the TVR for the provision of railway communication for the district to the south of Cowbridge, but the TVR was not in the least receptive; indeed, the rearrangement of the station layout at Cowbridge in 1886 does not suggest that the TVR was then contemplating an early extension of the Cowbridge branch.

The railway geography of the Vale of Glamorgan underwent a radical change with the opening of Barry Dock and its rail links in 1889. Attempts in the 1860s and 1870s to promote a dock at Barry, together with connecting railways, had all ended in failure. However, by the early 1880s, dissatisfaction with the increasingly congested facilities offered by the TVR and Cardiff Docks led certain South Wales coalowners and traders to consider the construction of a new port, which would be competitive with Cardiff and Penarth. A survey of six sites for such a port, including Barry, Aberthaw and Ogmore, was undertaken by H. M. Brunel, son of Isambard Kingdom Brunel. Brunel recommended Barry as the best location for the new dock. In 1884 an Act was obtained for the construction of Barry Dock, and for railways linking it with the coalfield areas; the undertaking opened for traffic on 18th July 1889.

The harbour at Aberthaw had declined in importance thoughout the nineteenth century, although even by the 1890s it was still visited by several small coasters each week. Apart from its harbour, Aberthaw was also famous for the quality of the lime which could be produced from locally obtained limestone. A bank of limestone pebbles, just off the foreshore near Pleasant Harbour, a house to the east of the village of East Aberthaw, provided the source from which the finest quality lime could be obtained. However, apart from some very minor local operations, the lime was not produced at Aberthaw. Instead, the pebbles were

either carted inland, or shipped from the harbour to be burnt for lime elsewhere. A growing demand for lime, coupled with restrictions on supply imposed by the small scale nature of its manufacture, resulted in its price remaining high, despite the fall in the costs of labour and coal which occured in the 1880s.

The potential of the Aberthaw limestone deposits was recognized by a Mr Stephen Collier, who conceived a scheme for the production of lime from the pebbles at the source of supply at Aberthaw. In 1881, Collier approached Daniel Owen of Ash Hall, near Ystradowen, with a proposition that Owen provide the backing for the construction of a limeworks at Aberthaw. Owen was joint proprietor of the *Western Mail*, and a notable South Wales businessman. He had made his fortune as a timber merchant in Australia, before returning to his home in South Wales, and was attracted to Collier's idea. A prospecting expedition was then organized to Aberthaw. Owen was accompanied on this outing by his partner, Mr Lascelles-Carr, Stephen Collier and Mr Hurman, Traffic Manager of the TVR. Although there was no immediate outcome as a result of this expedition, Owen was sufficiently impressed with the industrial prospects of Aberthaw to begin to advocate their exploitation, and the construction of a railway from Cowbridge to Aberthaw. Despite Owen's advocacy, however, the TVR was slow to respond and without a railway the industrial prospects of Aberthaw were somewhat limited.

Early in 1888, Owen invited Collier to Ash Hall to discuss his scheme for a limeworks at Aberthaw. Following this meeting, Collier and Owen, together with Lascelles-Carr, drove down to Aberthaw where it was agreed that if Collier could arrange suitable terms with the owner of the land, then a limeworks would be constructed. The landowner in question was approached, and satisfactory terms agreed, and work began immediately on the building of the limeworks. This was situated above the foreshore, near Pleasant Harbour, and was opened in December 1888. It consisted of kilns for burning the limestone pebbles, which were brought from the pebble bank by means of a cable-worked tramway, and a mill for crushing the lime. Tramways also connected the works with the road to East Aberthaw, and were used for bringing in coal and taking out the finished lime.

At Aberthaw, the railway continued beyond the station to serve the Aberthaw Lime Works, seen in this view.

C. Chapman

Standing in for diesel railcar No. 18, 'Metro' class 2-4-0T, No. 3586 waits in vain for passengers at Cowbridge in 1949.   *H. T. Hobbs*

The limeworks at Aberthaw formed one part of a larger scheme Owen had in mind for the industrial development of the Aberthaw area; this included the provision of a railway from Cowbridge and also vague ideas for the development of a port at Aberthaw. However, the construction of the railway required the support of the TVR. With work under way on the limeworks, early in 1888, it was essential that a rail link be provided as soon as possible. Although, at the time work commenced on the limeworks, there is no indication to suggest that the TVR was prepared to back Owen's proposal. Indeed, it was not until the opening of the works in December 1888, that Owen was able to announce that, after a long period of negotiation, the TVR was prepared to assist with the construction of the railway. Although the TVR had never been enthusiastic about such a railway, events elsewhere during 1888 had had a profound influence on their attitude towards Owen's scheme.

In June 1888, Colonel North's Western Navigation Syndicate, which later became 'North's Navigation Collieries', acquired the Llynfi & Tondu Company. The latter owned coal pits and iron works to the north of Bridgend, and had gone into liquidation in 1885. No.th was anxious to improve the transport links from his new acquisition, as the collieries to the north of Bridgend were relatively isolated from the main docks of South Wales, with the exception of the inadequate facilities offered by Porthcawl. They were also wholly dependent on the GWR for the transport of their coal. In August 1888, Mr Foster-Brown, North's financial adviser and engineer to the Barry Dock & Railway, approached Mr Lambert, the General Manager of the GWR. Their request was that the GWR reduce its gross rate on coal traffic, from the Bridgend Valleys to Barry Dock. When these negotiations failed in October 1888, Foster-Brown, acting on behalf of Colonel North, prepared plans for an independent railway from Bridgend to Barry, and in November 1888 plans were deposited for the Vale of Glamorgan Railway. Foster-Brown's initial thoughts had been for a direct line from Bridgend to Barry, via Cowbridge, but in response to pressure from the inhabitants of Llantwit Major and district, the Vale of Glamorgan Railway was routed via Ewenny and Llantwit Major instead.

53

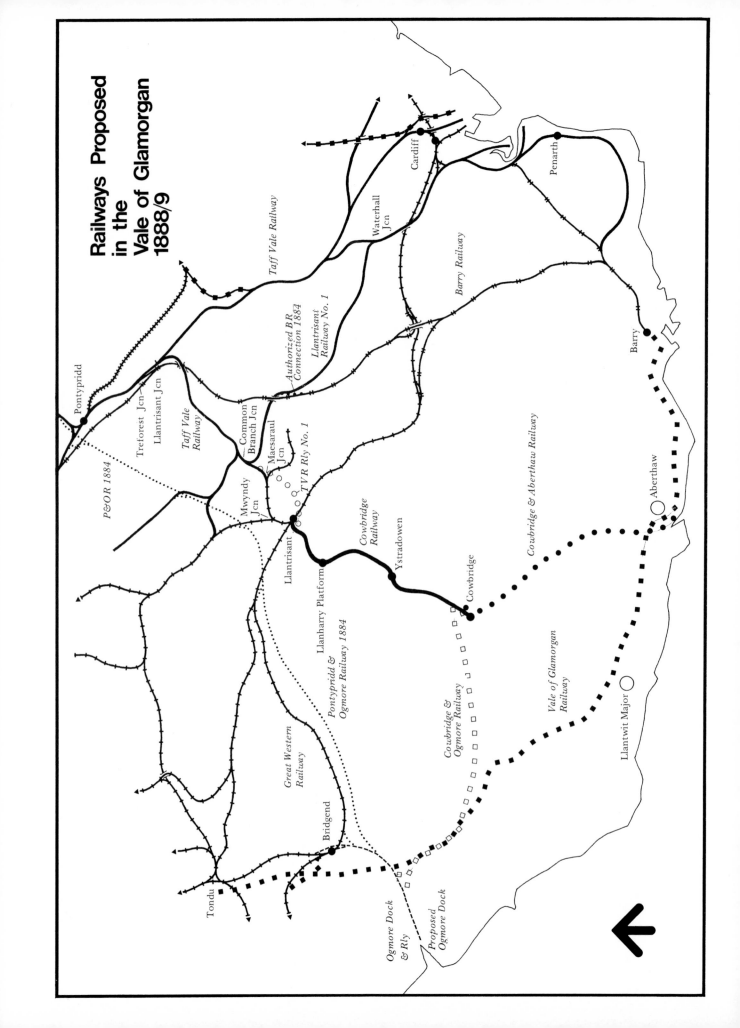

Railways Proposed in the Vale of Glamorgan 1888/9

Taff Vale Railway

Waterhall Jcn

Cardiff

Penarth

Barry Railway

Authorized BR Connection 1884

Llantrisant Railway No. 1

Pontypridd

Treforest Jcn

Llantrisant Jcn

Taff Vale Railway

P&OR 1884

Common Branch Jcn

Maesaraul Jcn

TVR Rly No. 1

Mwyndy Jcn

Barry

Cowbridge Railway

Aberthaw

Cowbridge & Aberthaw Railway

Llantrisant

Llanharry Platform

Ystradowen

Cowbridge

Pontypridd & Ogmore Railway 1884

Cowbridge & Ogmore Railway

Vale of Glamorgan Railway

Llantwit Major

Great Western Railway

Bridgend

Ogmore Dock & Rly

Proposed Ogmore Dock

Tondu

Whilst Foster-Brown was depositing plans for the Vale of Glamorgan Railway, Colonel North had also become vice-chairman of the Ogmore Dock & Railway Company. It had been incorporated in July 1883, to build a railway from Bridgend to the mouth of the River Ogmore, where a new dock was to be built. In addition to coal from the Bridgend Valleys, it was hoped that coal would be attracted from the Rhondda Valleys if, and when, the GWR built their authorized line of 1882 from Hendreforgan to Porth. In 1884, a Bill was promoted by Messrs Randall and Price-Williams, (engineer to the OD&R) for a Pontypridd and Ogmore Railway, from the authorized OD&R near Ewenny, to the TVR at Pontypridd. This railway would have provided access to the proposed dock at Ogmore, from the Merthyr and Aberdare valleys, but the Bill was withdrawn before its second reading. The necessary financial support for the OD&R was hard to come by and the GWR, who were to work the line, refused to guarantee a fixed dividend out of the receipts of the line. In 1887, an Act was obtained for the extension of the time allowed for the construction of the railway, but the GWR still refused to undertake the working of the completed railway.

North appears to have been keeping both options open by agreeing to become vice-chairman of the OD&R, whilst at the same time backing the promotion of the Vale of Glamorgan Railway. He asked Foster-Brown to report on the advantages and disadvantages of the competing schemes; Foster-Brown concluded that the Vale of Glamorgan Railway would be better for Colonel North than the OD&R, which he felt would be too dangerous because of the presence of Tusker Rock just outside the mouth of the Ogmore. He also considered that the Ogmore Dock would suffer from the limited export potential of the bituminous coal of the Bridgend Valleys. North accepted Foster-Brown's conclusions, and backed the Vale of Glamorgan Railway at the expense of the OD&R.

All this activity provides the background to the deposition of plans for the Cowbridge & Aberthaw Railway in November 1888. The TVR appears to have been aroused by the threat of incursion into its territory posed by the Vale of Glamorgan Railway, and to have appreciated the strategic value of a railway from Cowbridge to Aberthaw, in relation to the proposal for the Vale of Glamorgan Railway and the proximity of the Barry Dock. It appears to have felt that if it did not back Owen's scheme, then there was a possibility that another company might step into the breach, in its place. In addition, the rich agricultural area to the south of Cowbridge formed the source of much of the traffic of the Cowbridge branch. In December 1888, Sir Morgan Morgan, an associate of Owen and a fellow Director of the Aberthaw Lime Company, appeared before the TVR Board with the Draft Bill for the C&AR, which was approved. Later that month, at the opening of Aberthaw Limeworks, Owen was able to announce that the TVR was disposed to help with the construction of the railway to Aberthaw.

At the same time as plans were being deposited for the Vale of Glamorgan Railway and the C&AR, plans were also

Diesel railcar No. 22 is pictured at Cowbridge on 18th September 1943. The station nameboard has been removed as a wartime precaution. The 'down' starting signal was installed by the GWR following the withdrawal of the passenger service south of Cowbridge in 1930.

Ian L. Wright

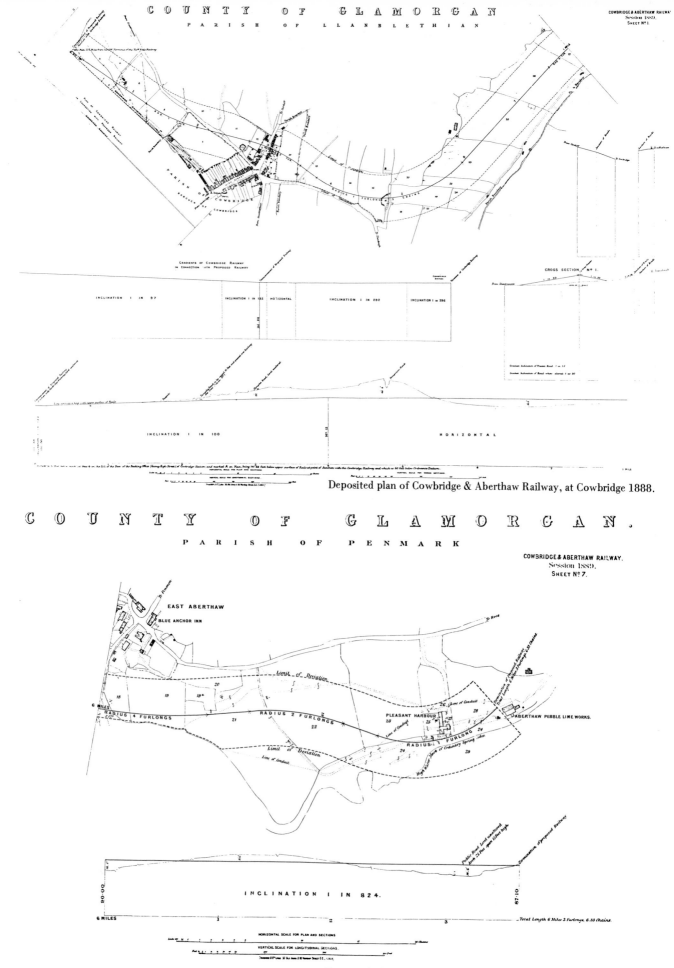

GRADIENTS OF COWBRIDGE RAILWAY
IN CONNECTION WITH PROPOSED RAILWAY

INCLINATION 1 IN 97

INCLINATION 1 IN 192   HORIZONTAL   INCLINATION 1 IN 292   INCLINATION 1 IN 396

CROSS SECTION No 1.

INCLINATION 1 IN 100   HORIZONTAL

Deposited plan of Cowbridge & Aberthaw Railway, at Cowbridge 1888.

COUNTY OF GLAMORGAN.
PARISH OF PENMARK

EAST ABERTHAW
BLUE ANCHOR INN

To Rhoos

Limit of Deviation

6 MILES
RADIUS 4 FURLONGS

RADIUS 2 FURLONGS

PLEASANT HARBOUR

Line of Conduit

ABERTHAW PEBBLE LIME WORKS.

RADIUS 1 FURLONG

Limit of Deviation

Line of Conduit

High Water Mark of Ordinary Spring Tides

INCLINATION 1 IN 824.

6 MILES   1   2   3

Total Length 6 Miles 3 Furlongs, 6.33 Chains.

HORIZONTAL SCALE FOR PLAN AND SECTIONS

VERTICAL SCALE FOR LONGITUDINAL SECTIONS.

Deposited plan of Cowbridge & Aberthaw Railway, at Aberthaw : 1888

deposited by Messrs Greathead and Price-Williams for a Cowbridge & Ogmore Railway. It would run from the Cowbridge line at a triangular junction, just north of its Cowbridge terminus, to another triangular junction with the authorized OD&R at Ewenny. The involvement of Mr Price-Williams, Engineer to the OD&R, suggests that the object of the C&OR was the provision of a connection between the proposed Ogmore Dock and the TVR. This link, although circuitous, would have performed a similar function to that intended for the abortive Pontypridd & Ogmore scheme of 1884, which was to attract coal from the TVR to Ogmore Dock. Thus the C&OR appears to have been a last desperate attempt to keep the Ogmore Dock proposal alive, and possibly to interest the TVR in the project at a time when it was feeling threatened by the opening of Barry Dock and by the scheme for the Vale of Glamorgan Railway. However, apart from the submission of notices relating to the intended Bill for the C&OR to the TVR Board on 10th January 1889, the TVR minutes are silent on the subject. North's decision to back the Vale of Glamorgan Railway instead of the OD&R dealt a fatal blow to the prospects for a dock at Ogmore, from which they did not recover. Although plans were deposited for the C&OR in November 1888, the Bill itself was not printed, and nothing more was heard of this proposal. The OD&R itself was finally abandoned in 1891.

The question of TVR support for the C&AR came up at a special general meeting of the shareholders, of the TVR, on 3rd May 1889, when a draft agreement for maintaining and working the C&AR was placed before the meeting. Under this draft agreement, the TVR would guarantee 3½ per cent return on the expenditure involved in the construction of the proposed railway. The chairman explained that the TVR had been asked, on a number of occasions, to provide a railway to Aberthaw to serve the lime trade and the agricultural district south of Cowbridge. The C&AR had been promoted by gentlemen who were largely interested in the limeworks and other property, who were prepared to construct the line if the TVR would guarantee the expenditure involved. A voice of dissent was raised by Major Brickman, a TVR shareholder, who owned land on the route of the C&AR, who asserted that the traffic on the new line would be infinitesimal and would not pay a couple of men for oiling the carriage wheels. In reply, the Chairman stated that the TVR Board felt that there was no doubt that the C&AR would be built, whether or not the TVR used it, and it was far more desirable for the TVR to have the line. It was the only way for the company to protect its interests, to serve the district completely and not to leave other people to intervene and make up the deficiency. The motion was carried with three dissentients.

The agreement between the TVR and the C&AR was signed on 25th May 1889. A further agreement was made between the Vale of Glamorgan Railway and the C&AR on 15th July 1889, covering the provision of a bridge for the Vale of Glamorgan Railway over the C&AR, at the intersection of the two railways near Aberthaw, and the delineation of the boundary between the two lines at Aberthaw. This agreement removed the threat of Vale of Glamorgan opposition to the C&AR Bill, which was passed unopposed; the C&AR Act received Royal Assent on 12th August 1889, with a capital of £90,000. The Act also confirmed the agreements between the C&AR and the TVR, and between the C&AR and the Vale of Glamorgan Railway.

The following month saw the Incorporation of the Vale of Glamorgan Railway with an authorized capital of £360,000 and empowered to make and maintain a railway from Bridgend to Barry, via Llantwit Major. It was to be worked by the Barry Company, which would retain 60 per cent of the gross receipts. However, circumstances were not favourable for the issue of new shares, and only half were sold, with the result that those subscriptions received had to be returned to those who had been prepared to invest in the undertaking.

The guarantee of the C&AR by the TVR gave rise to speculation that the TVR was thinking of using the C&AR as a means of obtaining access to Barry Dock from the west, having been thwarted in their attempt to get to the dock from the east, via Penarth. Barry Dock was only five miles from Aberthaw, and could be reached either via an extension of the C&AR, or by a junction with the Vale of Glamorgan Railway at Aberthaw. The TVR appears at least to have contemplated such a junction, for at the Vale of Glamorgan Railway Board Meeting on 25th October 1889, the solicitor to that company was instructed to prepare notices to be used, in the event of the TVR putting forward its scheme for a junction at Aberthaw. Although this junction would have been physcially straightforward, it, or an extension of the C&AR to Barry, would have entailed considerable legal difficulties, for if the TVR had wished to send coal to Barry Dock via this route, then the Barry Company could have invoked Clause 23 of its 1888 Act. This required the TVR to afford it facilities for the exchange of goods and mineral traffic at Treforest, with no discrimination as to the rates, which were to be no greater than the lowest TVR rate to Cardiff, Penarth or Barry.

At the same time, the Vale of Glamorgan Railway appears to have been toying with the idea of providing a junction of its own at Aberthaw. On 22nd November 1889, a report appeared in the *Barry Dock News*, stating that the Vale of Glamorgan Railway intended seeking authorization for a junction with the C&AR at Aberthaw. However, a week later it was reported that the Vale of Glamorgan Railway had decided not to proceed with this junction. After this decision, the uncertainty concerning the prospects for the construction of the Vale of Glamorgan Railway put any question of a junction at Aberthaw out of court for a number of years.

In contrast to the faltering progress of the Vale of Glamorgan Railway, work on the C&AR began almost before the ink was dry on its Act of Incorporation. By the end of September 1889, the entire route had been pegged out, the surveys had been completed and notices had been prepared for the land to be acquired. However, in order to proceed with the construction of the line, a siding was needed at Cowbridge. Provisional Board of Trade sanction was obtained, in February 1890, for a temporary junction about 200 yards to the north of Cowbridge Station, facing to 'up' trains. This required a number of modifications to the signalling, and resulted in all thirteen levers at Cowbridge cabin being brought into use. Formal Board of Trade sanction was not granted until after Colonel Rich had inspected the work, in June 1890, when he stipulated that all traffic on to the temporary siding should be worked from Cowbridge Station.

The temporary siding at Cowbridge allowed work to commence in earnest on the new railway. A ceremony for the cutting of the first sod of the C&AR was held on the site of the new station in Cowbridge on 7th February 1890.

An 0-4-2T, No. 1471 waits to depart from Cowbridge yard with an SLS tour on 13th July 1957. The rear elevation of the disused passenger station is visible on the right.

M. Hale

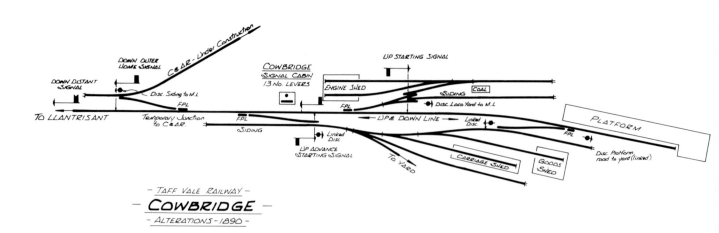

Signalling alterations at Cowbridge Station : 1890

Cowbridge Passenger Station and goods yard on 5th May 1951.   *R. C. Riley*

After the Half-Yearly Meeting of the C&AR Company, a procession formed up and was led by the Hungarian Band, followed by the Mayor and Corporation of Cowbridge, the Directors and shareholders of the company, and members of the general public. Unlike the similar ceremony for the Cowbridge Railway, nearly thirty years earlier, the C&AR Company was able to afford a proper silver shovel, which was presented by George Fisher for the company and the TVR to Mrs Naunton Davies, who cut the first sod of the C&AR.

In addition to the use made of the siding at Cowbridge, construction materials were also brought in by boat, up the River Thaw from Aberthaw. The contractor employed on the line was Mr Mathias, of Porth. Work proceeded without major incident, although the nature of the rock through which the cuttings had to be made was such that a great deal more work was needed, than had been anticipated. The arrival of the railway navvies in Cowbridge was treated with some trepidation, by the rather staid inhabitants of the Borough. In an attempt to promote the spiritual uplift of the navvies, a mission was established in the Dissenting Chapel in Cowbridge. Many of the navvies employed on the line were in fact local men, who were otherwise employed on a rather transient basis as agricultural labourers.

Whilst the construction of the C&AR forged ahead, the Vale of Glamorgan Railway had remained in a kind of limbo, after its failure to attract sufficient funds following its Act of Incorporation in 1889. Although there was no

immediate prospect of work starting on the line, an application was made to Parliament in 1892 for an extension of the time allowed for its construction. This Bill was examined before the Committees of the House, in May 1892. Giving evidence on behalf of the Vale of Glamorgan Railway, Mr Foster-Brown stated that it was anticipated that a junction would be provided by the Vale of Glamorgan Railway, between itself and the C&AR at Aberthaw. This would enable traffic from the coalfields of the Ely and Treferig valleys and the area served by the L&TVJR to be attracted via the C&AR on to the Vale of Glamorgan at Aberthaw, and thence to Barry Dock. Although the Barry Act of 1884 had contained powers for a junction between the Barry main line and the Common Branch Junction to Waterhall Junction section of the L&TVJR, usually known as Llantrisant Railway No. 1, and opened for freight traffic only on 11th September 1886, these had not been exercised. This was despite the fact that a temporary junction had been provided by the TVR at Creigiau, for construction traffic for the Barry line. Thus coal from the Llantrisant area served by the L&TVJR continued to be worked back to Treforest for exchange with the Barry Railway. A route via Aberthaw would have avoided this awkward working, according to Foster-Brown. The Vale of Glamorgan also sought powers in its 1892 Bill to enable it to enter into working agreements with any or either of the TVR, C&AR or GWR companies should this prove expedient. The Barry

An auto-train waits at Cowbridge Station in 1949 amidst signs of impending closure. The overbridge, in the background, carried the Cowbridge to Llantrisant road.

LGRP (Courtesy of David & Charles)

Company was not happy about the prospect of a junction at Aberthaw, nor did it relish the possibility of the Vale of Glamorgan Railway entering into working agreements with any of its enemies, and, as a result of its opposition, the Vale of Glamorgan Railway abandoned these proposals.

Despite the extension of time obtained under its 1892 Act, the future of the Vale of Glamorgan Railway remained uncertain until 1894 when the coal companies of the Bridgend valleys agreed to send 750,000 tons of coal each year to Barry Dock over the Vale of Glamorgan Railway. The Barry Railway guaranteed the Vale of Glamorgan Railway an annual income equal to 4 per cent of the money spent on making the railway. With such a firm commitment there was no difficulty in selling all the shares in the Vale of Glamorgan Railway, and construction commenced in August 1894. The railway opened to traffic on 1st December 1897.

By August 1892, the C&AR was complete and ready for Board of Trade Inspection. Unlike the unhappy outcome of the inspection of the Cowbridge Railway, nearly thirty years earlier, that of the C&AR by Major Yorke on 2nd September 1892 went well. Only a few minor defects were identified, the most serious of which concerned the new station at Cowbridge. At this date, the TVR appears to have intended to provide only pedestrian access to the new station from the old terminus. However, this idea did not meet with the approval of Major Yorke, who felt that a proper road access to the new station was necessary. The TVR accepted this point, but because of difficulties in obtaining the necessary land, the road approach was not completed until mid-1893. Board of Trade sanction, for the opening of the line to passengers, was granted subject to the detailed points identified by Major Yorke, and to an undertaking regarding the intended mode of working the railway.

The imminent opening of the C&AR, coupled with the continuing uncertainty over the future of the Vale of Glamorgan Railway, gave rise to renewed talk of an extension of the C&AR to Barry. This idea appears to have had a great attraction to Daniel Owen and other Directors of the C&AR. In September 1892, the *Barry Dock News* reported that the Directors of the C&AR had determined to extend their railway from Aberthaw to Font-y-gary, about a mile and a half along the coast towards Barry. The article went on to predict that 'this otherwise comparatively useless piece of railway' would eventually be extended from Aberthaw around the coast to Barry Dock. Although rumours of such an extension reached a peak in the following month, the authoritative *Western Mail* noted that although representations had been made on the subject, no decision had been reached. Whilst Owen and his associates were very vocal in their support of an extension, the attitude of the TVR was less clear, although, following the opening of the C&AR, it was reported that Mr Brewer, the joint engineer of the C&AR and TVR and others officially connected with the C&AR, were purchasing land along a route between Aberthaw and Barry. If the Vale of Glamorgan had not been constructed, then undoubtedly pressure would have increased for an extension of the C&AR to Barry. In the event, the guarantee of the Vale of Glamorgan by the Barry Railway in 1894, coupled with the financial difficulties then being encountered by the C&AR, and the death of Owen, in 1895, ended any thoughts about an extension to Barry. The Barry Company's opposition precluded any prospect of a junction between the two lines at Aberthaw.

The C&AR was opened to traffic on Saturday, 1st October 1892. The opening day was marred by heavy showers, and generally wintry weather, but this did not undermine the enthusiasm which attended the opening of the new railway. At 11.15 a.m. a special train, composed of the TVR Directors' saloon, a four wheel vehicle built in 1875, and a number of first class carriages left Queen Street Station in Cardiff for Pontypridd, carrying the official party. At Pontypridd the train reversed for its journey to Llantrisant, where another reversal was necessary before it could continued to Cowbridge. At the new station in Cowbridge, the train was met by the Mayor and Corporation of the town. After the speeches of welcome and well-wishing, the train continued over the new line to Aberthaw. At Aberthaw, the railway was declared open by Mrs Beasley, the wife of the General Manager of the TVR, after which the official party inspected the Aberthaw Lime Works, which was now connected to the railway. The party then rejoined the special train for the journey back to Cowbridge, where a celebratory dinner was held at the Bear Hotel. Amongst the many speeches of congratulation and hope, the Mayor of Cowbridge anticipated the extension of the railway from Aberthaw to Barry, a prospect shared by Daniel Owen and others. Sir Morgan Morgan spoke of the possibility of maritime development at Aberthaw, whilst Ammon Beasley was rather more circumspect, merely hoping that the traffic would be as 'substantial as the railway.'

The C&AR had been built at a cost of about £120,000, and had involved some 250,000 cubic yards of excavation. It was 6 miles 53 chains long, and single track throughout, with a goods loop at St. Mary Church Road Station. However, sufficient land had been acquired for doubling, should this prove necessary, and all the overbridges had been built with this in mind. The permanent way consisted of 82lb per yard bullhead rails in 30ft. lengths, with eleven sleepers per length, and it was well blasted with stone. The maximum gradient was 1 in 60, and despite the fact that the line followed the valley of the Thaw for most of its length, the earthworks were quite substantial, with a significant proportion of the line in cut or on embankment. There were eleven underbridges and twelve overbridges on the new line. Compared with the exceptionally light character of the Cowbridge Railway, the C&AR appeared to be engineered to heavy main line standards, a somewhat misleading impression as it was laid out on similar lines to other TVR branches of the period.

The C&AR left the Cowbridge line at Cowbridge Junction, about 200 yards north of the old terminus. The junction itself was a very straightforward affair, with the single line of the new railway branching off by means of a single turnout, under the control of a raised signal cabin of brick and timber construction to the characteristic TVR design. The junction was fully signalled, with McKenzie & Holland somersault signals, which the TVR employed from the mid-1880s. From the junction, the line climbed to the new Cowbridge passenger station, a single platform affair, with a single storey yellow and red brick building of a pattern much used by the TVR at this date.

On leaving Cowbridge Station, the line passed in quick succession under the Cowbridge to Llantrisant road and the Cardiff Road; the former crossed by means of a girder bridge, while the latter crossed by a stone arch bridge. The route of the C&AR out of Cowbridge differed radi-

Cowbridge Junction signal cabin in 1951. The cabin was opened in 1892 with ten working levers and had plan dimensions of only 11 ft. by 13 ft.

D. Chaplin

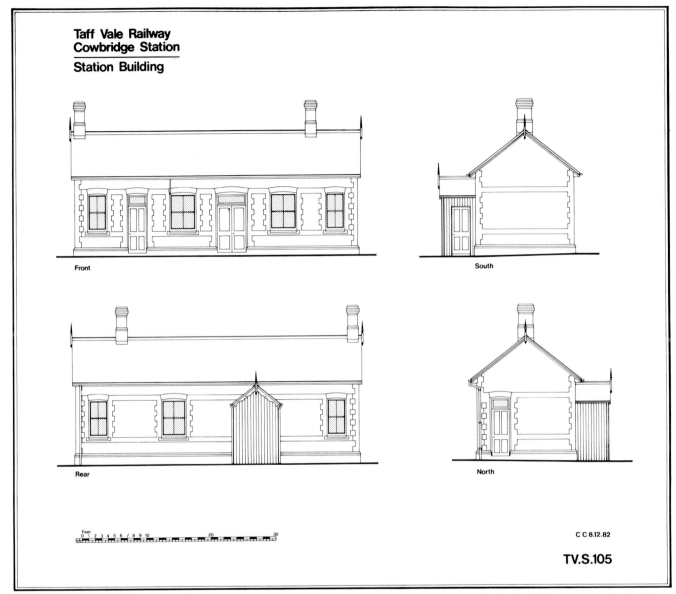

**Taff Vale Railway
Cowbridge Station**

Station Building

Front

South

Rear

North

Feet
0 1 2 3 4 5 6 / 8 9 10   20   30

C C 8.12.82

TV.S.105

Cowbridge Station : new station building

cally from earlier proposals for an extension to the south of the town which had envisaged either a tunnel under the Broadway, or a long detour via the valley of the Thaw through Llanblethian. The C&AR eschewed both these courses, and instead crossed an area of higher ground to the east of the town, before rejoining the Thaw Valley near St. Hilary. It then followed a route to the east of the Thaw, in contrast to the western routes of earlier proposals, through sparsely populated country to the first station, at St. Mary Church Road. This served the village of St. Mary Church, about a mile to the west, together with a number of other minor settlements, none of which was very near the rail-

way. The station consisted of a single platform, with the usual yellow and red brick building, albeit smaller than that at Cowbridge. It was also equipped with a goods loop opposite the platform. The station was fully signalled, with the signal cabin mounted on the platform next to the station building. The line below St. Mary Church Road was not signalled, and was worked on the one engine in steam principle. The goods yard followed a layout which was standard for all C&AR stations, consisting of two parallel sidings, one of which served a corrugated iron goods shed of the side loading type, and a set of cattle pens which adjoined the shed.

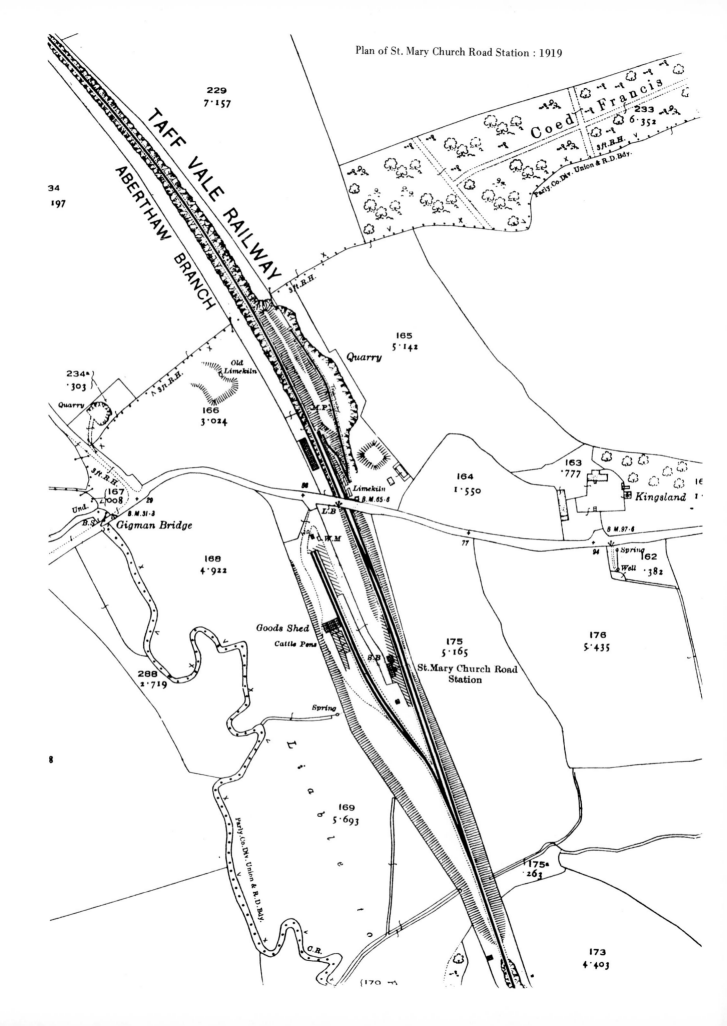

Plan of St. Mary Church Road Station : 1919

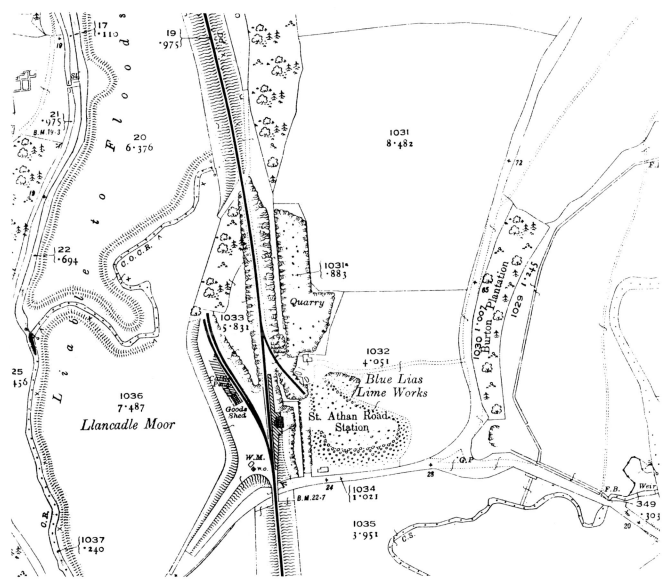

Plan of St. Athan Road Station : 1919

South of St. Mary Church Road, the railway crossed Flemingston Moor before turning due south at Llanbethery. For the following mile, the line ran on an embankment close to the River Thaw, before passing through a cutting and running into St. Athan Road Station. As with St. Mary Church Road, there was no settlement in the immediate vicinity of the station; St. Athan itself was about a mile to the west. The station also served the villages of Llancadle, West Aberthaw and Gileston, and enjoyed a similar layout and range of facilities to St. Mary Church Road, but without the loop or signalling.

From St. Athan Road, the line crossed the main road by means of a girder bridge, and continued over the flood plain of the Thaw on an embankment. The Vale of Glamorgan Railway, when opened, crossed the C&AR about a quarter

of a mile south of St. Athan Road Station, on a high embankment. Beyond this, the C&AR ran in a shallow cutting, before crossing a rough track from East Aberthaw to Aberthaw Well by means of a stone arch bridge, before running into Aberthaw Station.

Aberthaw Station possessed a single platform with the usual C&AR facilities. Beyond the station there was a run-round loop and a goods yard of standard C&AR design. The line then continued beyond the goods yard to serve the Aberthaw limeworks.

With the opening of the Aberthaw line, the original Cowbridge Railway terminus was retained as the town's goods station, with the old train shed continuing in use as a carriage shed.

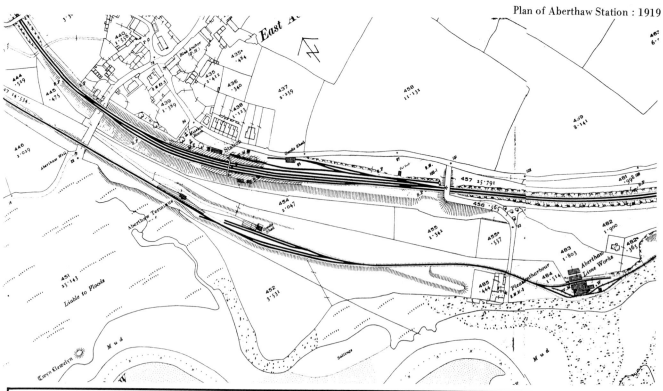

Taff Vale Railway
Aberthaw Station

Station Building

Front Elevation

East Elevation

Rear Elevation

West Elevation

Materials
_____
Yellow brick walls, red brick quoins etc,
timber lean-to, Welsh slate roof

Source : personal survey

C Chapman
October 1982

TV.S.120

Feet
0 1 2 3 4 5 6 7 8 9 10   20   30

Station building, Aberthaw Station

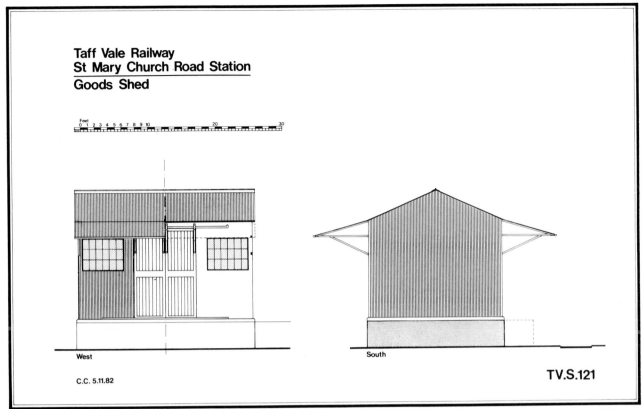

Taff Vale Railway
St Mary Church Road Station
Goods Shed

West

South

C.C. 5.11.82

TV.S.121

Goods shed, St. Mary Church Road Station

The cost of constructing the C&AR had exceeded its authorized capital by about £30,000. Without the prospect of an extension to Barry, or of the development of a port at Aberthaw, the traffic potential of the new line was limited to the requirements of the lime manufacturing industry at Aberthaw, and the agricultural produce of the lower part of the Vale of Glamorgan served by the railway. In July 1893, the Secretary of the C&AR suggested to the TVR Board that a formal lease be taken of the C&AR, but this was declined. However, a proposal by Sir Morgan Morgan, in December of that year, that the TVR acquire the C&AR proved more successful. So early in 1894, the TVR agreed to issue new stocks, and acquire the C&AR. This was confirmed by the TVR's Act of 17th August 1894, the reason given for the acquisition of this impecunious satellite being that its costs of construction had exceeded the amount authorized as capital, in the C&AR's Act of Incorporation of 1889. The C&AR was formally vested in the TVR from 1st January 1895.

Chapter Six
The Cowbridge Branch, Taff Vale Railway: 1889-1922

The amalgamation of the Cowbridge Railway with the TVR, in 1889, went largely unnoticed by the people of Cowbridge and district, as by that date, the line had become, to all intents and purposes, an integral part of the TVR. However, despite the improvements made by the TVR, and the introduction of their standard features, many aspects remained which distinguished the Cowbridge branch from the rest of the Taff system. These were partly a reminder of its very light standard of construction, in particular in the characteristic single track overbridges, and partly as a result of the rural environment, through which the railway followed its winding and undulating course.

The early 1890s saw a considerable amount of activity concerning new works on the branch. Apart from the new passenger facilities at Cowbridge, associated with the building of the C&AR, new passenger accommodation was also provided at Llantrisant and Llanharry, together with improved goods facilities at Llantrisant.

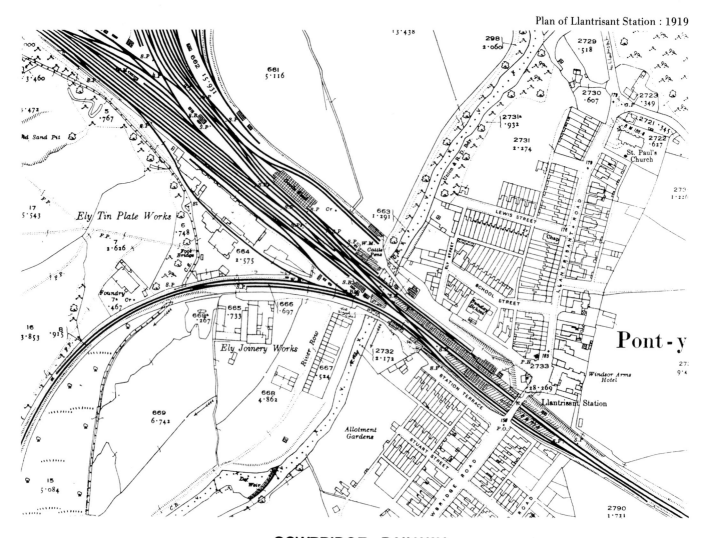

Pont-y

COWBRIDGE RAILWAY

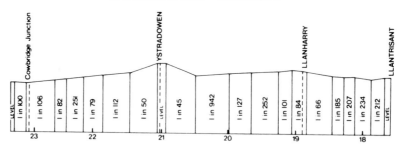

Gradient profiles for the Cowbridge Railway and the Cowbridge & Aberthaw Railway

COWBRIDGE & ABERTHAW RAILWAY

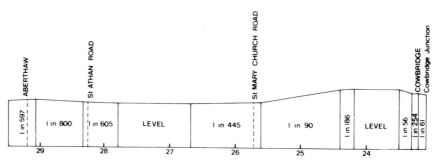

Llantrisant Station, looking from the west, circa 1910. TVR trains ran across the GWR South Wales main line to reach the Cowbridge bay on the right. The left-hand bay, together with the extended 'up' platform, was provided for the inauguration of the Great Western Railway's passenger service to Pen-y-graig, in 1901. TVR trains from Pontypridd, terminating at Llantrisant, did not use this bay, but ran across to the Cowbridge bay. Note the relatively lowly status granted to the Cowbridge and Taff Vale lines on the station nameboard.

Lens of Sutton

The rebuilding of Llantrisant Station, which was completed in 1890, had been foreshadowed in the agreement between the GWR and the TVR, which had been reached in March 1888. The rebuilding swept away the somewhat idiosyncratic layout, which had existed since the opening of the Cowbridge Railway, and considerably improved the operational efficiency of the station. The new works involved the reconstruction of the facilities used by both the GWR and the TVR to the benefit of both companies and their passengers. The platforms were extended to the west of the bridge carrying the Cowbridge to Llantrisant road, being raised in height in the process; the TVR dead-end line was extended under a new double track bridge of standard TVR design, which abutted rather incongruously up against the old SWR bridge with its graceful broad proportions; the turntable and waiting-room on the 'down' platform were removed and a new joint waiting-room was provided, being of timber construction with awnings on all four sides; and a footbridge was built linking the 'up'

and 'down' platforms, passengers previously having had to cross the line by the road bridge. The increased length of the run-round loop on the Cowbridge line greatly eased the operation of branch goods trains.

In addition, a number of alterations were carried out to the track layout to the west of the station, involving the abolition of Trecastle Junction and its associated signalling. In its place, the machine siding was extended to connect to Trecastle siding, and a new crossover, facing the 'down' trains, was laid in from the running line to join the machine siding, just before the divergence of the re-aligned Trecastle siding. These arrangements were inspected by the Board of Trade in June 1890, and found to be entirely satisfactory. However, their life span was extremely short, as the Trecastle mine was closed in 1891. The siding remained in place until 1896, when it was lifted from the TVR boundary, after which the machine siding was extended parallel to the running lines for some 150 yards.

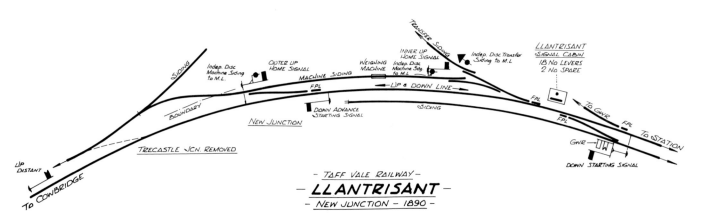

Signalling alterations at Llantrisant Station : 1890

69

A loaded iron-ore train is propelled from Llanharry towards Llantrisant. The locomotive is 0-6-0PT, No. 3656. In the foreground are the remains of the Llanharry Limeworks, which were originally connected to the Cowbridge branch by means of a private siding.

M. Hale

A further improvement to the passenger accommodation the line was initiated in January 1890, when the TVR Engineer was instructed to obtain tenders for the construction of a new station at Llanharry, to replace the old Llanharry Platform. The new station was on the north side of the Llanharry Road bridge, and was a considerable improvement on the spartan amenities of the old platform. It consisted of a single platform, with a yellow and red brick building of the same pattern as had been used on the C&AR. With the opening of the new station, all traces of the old platform to the south of the bridge were removed.

The residents of Ystradowen were not so lucky with regard to improvements at their station, however, as a request in November 1890 for better facilities was turned down by the TVR.

Further improvements were made at Llantrisant in 1892, this time involving the goods department. Up until then, the TVR goods facilities at that station had been restric-

ted to a single siding off the run-round loop. In 1892, a goods shed was provided alongside this siding; it was of corrugated iron to a design similar to those used on the C&AR, but with an arc roof in place of the pitched roofs used on the earlier sheds. An additional facility was provided in 1894, in the form of an end loading bay served by a short siding from the run-round loop. The goods station also possessed a set of cattle pens.

The opening of the C&AR in October 1892 did not lead to any major changes in the pattern of train working on the Llantrisant to Cowbridge section. The timetable retained its basic structure which, with certain alterations, had survived since 1878. The passenger service over the C&AR amounted to only three trains each way per day, with the first 'down' working extended to Aberthaw and the last 'up' train starting from the new terminus. An early afternoon service was provided by a mixed working between Cowbridge and Aberthaw.

Aberthaw	dep.		9.50 a.m.	2.10 p.m.			6.45 p.m.
Cowbridge	dep. 7.30 a.m.	10.06	2.40 arr.	2.53 p.m.	5.00 p.m.	7.15
Llantrisant	arr. 7.47	10.22		3.10	5.22	7.36
	dep. 7.52	10.27		3.28	5.27	7.41
Pontypridd	arr. 8.21	10.56		3.57	5.56	8.10
Pontypridd	dep. 8.32 a.m.	11.25 a.m.		4.20 p.m.	6.23 p.m.	8.21 p.m.
Llantrisant	arr. 9.01	11.52		4.50	6.51	8.51
	dep. 9.05	12.00		5.40	6.55	8.57
Cowbridge	arr. 9.26	12.17	1.15 p.m.	6.01	7.18	9.19
Aberthaw	arr. 9.42		1.43	6.20		

The Board of Trade had authorized mixed passenger and goods working on the 7.30a.m. Cowbridge to Pontypridd, 5.00p.m. Cowbridge to Llantrisant and 6.50p.m. Llantrisant to Cowbridge trains in August 1892. However, a request for such workings on the Aberthaw line did not meet with the full approval of the Board of Trade. The TVR wished to run the 1.15p.m. 'down' and the 2.10p.m. and 6.45p.m. 'up' trains on the Cowbridge to Aberthaw section as mixed trains, but the Board of Trade felt that this was unacceptable, in view of the very limited service which was to be provided on the line, and was prepared to sanction only one mixed train in each direction. In response, the TVR elected to work the 1.15p.m. from Aberthaw and the 2.10p.m. from Cowbridge as mixed trains. Such trains were restricted to a load of eight wagons at the rear of the passenger carriages, with a brake van at the tail, with a guard riding in it. In common with passenger trains throughout the TVR, those between Pontypridd and Aberthaw required a brake van at either end, with a guard in one and a brakesman in the other.

The new station at Cowbridge was less convenient for passengers than the old terminus in Eastgate Street, and involved a 300 yard walk to the main road. It also brought some operational disadvantages, as the lack of a run-round loop at either the station or Cowbridge Junction meant that any passenger trains terminating at Cowbridge had to set back to the junction, before proceeding to the old station for reversal or stabling. It is possible that the TVR had originally intended to provide a loop alongside the station

platform, as the formation was laid out for double track through the station, complete with ballast on the loop side. Goods trains were able to proceed directly to the goods yard from Cowbridge Junction. Although the lack of a loop at the junction did not cause many problems at first, because of the limited service provided, it became a serious handicap to the running of additional passenger trains in later years.

The initial pattern of service on the C&AR did not remain unaltered for long. In 1894, the mixed workings to and from Aberthaw were integrated in the main Pontypridd to Cowbridge service, and thereafter the 11.25a.m. 'down' passenger from Pontypridd continued to Aberthaw, and returned as the 2.35p.m. 'up' to Pontypridd.

In addition to the new passenger facilities provided in the early 1890s, the TVR also made a number of improvements to the accommodation provided for staff on the line. In 1893, a house in Aberthaw was altered to provide a home for the Aberthaw station master. The following year, two cottages, known as the Taff Cottages, were erected near Llanharry Station to house the Llanharry station master and another member of staff. Rather less well appointed were two single storey dwellings at St. Mary Church Road. These were acquired in 1895 from Mr Mathias, the contractor of the C&AR, and provided accommodation for staff at that station.

The cattle market at Cowbridge was an important part of the life of the town, and provided a valuable source of traffic for the line. However, the facilities for loading cattle

TVR Class M, 0-6-2T engines were introduced in 1885 and made their first appearance on the Cowbridge line in the early 1890s.
Locomotive Publishing Co.

at the station were decidedly limited, consisting of only three loading pens. This led to a great deal of shunting when there were many cattle wagons to load, something which could result in delays in despatching livestock after the weekly market. This problem was brought up at a meeting of the Cowbridge Borough Council in November 1895, when the matter was referred to the TVR. The TVR responded speedily, by installing four pens in the goods yard so that cattle could be held clear of the loading pens. The loading pens were of typical TVR design, with removable horizontal bars to the rail side, in place of the more usual double gates.

The passenger service between Cowbridge and Pontypridd was improved in July 1896, when an additional round trip was introduced, leaving Cowbridge at 11.43 a.m. and leaving Pontypridd at 1.50 p.m. It arrived back at Cowbridge at 2.43 p.m. This revision was facilitated by the use of the second set of carriages, which had previously been restricted to the early evening short working to Llantrisant and back.

Further improvement to the service were hampered by the lack of passing loops for passenger trains, on both the Llantrisant Junction to Maesaraul Junction section, and the Cowbridge branch. The lack of a loop at Cowbridge was an obvious defect, in view of the concentration of train working at that point. The loop at St. Mary Church Road Station was of little use, given the sparse traffic of the Aberthaw line, and was hardly ever used for passing trains. Even so, the cabin at that station was in use from 8.30 a.m. until 7.00 p.m. every weekday. It was possible to shunt a train clear of the main line at Cowbridge Junction, so that another train might cross its path, but although this was a regular feature of operation, it was not entirely satisfactory for passenger trains.

It was in order to overcome this deficiency that the TVR authorized the provision of a loop siding at Cowbridge Junction, in April 1896. This allowed two goods trains or a goods and a passenger train to cross, whilst goods trains terminating at Cowbridge Goods could still run directly to the yard. The completed loop was inspected by Colonel Yorke for the Board of Trade on 4th January 1897. However, by that date, the TVR had had a change of mind regarding the use it wished to make of the loop, and requested instead that sanction be granted for its use for passing two passenger trains. This was something the Board of Trade was not prepared to countenance until the proper safeguards for passenger use had been provided. This the TVR agreed to do, and the alterations were carried out

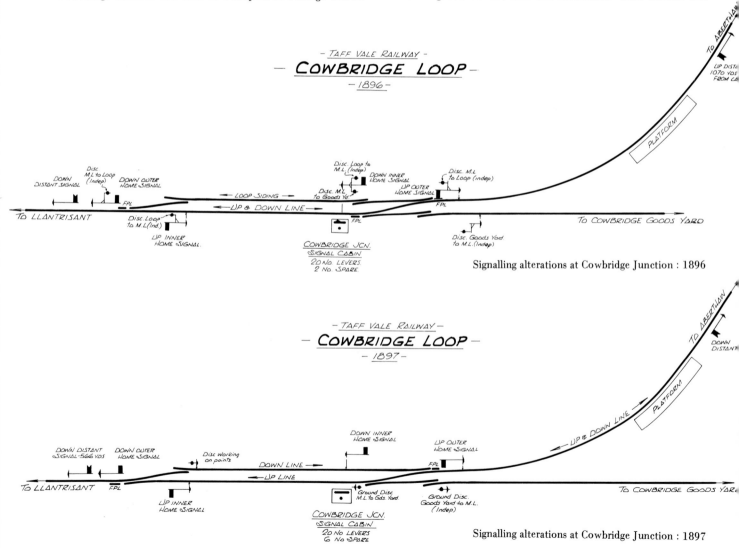

Signalling alterations at Cowbridge Junction : 1896

Signalling alterations at Cowbridge Junction : 1897

shortly after Yorke's inspection. The loop ceased to be a bi-directional goods siding, and became instead a passing loop, with 'up' and 'down' lines suitable for passenger use. The new layout required complete resignalling, with the line to the goods yard becoming a trailing connection from the 'up' line of the loop.

The revised arrangements at Cowbridge Junction were re-inspected, in October 1897, by Colonel Yorke. He was satisfied with the alterations, and recommended that the Board of Trade approve the new works. With the provision of the loop at Cowbridge Junction, the cabin at Cowbridge yard, which had been retained since the opening of Cowbridge Junction cabin in 1892, was abolished.

Although the new loop did not result in an immediate increase in the number of trains on the branch, it did enable the existing timetable to be worked more efficiently, even though terminating trains from Llantrisant still had to set back to the junction before their engines could run-round.

By 1897, goods traffic over the Aberthaw line had increased to an extent sufficient to justify the running of separate goods trains over the line: the 12.22p.m. from Cowbridge, and the 2.30p.m. from Aberthaw, although nominally 'mixed', were accelerated to passenger speeds. The carriages of the 12.22p.m. 'mixed' 'down' train were left at Aberthaw, while the engine returned with the 12.50p.m. goods train from Aberthaw. At Cowbridge, it crossed the 8.08a.m. Coke Ovens (Pontypridd) to Aberthaw local goods train. This train, having sorted the yard at Aberthaw, worked back as the 2.30p.m. mixed to Cowbridge.

Goods workings on the line at this date consisted of an early morning train from Cowbridge to Pontypridd Coke Ovens, returning as the 8.08a.m. to Aberthaw, a 'down' goods, hauled by a Coke Ovens engine, which left Coke Ovens at 5.10a.m., arriving at Cowbridge yard at 8.30a.m., and returning to Coke Ovens at 10.15a.m. A 12.50p.m. goods from Aberthaw remained at Cowbridge until 3.05p.m., when it continued to Llantrisant as a through goods, returning to Cowbridge at 4.00p.m.

The opening of the Vale of Glamorgan Railway in 1897 appears to have led to a decline in goods traffic on the Aberthaw line, as in 1898 the separate goods trains were withdrawn, and the mixed workings reintroduced with extended journey times.

A further improvement to the signalling facilities of the line was provided in 1897, in the form of a new signal cabin at Llantrisant, replacing an earlier cabin at the same place. The new cabin was very close to that of the GWR, and communication between the two was by means of a speaking tube connection.

The building of this new cabin foreshadowed a major improvement to the signalling arrangements of the line, when in June 1897 the TVR authorized the provision of the Electric Train Staff (ETS) mode of operating single lines for the Llantrisant to Cowbridge section. ETS replaced the train staff and ticket method, and had been provided between Llantrisant Junction and Maesaraul Junction since 1894. The introduction of ETS, between Llantrisant and Cowbridge, in 1897, allowed the abolition of the small signal cabins at Llanharry and Ystradowen. They were replaced by ground frames, unlocked by the train staff, the colour for this section being red. The train staff and ticket system was retained between Cowbridge and St. Mary Church Road, with one engine in steam operation from there to Aberthaw.

Cowbridge Junction 'up' home signal in 1951. This was a standard TVR McKenzie & Holland somersault signal, probably dating from the resignalling of the Cowbridge Junction loop in 1897. The original double white stripes can be seen through the flaking paint on the signal arm.

D. Chaplin

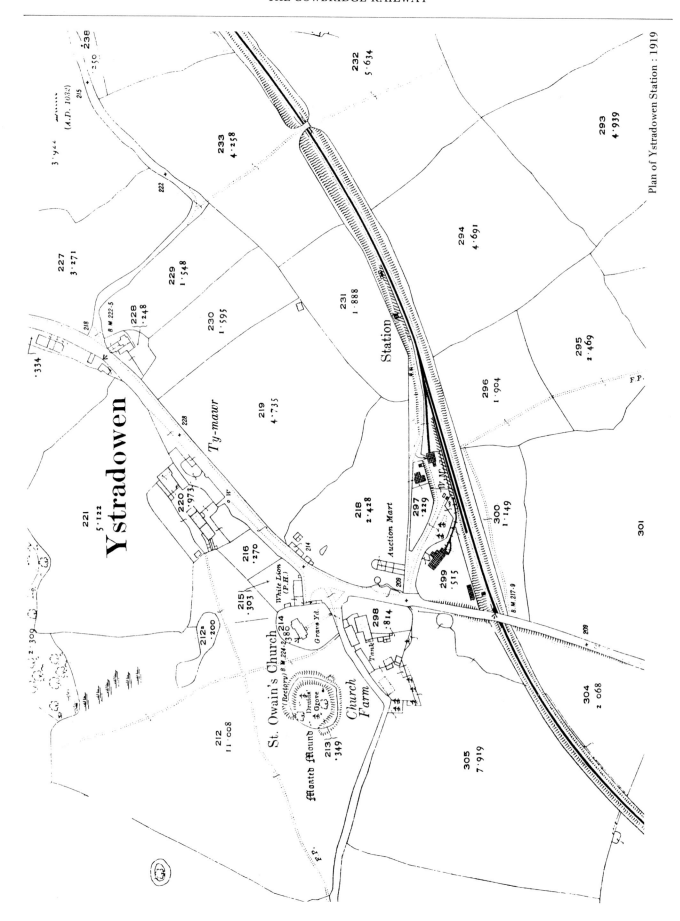

Plan of Ystradowen Station : 1919

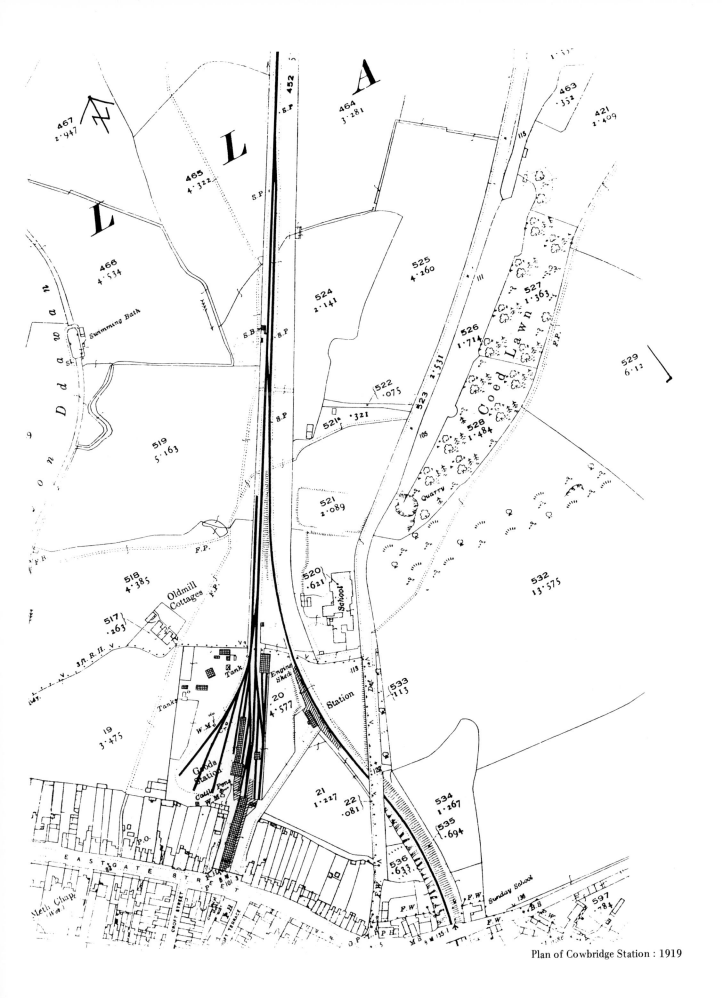

Plan of Cowbridge Station : 1919

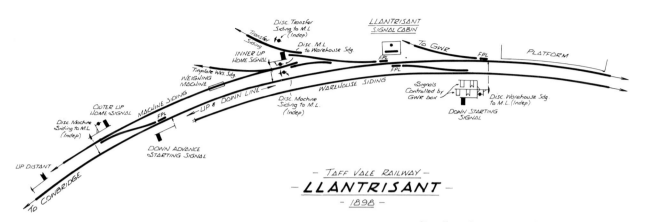

- TAFF VALE RAILWAY -
- LLANTRISANT -
- 1898 -

Signalling alterations at Llantrisant Station : 1898

The very limited goods traffic of the C&AR was augmented, in 1898, when a private siding was provided to serve the lime works of L. Williams & Son, just north of St. Athan Road Station. The siding connection was facing the 'down' trains, and was controlled by a new two-lever ground frame. The lime works pre-dated the siding by a number of years, and was originally served by a tramway from the St. Athan Road, from where the finished lime was carted to the station yard. Five wagons, owned by L. Williams & Son, were passed for service on the TVR in 1897.

Although the TVR and Vale of Glamorgan Railway stations at Aberthaw were almost back to back, there was no direct communication between the two for passengers wishing to change trains; these passengers were faced with a ¼ mile walk between the two stations. This deficiency was raised by the Cowbridge Borough Council in August 1899, when it drew attention to the difficulties encountered by passengers travelling from Cowbridge to Barry, or other stations on the Vale of Glamorgan Railway or the Barry Railway. It also pointed out that certain people were taking a short cut between the two stations, which involved not only trespass, but also danger to life and limb, and requested that the TVR and the Vale of Glamorgan Railway provide a footpath between the two stations. However, the TVR was not impressed by the case for the footpath, and responded by stating that the traffic was not large enough to justify the cost of its construction. This attitude was not shared by the Vale of Glamorgan Railway, which was prepared to build that part of the footpath which fell within its ownership.

L. Williams & Son acquired five wagons, in 1897, for their limeworks, which adjoined St. Athan Road Station. This wagon was used for the transport of coal to the works for the burning of lime.

Gloucester Railway Carriage & Wagon Company (Courtesy of the Historical Model Railway Society)

'Metro' class 2-4-0T, No. 3586 waits at Cowbridge in 1949. In the foreground is the footpath which connected the station to the Llantrisant Road.

H. T. Hobbs

The reluctance of the TVR to provide a footpath at Aberthaw did not extend to the provision of a similar facility at Cowbridge Station, the following year. This connected the Aberthaw end of the station platform to the Llantrisant Road near the point at which that road crossed the railway, and improved access to the station from the east end of the town.

With traffic on the Aberthaw line showing no signs of a significant upturn, and with the availability of the new loop at Cowbridge Junction, the loop and signalling at St. Mary Church Road was largely redundant. A proposal to close St. Mary Church Road signal cabin, and to remove the signalling at the station was agreed by the TVR Traffic Committee in February 1900. The loop was retained as a

loop siding, controlled by new ground frames at each end. The ground frame at the southern end contained 4 levers, and also controlled access to the goods yard.

The last in the series of improvements to stations on the Cowbridge branch was carried out in 1901, when Ystradowen was brought up to the standard of the other stations on the line. The platform was lengthened and raised in height, and other improvements were carried out.

The ordered existence of Cowbridge Station was disturbed on 20th June 1902, when the booking office was broken into and a total of £8 11s 0d was stolen. Investigations continued until January 1903, when a booking clerk at Cowbridge confessed to stealing the Llantrisant cash bag, containing £1 9s 5d on 15th December 1902. He

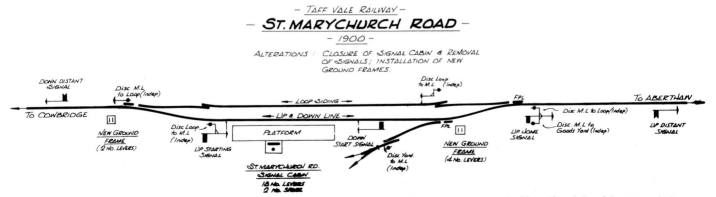

Signalling arrangements at St. Mary Church Road Station : 1900

also admitted the burglary at Cowbridge the previous June, together with other thefts. The booking clerk was dismissed and prosecuted, whilst the Cowbridge station master, Mr Glastonbury, was ordered by the TVR to make up the cash shortfall out of his own pocket. However, Glastonbury's ill luck did not abate, as in January 1904 he was reported for irregularities in the cash account at the station, and was demoted to the lesser post of station master at Cross Inn Station.

A couple of rather less impressive thefts took place at St. Athan Road Station in 1906, when in March of that year the grand sum of 4½d was stolen, and in June the station master's watch went missing! A somewhat more significant theft took place at Llantrisant in May 1914, when the booking office of the GWR station was broken into and £70 10s 8d stolen, £4 2s 0d of which belonged to the TVR.

Vandalism is often thought of as a malaise of the latter part of the present century. However, a number of incidents on the Cowbridge branch show that it was also a feature of life around the turn of the century. On 18th August 1896, 'some evil-disposed person or persons' placed two pieces of iron on the line near Llanharry Station. Luckily, this did not result in any damage or threat to life, but it did prompt the TVR to offer a reward of £10 for information concerning the perpetrators of this outrage. Llanharry appears to have been a particular trouble spot for vandalism of this sort, as two incidents in 1912 show; on 12th July of that year a train between Llanharry and Ystradowen ran into a sleeper which had been placed across the track; a similar occurrence took place at the same spot on 19th July 1912, causing the TVR to offer a reward of £25.

The opening of the C&AR gave the people of Cowbridge the opportunity to partake in relatively quick and easy visits to the seaside around Aberthaw. In earlier years, such trips had involved long and bumpy rides on wagonettes. Trips to the Leys, the headland to the west of the mouth of the River Thaw, were a favourite for Sunday school outings from Cowbridge and further afield. They terminated at St. Athan Road Station, from where the Sunday scholars had to walk about a mile to the sea-shore. Aberthaw was also a common destination: one such outing from Cross Inn Station for Llantrisant Sunday School in July 1902 involved some 500 children, and required the sending of three extra carriages from Cowbridge to Cross Inn, to be attached to the 8.54 a.m. 'down' train from that station. The excursion returned home in the evening as a special train, with the carriages being worked back to Cowbridge from Cross Inn as empty stock. Excursionists to Barry Island, that mecca of South Wales resorts, had to trudge up the hill to the Vale of Glamorgan Station at Aberthaw, in order to continue their journey. As well as excursions to Cowbridge Races, special trains for passengers and stock were run in connection with the annual Cowbridge Show, which was first held on 22nd September 1892. On one such occasion, a special horse-box train is known to have worked through from Cowbridge to Peterborough, via the Severn Tunnel and Oxford.

Other excursions which were regularly worked on to the Cowbridge line, albeit for a very short distance, were the many trips from Pontypridd and the valleys to Porthcawl. These ran into the Cowbridge bay at Llantrisant, before reversing and continuing their journeys over the GWR. Excursions from the Cowbridge line could often involve rather circuitous routes. For example, an excursion for the employees of the Ely Tinplate Works at Llantrisant to Penarth, in 1889, stuck rigidly to TVR metals for its route, which was via Treforest and Radyr.

Ex-GWR 0-4-2T, No. 1471 is pictured with the SLS tour, in the Cowbridge bay at Llantrisant Station, on 13th July 1957. *M. Hale*

Taff Vale Railway.

NOTICE.

£10 REWARD

WHEREAS on Tuesday, the 18th August, 1896, some evil=disposed Person or Persons placed Two Pieces of Iron on the Rail near Llanharry Station of the Cow=bridge Railway, with the object, it is believed, of throwing a Train off the Line.

The above Reward will be paid for such information as will lead to the discovery and conviction of the Person or Persons by whom the Pieces of Iron were so placed.

A. BEASLEY,

CARDIFF, *September 2nd, 1896.* *General Manager.*

TVR notice of reward for information : 1896

Public Record Office

No. 6558.

Taff Vale Railway.

WEEK-END MARKET TICKETS

— AND —

TOURIST ARRANGEMENTS

Nov. 1st, 1912 to April 30th, 1913.

Full Particulars of Arrangements may be obtained on application to the Superintendent of the Line, or at the respective Booking Offices.

A. BEASLEY,
General Manager.

Cardiff, October, 1912.

THIS CANCELS ALL PREVIOUS ANNOUNCEMENTS.

A. M'LAY & CO., LTD. Railway and Commercial Printers, 20, Womling Street, Cardiff.

TVR weekend market tickets and tourist arrangements : 1912

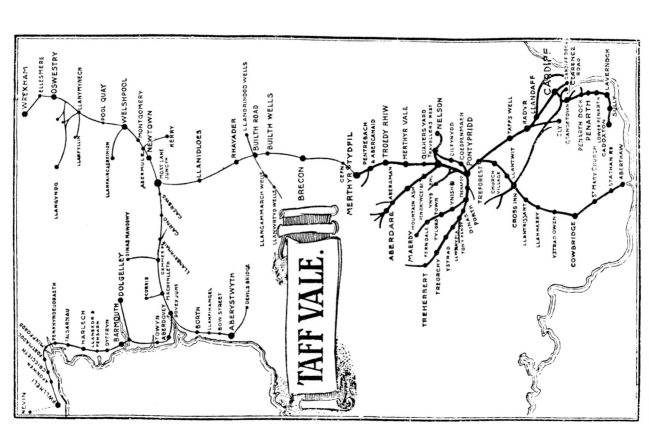

TVR plan of network used on publicity material

An additional service from Llantrisant was provided on 1st May 1901, when the GWR introduced passenger trains between Llantrisant and Pen-y-graig, on the Ely Valley line, using a new bay which it had constructed on the north side of the 'up' platform at Llantrisant.

By 1902, an extra early evening passenger train had been introduced between Cowbridge and Llantrisant, bringing the total to seven trains each way. In addition, a late evening round trip, known locally as the 'Rodney' was introduced on Saturdays, for the benefit of revellers returning from Llantrisant to Cowbridge.

Despite the gradual improvement in frequency, the passenger service was still a cause of much complaint. Most of the branch trains worked through to Pontypridd, where good connections were usually available for the towns of Merthyr, Aberdare and the Rhondda Valley, and even minor destinations such as Ynysybwl and Nelson, in later years. However, many of the passengers wished to go to Cardiff or Bridgend, which involved a change to GWR trains at Llantrisant. As the TVR trains were timed with Pontypridd connections in mind, a convenient connection at Llantrisant was often a matter of luck, and some very lengthy waits at Llantrisant could feature in journeys between Cowbridge and Cardiff.

The TVR had always responded to requests for improved services by pointing out that the traffic on the line was insufficient to justify more intensive working. However, from 1903 onwards, an attempt was made to develop new traffic, and to reduce the operating costs of certain services throughout the TVR network with the introduction of steam railcars, called 'motor cars' on the TVR. The Cowbridge line was one of those selected for such a service, and halts, or platforms, as they were known to the TVR, were planned at Trerhyngyll & Maendy and Aberthin, between Llantrisant and Cowbridge, and at St. Hilary and Llanbethery on the Aberthaw line. Initially, consideration

was given to two alternative types of platform, either ground level or normal height. The use of ground level platforms depended on the satisfactory operation of movable steps, fitted to the cars. Evidently, these were not found to be sufficiently reliable and it was decided to go for raised platforms, albeit at a lower cost than those originally proposed. These were of standard design, 40 ft. long without any form of shelter; intending passengers were confined to a fenced enclosure at the rear of the platform, from which they were released by the motor car conductor on the arrival of the car.

Trerhyngyll & Maendy Platform was quite reasonably situated for the villages it served, whereas Aberthin Platform was about half a mile from the village, and was reached by means of a footpath across the intervening fields. St. Hilary Platform was also some way from its village, at the foot of a long steep hill. Passengers arriving at Llanbethery were faced with a similar climb to that village.

The introduction of the motor car service on the Cowbridge branch was delayed until the second batch of cars was available, in 1905. They appear to have been awaited with some impatience, for in October 1904, Llantwit Fardre Parish Council pressed the TVR for an early date for the start of the new service. In his reply, Ammon Beasley pointed out that as there were only five cars in use on the TVR, with another two under construction, it would not be possible to introduce the cars on the Pontypridd to Aberthaw service until the following spring, when a further six cars would be available. He also noted that the passenger traffic on the branch was very slight, and was then being operated at a loss; it was hoped that the cars would enable the company to provide for a greater traffic at a lower cost. The fact that these cars were equipped with heating was a great attraction, this being in sharp contrast to the four-wheeled carriages then used on the line.

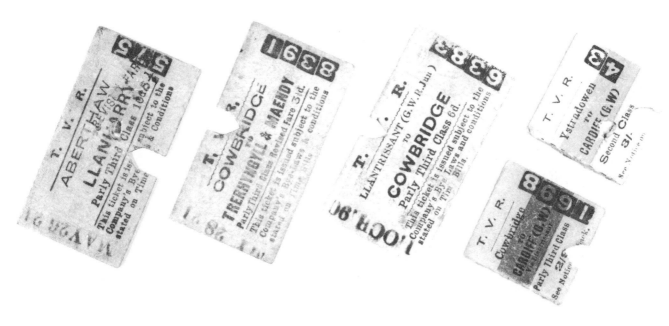

A selection of tickets   *C. W. Harris Collection*

TVR steam railcar No. 9 was one of the batch of six cars built by Kerr Stuart & Co. in 1905. No. 9 failed in service on the Cowbridge branch on 5th June 1907. *R. F. Wilding*

The new steam motor car service between Pontypridd, Llantrisant, Cowbridge and Aberthaw opened on 1st May 1905, together with the motor car platforms. The revised timetable provided a significant improvement in frequency, with nine round trips per day between Cowbridge and Pontypridd, and no less than six each way on the Aberthaw line. Two cars were used for the service, together with an engine and coaches working, which was retained to cover the first trip of the day to Pontypridd and back. A mixed passenger and goods working between Cowbridge and Aberthaw was retained for the goods traffic of that section. These trains did not call at any of the motor car platforms.

May 1905 Timetable

				m.c.	m.c.		m.c.	m.c.	m.c.	m.c.	m.c.	m.c.	WSO
Pontypridd	dep.		8.31	10.05	11.20		1.47	3.15	4.58	6.35	8.20	9.53	
													m.c.
Llantrisant	dep.		9.05	10.45	12.10		2.19	3.48	5.40	7.25	8.53	10.22	11.10
		m.c.				mix							
Cowbridge	dep.	7.45	9.22	11.08	12.29	12.40	2.39	4.10	6.08	7.45	9.13	10.42	11.30
Aberthaw	arr.	8.02	9.35	11.25		1.09		4.27	6.25				

			m.c.			m.c.		mix		m.c.	m.c.		WSO
Aberthaw	dep.		8.10	9.45		12.05		2.10		4.40	6.30		
					m.c.		m.c.		m.c.			m.c.	m.c.
Cowbridge	dep.	7.15	8.30	9.59	10.09	12.27	1.35	2.34	2.48	5.00	6.50	8.25	10.50
Llantrisant	dep.	7.37	8.53		10.30	12.47	1.53		3.28	5.23	7.20	9.02	11.08
Pontypridd	arr.	8.07	9.13		10.51	1.20	2.51		3.58	6.00	7.49	9.30	

Key: *m.c. = motor car*
mix = mixed train

Motor car No. 17 was one of the larger units built by Manning Wardle in 1906, with the coach section by Brush of Loughborough. They shared the Cowbridge service with the smaller cars until the arrival, in 1907, of the auto-train, when the use of a larger car alongside an auto-train became the rule. The coach units were freely exchanged with those of the smaller cars.

R. C. Riley

4

MARKET TICKETS.

MARKET TICKETS are issued as under.   They are only available by the trains named and on the day of issue, if used otherwise the ordinary fare will be charged.

Each holder of a Market Ticket is allowed to carry a basket or package not exceeding 60 lbs. in weight free ; all goods in excess of this weight must be paid for at the rate of 1s. 2d. per cwt.

To	From	3rd Class return fare	Market Days.	Trains by which the Tickets are available.						
				Forward Journey.						Return Journey.
		s. d.		A.M.	P.M.			P.M.		
Cardiff	Cross Inn ...	1 7	Saturdays	10 37	12 57			3 48		2 28, 4 0, 6.0, 7 55, 9 40 p.m.
,,	Llantwit ...	1 6	,,	10 46	1 6			3 58		
,,	Church Village ...	1 4	,,	10 49	1 9	P.M.		4 1		
,,	Pontypridd ...	1 4	,,	9 9	1 28	4 59		6 9		
,,	Treforest ...	1 3	,,	9 58	1 48	5 3		6 30		3 0 p.m. 5 40 p.m. 7 35 p.m.
,,	Taffs Well	0 9	,,	9 20	1 58	5 13		6 40		9 40 p.m. 10 45 p.m. 10 58 p.m.
,,	Radyr ...	0 6	,,	9 25	1 42	5 18		6 45		
,,	Llandaff ...	0 5	,,	9 31	1 48	5 25		6 51		
	for Whitchurch			A.M.	A.M.			P.M.		
Pontypridd	Cowbridge ...	1 7	Wednesdays	7 0	10 0			5 0		
,,	Ystradowen	1 5	and	7 10	10 10			5 10		
,,	Llanharry ...	1 2	Saturdays	7 15	10 15			5 15		11 28 a.m. and any ordinary train
,,	Llantrisant ...	1 1	,,	7 25	10 30	P.M.		5 23		after 12.0 noon.
,,	Cross Inn...	0 10	,,	7 34	10 37	2 25		5 30		
,,	Llantwit ...	0 7	,,	7 45	10 46	2 34		5 42		
,,	Church Village	0 6	,,	7 48	10 49	2 37		5 45		12.30., 2.49, 6.9, 8.12, 9.44 and
,,	Taffs Well	0 9	,,	8 8	9 16	..	1 16	5 56		11.34 p.m.
,,	Treherbert	1 3	,,	7 35	10 30	11 50	3 31	4 15		
,,	Treorchy ...	1 1	,,	7 40	10 35	11 55	3 36	4 20		
,,	Ystrad ...	0 11	,,	7 45	10 40	11 59	3 41	4 25		
,,	Llwynypia ...	0 9	,,	7 50	10 45	12 4	3 46	4 30		
,,	T'pandy & Trealaw	0 8	,,	7 54	10 49	12 9	3 50	4 34		
,,	Dinas ...	0 7	,,	7 57	10 52	12 12	3 53	4 37		11 23 a.m. and any ordinary train
,,	Porth ...	0 5	,,	8 6	11 1	12 18	4 2	4 46		after 12 noon.
,,	Maerdy ...	1 1	,,	7 35	10 25	11 48	3 20	4 13		
,,	Ferndale ...	0 11	,,	7 42	10 32	11 54	3 26	4 19		
,,	Tylorstown	0 8	,,	7 48	10 38	12 0	3 32	4 25		
,,	Ynyshir ...	0 6	,,	7 53	10 43	12 3	3 40	4 33		
,,	Mountain Ash	0 11	,,	8 0	10 45	...	2 16	4 1		
,,	Penrhiwceiber	0 9	,,	8 4	10 49	...	2 20	4 5		11 23 a.m. and any ordinary train
,,	Abercynon	0 6	,,	8 18	10 57	...	2 39	5*45		after 12.0 noon.
,,	Quakers Yard	0 8	,,	8 8	10 58		2 30	5*37		11 18 a.m. and any ordinary train after 12.0 noon.
,,	Ynysybwl...	0 6	,,	7 49	10 44		2 22	4 6		11 27 a.m. and any ordinary train after 12.0 noon.
,,	Nelson ...	0 9	,,	7 48	9 13, 10 38, 12 58, 4 3, 5 51					11 25 a.m. and any ordinary train train after 12.0 noon.
Cowbridge	Pontypridd ...	1 7	Tuesdays	A.M. 8 36	A.M. 10 0	A.M. 11 28				
,,	Treforest ...	1 6	,,	8 40	10 4	11 32				
,,	Church Village	1 4	,,	8 51	10 15	11 43				
,,	Llantwit ...	1 2	,,	8 56	10 18	11 46				
,,	Cross Inn...	0 11	,,	9 5	10 27	11 55				12 5 p.m. 1 38 p.m. 3 55 p.m. 5 0 p.m.
,,	Llantrisant	0 9	,,	9 15	10 45	P.M. 12 27				
,,	Llanharry	0 6	,,	9 21	10 51	12 33				
,,	Ystradowen	0 4	,,	9 26	10 56	12 38				
,,	Aberthaw	0 9	,,	7 55	11 40	...				
,,	St. Athan Road	0 8	,,	7 58	11 43	...				11 8 a.m. 4 11 p.m. 7 52 p.m.
,,	St. Mary Church Rd	0 3	,,	8 7	11 52	...				
Merthyr	Abercynon	1 1	Fridays	A.M. 8 36	A.M. 9 42					
,,	Quakers Yard	0 10	,,	8 44	9 50					2 10 p.m. and 3 50 p.m
,,	Merthyr Vale	0 7	,,	8 50	9 56					
,,	Troedyrhiw	0 5	,,	8 55	10 1					
Merthyr	Abercynon	1 1	Saturdays	A.M. 11 28	P.M. 4 18					
,,	Quakers Yard	0 10	,,	11 36	4 26					3 50 p.m. 5 45 p.m. 7 25 p.m.
,,	Merthyr Vale	0 7	,,	11 42	4 32					9 5 p.m. and 10.25 p.m.
,,	Troedyrhiw	0 5	,,	11 47	4 37					
Aberdare	Abercynon	0 11	Saturdays	A.M. 11 33	P.M. 3 46	P.M. 4 42				
,,	Penrhiwceiber	0 8	,,	11 41	3 55	4 50				3 5 p.m. 5 50 p.m. 7.25 p.m
,,	Mountain Ash	0 6	,,	11 45	3 59	4 54				and 9 5 p.m.
,,	Aberaman	0 3	,,	11 52	4 6	5 1				

* Saturdays only.

TVR market tickets notice : 1912

In October 1905, the TVR authorized the introduction of the ETS system on the Cowbridge to Aberthaw section. This allowed a goods train to be sent down the line to Aberthaw, where it was locked out of section, making it possible to work a motor car to Aberthaw and back, whilst the goods shunted at Aberthaw. A blue train staff was used for this section, unlocking the ground frames at St. Mary Church Road, Williams Siding, St. Athan Road and Aberthaw. Following the introduction of ETS, the mixed passenger and goods working between Cowbridge and Aberthaw was replaced by a separate goods train. The engine and coaches working was also revised; the 9.45 a.m. from Aberthaw was extended to Pontypridd, returning to Cowbridge at 11.27 a.m. where a connection was made with a car for Aberthaw.

June 1906 Timetable

			m.c.			m.c.	m.c.	m.c.	m.c.	m.c.	m.c.
Pontypridd	dep.	8.31	10.03	11.27		1.46	3.14	4.55	6.25	8.20	10.05
Llantrisant	arr.	8.58	10.33	11.55		2.16	3.34	5.26	6.50	8.51	10.35
	dep.	9.05	10.45	12.27		2.19	3.48	5.45	6.55	9.03	10.40
Cowbridge	arr.	9.20	11.04	12.43		2.38	4.07	6.04	7.45	9.22	10.59
		m.c.			m.c.						
	dep. 7.45	9.22	11.08*		12.48		4.11		7.48		
Aberthaw	arr. 8.04	9.35	11.27*		1.07		4.30		8.07		
		m.c.		m.c.	m.c.		m.c.		m.c.		
Aberthaw	dep.	8.08	9.45	11.40*	1.14		4.37		8.13		
Cowbridge	arr.	8.28	9.59	11.55*	1.34		4.57		8.33		
						m.c.		m.c.			
	dep. 7.15	8.30	10.03	12.05	1.38	2.55	5.00	6.45	8.36		
Llantrisant	arr. 7.30	8.49	10.18	12.24	1.57	3.14	5.19	7.04	8.55		
	dep. 7.37	8.53	10.28	12.50	2.32	3.40	5.23	7.25	9.00		
Pontypridd	arr. 8.07	9.25	10.57	1.20	3.02	4.14	5.57	7.54	9.31		

Key: *m.c. = motor car*
* = Tuesdays only

In spite of, or because of, the improvement in the accessibility of the railway passenger service, which the motor car platforms provided, there were still requests for extra stops. An approach from Lady Quin for a platform at Beaupre, between Cowbridge and St. Hilary Platform, was rejected by the TVR in January 1906. A request from the residents of Ystradowen and district for a platform at Rhydhalog Bridge was also refused in October 1913.

The capacity of the single track section between Llantrisant Junction and Mwyndy Junction was increased in 1906, when the loop at Maesaraul Junction was upgraded to passenger status. A similar modification was undertaken at Llantwit Station in 1910, when the former goods loop siding was converted to an 'up' passenger loop.

A further improvement to the working of Cowbridge branch trains came with the rebuilding of Pontypridd Station, which commenced in 1907. The old 'up' and 'down' platforms, with their 'up' and 'down' bays, were replaced by a new island platform, having a total of five inset bays, although only one was provided at the south end of the station. It was this bay into which the Cowbridge service usually worked. Nevertheless, the reversal of these trains, or cars, over the North Curve still took place as necessary.

The branch timetable was revised in May 1908, following the replacement of one of the motor cars by an auto-train At the same time, the engine and coaches working was withdrawn and, henceforth, all trains and cars called at all stations and motor car platforms, between Aberthaw and Pontypridd.

May 1908 Timetable

Pontypridd	dep.	8.31	10.03	11.27	1.46	3.15	5.12	6.25	8.20	10.05	
Llantrisant	arr.	9.01	10.33	11.57	2.16	3.45	5.46	6.55	8.51	10.35	
	dep.	9.05	10.45	12.27	2.19	3.51	5.51	7.26	9.03	10.40	
Cowbridge	arr.	9.24	11.04	12.46	2.38	4.07	6.10	7.45	9.22	10.59	
	dep. 7.40	9.26	11.08*	12.48		4.11		7.48			
Aberthaw	arr. 7.59	9.45	11.27*	1.07		4.30		8.07			
Aberthaw	dep.	8.05	9.47	11.40*	1.14		4.37		8.13		
Cowbridge	arr.	8.25	10.07	12.00*	1.34		4.57		8.33		
	dep. 7.10	8.28	10.09	12.05	2.55	5.00	6.45	8.36			
Llantrisant	arr. 7.29	8.47	10.27	12.24	1.57	3.14	5.19	7.04	8.55		
	dep. 7.37	8.52	10.30	12.50	2.32	3.40	5.23	7.24	9.00		
Pontypridd	arr. 8.07	9.23	11.00	1.20	3.02	4.14	5.57	7.54	9.31		

Key: ** = Tuesdays only*

A Llantrisant branch auto-train waits in the 'down' bay at Pontypridd Station in 1949. This bay was formerly used by Cowbridge trains when working through to Pontypridd after the rebuilding of that station. The auto-car is a conversion from one of the Taff Vale Railway's small railcars.

LGRP (Courtesy of David & Charles)

Auto-fitted Class I, 4-4-0T, No. 287 (formerly No. 69) is seen sandwiched between two auto-cars, which were built in 1907, in the early years of auto-working on the TVR.

P. Korrison

ABERTHAW, COWBRIDGE, LLANTRISANT AND PONTYPRIDD.

WEEKDAYS.

		a.m	a.m	a.m	a.m	a.m	a.m	p.m	p.m	p.m	p.m	p.m	p.m	p.m	p.m
		W	Car	Car	Car	Car	Car	Car	Car	Car	Car	Car	Car	Car	Car
Aberthaw ...	dep	W	...	8 5	...	10 5	1140	...	1 38	2 55	4 37	5 0	...	8 13
St. Athan Road	,,		...	8 8	...	10 8	1143	...	1 41	2 58	4 40	5 5	...	8 16
Llanbethery Platform	,,		...	8 11	...	1010	1146	...	1 43	3 0	4 43	5 5	...	8 19
St. Mary Church Road	,,		...	8 17	...	1015	1152	...	1 48	8 5	4 49	5 10	...	8 25
St. Hilary Platform	,,		...	8 20	...	1020	1155	...	1 53	8 10	4 52	5 15	...	8 28
Cowbridge ...	arr		...	8 25	...	1023	12 0	...	1 57	8 14	4 57	5 19	...	8 33
Cowbridge ...	dep		7 10	8 28	...	1030	12 5	1 33	2 25	3 40	5 0	5 23	6 45	8 41
Aberthin Platform	,,		7 13	8 31	...	1037	12 8	1 41	2 33	3 48	5 5	5 31	6 48	8 43
Trerhyngyll & Maendy	,,		7 15	8 33	...	1042	1210	1 43	2 38	3 53	5 5	5 36	6 50	8 48
Ystradowen	,,		7 20	8 38	...	1046	1215	1 48	2 43	3 58	5 10	5 41	6 55	8 58
Llanharry	,,		7 25	8 43	...	1049	1220	1 53	2 46	4 5	5 15	5 48	7 0	8 67
Llantrisant for G.W.R.	arr		7 29	8 47	...	1053	1224	1 57	2 50	4 11	5 19	5 54	7 4	8 67
Llantrisant for G.W.R.	dep		7 37	...	8 52	1030	1250	...	2 55	3 40	5 23	8 7	...	9 0
Cross Inn for Llantris't	,,		4 177	45 8	8 59	1087	1257	...	2 58	3 48	5 31	8 107	34	9 7
Llantwit	,,			50 8	10 9	1042	1 2	...	8 0	3 53	5 36	8 157	39	9 12
Church Village	,,		4 247	54 8	14 9	1046	1 6	...	8 3	3 58	5 41	8 197	43	9 16
Tonteg Platform	,,		4 277	57 8	17 9	1049	1 11	...	8 10	4 5	5 44	8 227	46	9 23
Treforest	,,		4 358	18 9	1053	1 15	...	8 14	4 11	5 48	8 267	50	9 28
Pontypridd Junction	arr		4 388	259	23	1058	1 18	...	8 14	4 14	5 57	8 327	58	9 32

W Workmen's Train not run on Bank Holidays.

NO SUNDAY SERVICE.

PONTYPRIDD, LLANTRISANT, COWBRIDGE AND ABERTHAW.

WEEKDAYS.

		a.m	a.m	a.m	a.m	p.m	p.m	p.m	p.m	p.m	p.m	p.m
		Car	Car	Car	Car	Car	Car	Car	Car	Car	Car	Car
Pontypridd Junction	dep	...	8 33	10 0	1125	1 48	3 12	335	5 10	6 25	8 18	10 5
Treforest	,,	...	8 37	10 4	1129	1 52	3 16	375	5 14	6 29	8 22	10 9
Tonteg Platform	,,	...	8 48	1011	1130	1 50	3 23	375	5 21	6 36	8 29	1016
Church Village	,,	...	8 48	1018	1140	2 7	3 27	485	5 25	6 40	8 34	1020
Llantwit	,,	...	8 58	1022	1148	2 12	3 30	515	5 28	6 43	8 37	1023
Beddau Platform	,,	...	9 5	1027	1152	2 16	3 34	555	5 32	6 47	8 41	1027
Cross Inn for Llantris't	,,	...	9 10	1033	1157	2 21	3 38	595	5 41	6 52	8 46	1031
Llantrisant for G.W.R.	arr	...	...	...	...	...	3 43	5 46	...	6 57	8 51	1036
Llantrisant for G.W.R.	dep	...	9 21	1045	1227	2 24	3 48	4 6	5 51	7 36	9 3	1040
Llanharry	,,	...	9 25	1051	1238	2 30	3 54	5 57	7 32	9 4	1046
Ystradowen	,,	...	9 26	1056	1285	2 35	3 59	6 2	7 40	9 14	1051
Trerhynygyll & Maendy	,,	...	9 29	1059	1241	2 38	4 2	6 5	7 44	9 17	1054
Aberthin Platform	,,	...	9 31	11 1	1243	2 40	4 5	6 7	7 46	9 19	1056
Cowbridge	,, arr	...	9 34	11 4	1246	2 43	4 7	6 10	7 49	9 22	1059
Cowbridge ...	dep	7 40	...	11 8	...	...	4 11	...	7 52	...
St. Hilary Platform	,,	7 45	...	1113	...	...	4 16	...	7 57	...
St. Mary Church Rd.	,,	7 48	...	1116	...	...	4 19	...	8 0	...
Llanbethery Platform	,,	7 54	...	1122	...	...	4 25	...	8 6	...
St. Athan Road	,,	7 57	...	1125	...	...	4 28	...	8 8	...
Aberthaw ...	arr	7 59	...	1127	...	...	4 30	...	8 11	...

NO SUNDAY SERVICE.

ABERTHAW, COWBRIDGE, LLANTRISANT AND PONTYPRIDD.

WEEKDAYS.

		a.m	a.m	a.m	a.m	a.m	a.m	p.m	p.m	p.m	p.m	p.m	p.m	p.m	p.m
		Car	Car	Car	Car	Car	Car	Car	Car	Car	Car	Car	Car	Car	Car
Aberthaw ...	dep		8 5	...	9 45	1140	...	1 14	2 55	4 37	5 0	...	6 45	8 13
St. Athan Road	,,		8 8	...	9 48	1143	...	1 17	2 58	4 40	5 5	...	6 48	8 16
Llanbethery Platform	,,		8 11	...	...	1146	...	1 20	3 0	4 43	5 5	...	6 50	8 19
St. Mary Church Road	,,		8 17	...	9 54	1152	...	1 26	8 5	4 49	5 10	...	6 55	8 25
St. Hilary Platform	,,		8 20	...	...	1155	...	1 29	8 10	4 52	5 15	...	7 0	8 28
Cowbridge ...	arr		8 25	...	9 59	12 0	...	1 34	8 14	4 57	5 19	...	7 4	8 33
Cowbridge ...	dep	7 15	8 28	...	10 3	12 5	...	1 38	2 55	3 40	5 0	...	6 45	8 36
Aberthin Platform	,,		8 31	...	...	12 8	...	1 41	2 58	3 48	5 5	...	6 48	8 39
Trerhyngyll & Maendy	,,		8 33	...	...	1210	...	1 43	3 5	3 53	5 5	...	6 50	8 41
Ystradowen	,,	7 21	8 38	...	10 9	1215	...	1 48	3 8	3 58	5 10	...	6 55	8 46
Llanharry	,,	7 27	8 43	...	1015	1220	...	1 53	3 10	4 5	5 15	...	7 0	8 51
Llantrisant for G.W.R.	arr	7 30	8 47	...	1018	1224	...	1 57	3 14	4 11	5 19	...	7 4	8 55
Llantrisant for G.W.R.	dep	7 37	8 52	...	1025	1250	...	2 32	3 40	5 23	...	9 0
Cross Inn for Llantris't	,,	7 45	40 9	1035	1257	...	2 39	3 50	5 33	6 107	31	9 7
Llantwit	,,	7 53	50 9	8	1043	1 5	...	2 47	3 58	5 41	6 187	39	9 15
Church Village	,,	7 56	8 539	11	1046	1 8	...	2 50	4 5	5 44	6 217	42	9 18
Tonteg Platform	,,		57 9	15	1 12	...	2 54	4 5	5 48	6 257	46	9 22
Treforest	,,	4 9	9 20	1054	1 17	...	2 59	4 11	5 54	6 317	51	9 28
Pontypridd Junction	arr	8 7	9 9 23	1057	1 20	...	3 2	4 14	5 57	6 347	51	9 31

NO SUNDAY SERVICE.

PONTYPRIDD, LLANTRISANT, COWBRIDGE AND ABERTHAW.

WEEKDAYS.

		a.m	a.m	a.m	a.m	a.m	a.m	p.m	p.m	p.m	p.m	p.m	p.m	p.m
		Car	Car	Car	Car	Car	Car	Car	Car	Car	Car	Car	Car	Car
Pontypridd Junction	dep		8 10	8 31	...	1127	...	1 46	3 15	4 35	5 16	5 17	6 52	8 20	10 5
Treforest	,,		8 14	8 35	...	1131	...	1 50	3 19	4 39	5 19	5 77	56	8 24	10 9
Tonteg Platform	,,		8 22	...	1139	...	1 57	3 26	4 46	6 2	8 31	1016
Church Village	,,		8 25	8 43	...	1142	...	2 1	3 30	4 50	5 26	6 4	6 7	8 36	1020
Llantwit	,,		8 28	8 46	...	1149	...	2 11	3 33	4 53	5 31	6 7	6 107	41	8 39	1023
Cross Inn for Llantris't	,,		8 33	8 52	...	1155	...	2 16	3 40	5 4	5 41	...	7 45	8 46	1030
Llantrisant for G.W.R.	arr		8 35	8 58	...				3 45	5 46	46 5	6 55	8 51	1035
Llantrisant for G.W.R.	dep		9 5	...	1227	...	2 19	3 48	5 17	7 26	9 3	1040
Llanharry	,,		9 9	...	1231	...	2 25	3 54	5 77	32	9 9	1046
Ystradowen	,,		9 15	...	1237	...	2 33	3 59	6 7	7 40	9 14	1051
Trerhvngyil & Maendy	,,		...	1243	...	2 35	4 2	6 7	7 42	9 17	1054
Aberthin Platform	,,	9 20	...	1248	...	2 38	4 7	6 107	45	9 19	1056
Cowbridge	,, arr	9 22	...	1250	...	...	4 11	7 48	9 22	1059
Cowbridge ...	dep	7 40	...	11 8	...	...	4 16	7 53	...
St. Hilary Platform	,,	7 45	...	1113	...	...	4 19	7 56	...
St. Mary Church Rd.	,,	7 48	9 27	1116	...	...	4 22	8 2	...
Llanbethery Platform	,,	7 54	...	1122	...	...	4 25	8 6	...
St. Athan Road	,,	7 57	9 33	1125	...	...	4 28	8 6	...
Aberthaw ...	arr	7 59	9 35	1127	...	...	4 30	8 7	...

NO SUNDAY SERVICE.

TOURIST TICKETS

AVAILABLE FOR SIX MONTHS,

ARE ISSUED DAILY (EXCEPT SUNDAYS) TO

BUILTH, LLANDRINDOD, LLANWRTYD, AND LLANGAMMARCH WELLS,

Via MERTHYR and TALYLLYN,

AS UNDER :—

STATIONS TO ☞	BUILTH WELLS		LLANDRINDOD		LLANWRTYD or LLANGAMMARCH	
STATIONS FROM	Classes		Classes		Classes	
	1st	3rd	1st	3rd	1st	3rd
	s. d.	s. d.	s. d.	s. d.	s. d.	s. d.
ABERDARE	16 10	9 0	16 10	9 3	18 5	10 0
Aberaman	16 10	9 0	16 10	9 3	18 5	10 0
Abercynon	15 3	8 3	16 4	9 0	17 11	9 9
CARDIFF (Queen Street) ...	18 9	10 3	20 11	10 6	22 6	11 9
Cowbridge	20 9	10 6	21 11	12 6	23 6	12 9
Cross Inn (for Llantrisant)...	18 7	9 6	19 9	10 6	21 4	11 9
Cilfynydd...	16 10	8 6	17 10	9 6	19 5	10 6
Dinas	17 7	9 6	18 9	10 6	20 4	11 9
Ferndale	18 8	9 6	19 10	10 6	21 5	11 9
Llandaff (for Whitchurch) ...	18 9	9 6	20 0	10 6	21 7	11 9
Llwynypia	18 2	9 6	19 4	10 6	20 11	11 9
Maerdy	19 4	9 6	20 6	10 6	22 1	11 9
Merthyr Vale	14 6	8 0	15 8	9 0	17 3	9 9
Mountain Ash	15 6	8 3	16 8	9 0	18 3	9 9
Penarth Town	19 11	10 6	22 5	11 9	24 0	12 9
Penarth Dock	19 11	10 6	22 4	11 9	23 11	12 9
Penrhiwceiber	16 2	8 3	16 4	9 0	17 11	9 9
PONTYPRIDD	16 6	8 6	17 8	9 6	19 3	10 6
Porth	17 3	9 3	18 5	10 6	20 0	11 6
Quakers Yard	14 11	8 0	16 1	9 0	17 8	9 9
Radyr	18 9	9 6	20 0	10 6	21 7	11 9
Taff's Well	18 2	9 6	19 4	10 6	20 11	11 9
Tonypandy and Trealaw ...	17 11	9 6	19 1	10 6	20 8	11 9
Treforest...	16 9	8 6	17 11	9 6	19 6	10 6
Trehafod	17 0	9 0	18 2	10 6	19 9	10 6
Treherbert	19 6	10 3	20 8	11 9	22 3	11 9
Treorchy...	19 0	9 6	20 2	11 6	21 9	11 9
Troedyrhiw	13 10	8 0	15 0	9 0	16 7	9 9
Tylorstown	18 2	9 6	19 4	10 6	20 11	11 9
Ynyshir	17 7	9 6	18 9	10 6	20 4	11 9
Ystrad	18 8	9 6	19 10	10 6	21 5	11 9
Ynysybwl	17 0	8 6	17 7	9 6	19 2	10 6

For General Conditions see Page 2.

TVR tourist tickets notice : 1912

(182)

ABERTHAW, COWBRIDGE, LLANTRISANT, TREFERIG, AND LLANTRISANT JUNCTION.—UP.

Single Line ... ... Aberthaw to Cowbridge—Train Staff and one Engine in steam.
" ... ... Cowbridge to Llantrisant—Electric Train Staff.
Double Line ... ... Llantrisant to Cowbridge Road Crossing.—Block Telegraph.
Single Line ... ... Cowbridge Road Crossing to Llantrisant Junction—Electric Train Staff.

Distance from Aberthaw	STATIONS AND SIDINGS / No.	1		3	5		7		9		11		13		15		17		19		21	
	Description of Trains.	Coke Ovens Express Goods Z 1		Car'ges. X 1	Pontypridd Passenger and Goods. Z 2		Glyn Through Goods X 1		Pontypridd Passenger. X 4		Coke Ovens. Local Goods X 1		Pontypridd Passenger. Z 1		Pontypridd Passenger. Z 2		Workmen's Train. C 41					
		arr	dep.	dep	arr.	dep.	arr.	dep.	arr.	dep.	arr.	dep.	arr.	dep.	arr.	dep.	arr.	dep.	arr.	dep.	arr.	dep.
M.CH.		a.m.	a.m.	a.m.	a.m	a.m.	a.m.	a.m.	a.m.	a.m.	a.m.	a.m.	p.m.	p.m.	p.m.	p.m.	p.m.	p.m.				
—	ABERTHAW								—	9 55					—	2 15						
0 67	ST. ATHAN ROAD								9 57	9 58					2 18	2 20						
8 37	ST. MARY CHURCH ROAD								10 3	10 4					2 27	2 31						
5 67	COWBRIDGE STATION				—	7 20			10 9	10 12			—	12 20	2 39	2 48						
	Cowbridge Goods	—	4 10																			
6 10	Cowbridge Junction	S	T		S	T			S	T			S	Tx	2 49x	2 51						
8 8	YSTRADOWEN				7 25	7 26			10 17	10 18			12 25	12 26	2 55	2 56						
10 11	LLANHARRY				7 31	7 32			10 23	10 24			12 31	12 32	3 1	3 2						
11 36	LLANTRISANT STATION	4 30	5A30		7 35	7 42			10 27	10 32			12 35	12 47	3 5¶	3 25						
	Mwynddy Junction	—	—		—	—			—	—			—	—	—	—						
12 77	Cowbridge Road Crossing	S	T		S	T			S	T			S	T	S	T						
	Maesaraul Junction	—	—		—	—			—	—			—	—	—	—						
	Brofiskin										—	10 0										
	Mwynddy Siding										10 5	10 10										
	Bute Siding										10 15	10 20										
13 18	Maesaraul Junction	5 36	ST 5 38		S T	7 46			S T ¶	10 36	10 25§	10 42	S T	12 51	S T	3 29						
13 46	Cottage Siding				—	—			—		—	—	—	—	—	—						
	CROSS INN STATION				7 49	7 50			10 38	10 39	—	—	12 53	12 54	3 31	3 32						
From Glyn.	Glyn Colliery	Assisted by X 7 from Maesaraul	Junction to Coke Ovens.	6 50			—	7 55									S O	3 15				
— 52	Treferig Old Mill Siding			—			—	—									3 20	3 22				
	Llan. Common Junction																					
1 57	Castellau Siding			—			—	—									—	—				
2 39	Treferig Siding			—			—	—									—	—				
2 56	Treferig Junction			7 5			8 15	8 30									—	—				
2 77	Gelynog Colliery																—	—				
3 5	Common Road Bridge																3 36	3†39				
14 11	Common Branch Junction	S T x	5 44		S T	7 53	8 35	x9 0	S T	10 41	10 47	11 10	S T	12 56	S T	3 34	3†45	—				
14 55	Wallsend Siding	—	—		—	—	To	Brofiskin.	—	—	—	—	—	—	—	—						
15 54	LLANTWIT STATION	5 50	5 53		7 57x	7 58			10 45	10 46	11 20x	12 30	1 0	1 1	3 38	3 39						
16 28	CHURCH VILLAGE	—	—		8 0	8 1			10 48	10 49	—	—	1 3	1 4	3 41	3 42						
18 17	Llantrisant Junction	6 3	6 5		S T	8 6			S T	10 54	12 50	1 35	S T	1 9	S T	3 47						
	Arrival at Destination	6 21	—		8 12	—			11 0	—	2 14	—	1 15	—	3 53	—						

▲ To pick up and start from G.W.R. Yard at 5 30 a.m.

(184)

ABERTHAW, COWBRIDGE, LLANTRISANT, TREFERIG, AND LLANTRISANT JUNCTION.—UP.

STATIONS AND SIDINGS. / No.	23		25		27		29		31		33		35		37		39		41		43	
Description of Trains.	Glyn Mineral. C 41		Coke Ovens Local Goods. Z 3		Pontypridd Passenger. Z 1		Passenger. Z 2		Pontypridd Passenger. Z 2 & 1		Glyn Mineral. C 41		Pontypridd Passenger. Z 2 & 1		Merthyr Through Goods. M 8							
	arr.	dep.	arr.	dep.	arr	dep.	arr.	dep.	arr.	dep.	arr.	dep.	arr.	dep.	arr.	dep.	arr.	dep.	arr.	dep.	arr.	dep.
	p.m.	p.m.	p.m.	p.m.	p.m.	p.m.	p.m.	p.m.	p.m.	p.m.	p.m.	p.m.	p.m.	p.m.	p.m.	p.m.						
ABERTHAW									—	6 45												
ST. ATHAN ROAD									6 47	6 48												
ST. MARY CHURCH ROAD									6 53	6 54												
COWBRIDGE STN.					—	5 5	—	5 25	6 59	7 2			S O	8 27								
Cowbridge Goods			—	12 50																		
Cowbridge Jc.			S	T	5 6x	5 8	S	T	S	T			S	T								
YSTRADOWEN			1 0	1 10	5 12	5 13	5 30	5 31	7 7	7 8			8 32	8 33								
LLANHARRY			1 18	1 35	5 18	5 19	5 36	5 37	7 13	7 14			8 38	8 39								
LLANTRISANT STN.			1 40§	3 40	5 22	5 25	5 40	—	7 17x	7C22			8 42x	9C2								
Mwynddy Jc.			—	—	—	—			—	—			—	—								
Cowbridge Road Crossing			S	T	S	T			S	T			S	T								
Maesaraul Jc.			S T	3 50	—	—	29 a		—	—			—	—								
Brofiskin																						
Mwynddy Sdg.							Work men's Train.															
Bute Sdg.							C 41															
Maesaraul Jc.			—	—	S T	5 30			S T	7 26			S T	9 6								
Cottage Sdg.			—	—	—	—			—	—			—	—								
CROSS INN STN.			3 55	4 5	5 33	5 35	p.m.	p.m.	7 28	7 29			9 8	9 9								
Glyn Colly.	X S	4 0					X S	5 40			—	7 15										
Treferig Old Mill Sdg.	—	—					5 44	5 46			—	—										
Llan. Common Jc.															—	10 45						
Castellau Sdg.	—	—					—	—			—	—			—	—						
Treferig Sdg.	—	—					—	—			—	—			—	—						
Treferig Jc	4 20	4 25					—	—			7 35	7 45			10 55	11 30						
Gelynog Colly.	—	—					—	—			—	—			—	—						
Common Road Bridge	—	—					6 1	6†4			—	—			—	—						
Common Branch Jc.	4 35	—	4 10x	4 40	S T	5 37	6†10	—	S T	7 31	7 55	8 15	S T	9 11	11 40	11 50						
Wallsend Sdg			—	—	—	—			—	—			—	—								
LLANTWIT STN.			4 50	5 10	5 41	5 42			7 35x	7 36			9 15	9 16	12 0	12 20						
CHURCH VILLAGE			—	—	5 45	5 46			7 38	7 39	To Waterhall		9 18	9 19	—	—						
Llantrisant Jc.			5 30	5 35	S T	5 51			S T	7 44			S Tx	9 24	12 40	1 10						
Arrival at Destination			5 53	—	5 58	—			7 50	—			9 30	—	3 5							

C Change Engines

(185)

LLANTRISANT JUNCTION, TREFERIG, LLANTRISANT, COWBRIDGE, AND ABERTHAW.—DOWN.

STATIONS AND SIDINGS. / No.	22		24		26		28		30		32		34		36		38		40		42	
Description of Trains.	1.0 p.m. Cathays Local Goods. C 41		4.20 p.m. Pontypridd Passenger. Z 2		Workmen's Train. C 41		Glyn Empties. C 41		6.35 p.m. Pontypridd Passenger. Z 1 & 2		6.20 p.m. Coke Ovens Through Goods. Z 3		8.17 p.m. Pontypridd Passenger. Z 1		5.30 p.m. Merthyr Through Goods. M 8		9.50 p.m. Pontypridd Passenger. Z 1					
	arr.	dep.	arr.	dep.	arr.	dep.	arr.	dep.	arr.	dep.	arr.	dep.	arr.	dep.	arr.	dep.	arr.	dep.	arr.	dep.	arr.	dep.
	p.m.	p.m.	p.m.	p.m.	p.m.	p.m.	p.m.	p.m.	p.m.	p.m.	p.m.	p.m.	p.m.	p.m.	p.m.	p.m.	p.m. S	p.m. O				
Llantrisant Jc.			S T	4 26					S T	6 41	6 44	7 0	S T	8 23	8 48x	9 25	S T	9 56				
CHURCH VILLAGE			4 31	4 32					6 46	6 47	—	—	8 28	8 29	—	—	10 1	10 2				
LLANTWIT STN.			4 34	4 35					6 49	6 50	7 15x	7 40	8 31	8 32	9 40	9 45	10 4	10 5				
Wallsend Sdg.	X	S	—	—					—	—	—	—	—	—	—	—	—	—				
Common Branch Jc.	3 5	3 10	S T	4x38	X S	5†5	—	6 35	S T	6 53	S T	7 50	S T	8 35	9 50	9 55	S T	10 8				
Common Road Bridge	—	—			5†8	5 10	—	—							—	—						
Gelynog Colly	—	—			—	—	—	—							—							
Treferig Jc.	3 18	3 25			—	—	—	—							10 5	10 20						
Castellau Sdg.	—	—			—	—	—	—							—	—						
Llan. Common Jc.															10 30	—						
Treferig Old Mill Sdg.	—	—			5 25	5 28	—	—														
Glyn Colly.	3 45	—			5 35	—	7 0	—														
CROSS INN STN.			4 40	4 41					6 55	6 56	C	R	8 37	8 38			10 10	10 11				
Cottage Sdg.			—	—					—	—	—	—	—	—			—	—				
Maesaraul Jc.			—	—					—	—	8 0	—	—	—			—	—				
Bute Sdg.																						
Mwynddy Sdg.					26 a																	
Brofiskin					Passenger.																	
Maesaraul Jc.			S T	4 43	p.m.	p.m			S T	6 58	S T	8 20	S T	8 40			S T	10 13				
Cowbridge Road Crossing			S	T	Z 2				S	T	S	T	S	T			S	T				
Mwynddy Jc.			—	—					—	—	—	—	—	—			—	—				
LLANTRISANT STN.			4 47	4 52	—	5 50			7 2x	7 25	8 30§	9 30	8 44x	8 50			10 17	10 22				
LLANHARRY			4 55	4 56	5 53	5 54			7 28	7 29	9 35	9 45	8 53	8 54			10 25	10 26				
YSTRADOWEN			5 1	5 2	5 59	6 0			7 34	7 35	9 55	10 10	8 59	9 0			10 31	10 32				
Cowbridge Jc.			S	Tx	S	T			S	T	S	T	—	—			S	T				
Cowbridge Goods											10 20	—						—				
COWBRIDGE STN.			5 7	—	6 5	6 10			7 40	—			9 5				10 37	—				
ST. MARY CHURCH ROAD					—	6 15								—								
ST. ATHAN ROAD					6 20	6 21																
ABERTHAW					6 24	—																

† Empty Train.

(188)

LLANTRISANT JUNCTION, TREFERIG, LLANTRISANT, COWBRIDGE, AND ABERTHAW.—DOWN.

Distance from Llantrisant Jnc.	STATIONS AND SIDINGS. / No.	2		4		6		8		10		12		14		16		18		20		20a
	Description of Trains.	Glyn Empties. X 1		4.55 a.m. Coke Ovens Engine. X 7		Glyn Workmen X 1		Glyn Empties. X 1		6.40 a.m. Coke Ovens Through Goods. Z 1		8.33 a.m. Pontypridd Passenger. X 4		Through Goods. X 1		11.20 a.m. Pontypridd Passenger. Z 2		2.0 p.m. Pontypridd Passenger. Z 1		Workmen's Train. C 41		
		arr.	dep.	arr.	dep.	arr.	dep.	arr.	dep.	arr.	dep.	arr.	dep.	arr.	dep.	arr.	dep.	arr.	dep.	arr.	dep.	
M.CH.		a.m.	a.m.	a.m.	a.m.	a.m.	a.m.	a.m.	a.m.	a.m.	a.m.	a.m.	a.m.	a.m.	a.m.	a.m.	a.m.	p.m.	p.m.	p.m.	p.m.	
—	Llantrisant Jc.	4 34	5 4	5 3	5 4					7 5	7 35	S T	8 39			S T	11 26	S T	2 6			
1 69	CHURCH VILLAGE	—	—	—	—					—	—	8 44	8 45			11 31	11 32	2 11	2 12			
2 43	LLANTWIT STN.	5 19	5 34	5 19	5 23					7 50	x8 5	8 47	8 48			11 34x	11 35	2 14	2 15			
3 42	Wallsend Sdg.	—	—	—	—					—	—	—	—			—	—	—	—			
4 6	Common Branch Jc.	5 44	x6 0	S T	5 26					S T	8 15	S T¶	8 51	8 35§	9 0	S T	11 38	S T	2 18	S O	2†45	
4 76	Common Road Bridge	—	—	To assist X 1 Llantrisant	Jc. to Llantwit.															2†48	2 50	
5 4	Gelynog Colliery	—	—																	—	—	
5 27	Treferig Jc.	6 10	—			—	6 20	—	7 20											—	—	
6 27	Castellau Siding					—	—	—	—											—	—	
6 36	Llan. Common Jc.																					
7 31	Treferig Old Mill					—	—	—	—											3 0	3 2	
8 3	Glyn Colly.					6 40	—	7 40	—											3 14	—	
4 50	CROSS INN STN.									C	R	8 53	8 54	9 5	9 10	11 40	11 41	2 20	2 21			
4 79	Cottage Sdg.									—	—	—	—	9 12	9 17	—	—	—	—			
5 20	Maesaraul Jc.									—	—	—	—	9 20	9 30	—	-	—	—			
	Bute Sdg.													9 35	9 40							
6 58	Mwynddy Sdg.													9 45	9 50							
7 15	Brofiskin													9 55	—							
5 20	Maesaraul Jc.			5 31	—					S T	8 28	S T	8 56			S T	11 43	S T	2 23			
	Cowbridge Road Crossing									S	T	S	T			S	T	S	T			
	Mwynddy Jc.									—	—	—	—			—	—	—	—			
6 61	LLANTRISANT STN.									8 38	§9 20	9 0¶	9 5			11 47	12 5	2 27	2 35			
8 6	LLANHARRY									—	—	9 8	9 9			12 8	12 9	2 38	2 39			
10 13	YSTRADOWEN									C	R	9 14	9 15			12 14	12 15	2 44	2 45			
12 27	Cowbridge Jc.									—	—	S	T			12 19	12 21	2 49x	2 50			
12 30	Cowbridge Goods									9 53	—					—	M					
12 30	COWBRIDGE STN.											9 20	9 22			12 22	12 30	2 54	—			
14 60	ST. MARY CHURCH ROAD											—	9 27			12 37	12 42					
17 30	ST. ATHAN ROAD											9 32	9 33			12 50	12 55					
18 17	ABERTHAW											9 35	—			12 59	—					

M Passenger and Goods Cowbridge to Aberthaw.

TVR working timetable, Aberthaw to Llantrisant Junction : 1903

The Glamorgan Hematite Iron Ore Company became a subsidiary of the Guest Keen & Nettlefold empire in the 1920s. Hopper wagons of this type were used to convey iron ore from Llanharry to GKN's Dowlais Works, and later to the East Moors Works in Cardiff.
R. Y. Pickering & Company, Wishaw Collection *(Courtesy of the Historical Model Railway Society)*

The level of service between Cowbridge and Aberthaw evidently proved too lavish for the traffic on offer, as by September 1910, it had been cut to four trains each way. The service on this section between 1905 and 1917 was, for the first time, convenient for scholars attending school in Cowbridge, who came from the area served by the Aberthaw line. Some children walked considerable distances to reach the branch stations. It also allowed a number of reasonably-timed connections with Barry trains at Aberthaw, although the long walk between the two stations at Aberthaw must have been something of a disincentive for those unwilling, or unable, to take a short cut.

The years up to World War I saw a considerable increase in freight traffic over the Cowbridge branch, as a result of the opening of a number of private sidings. The first of these was a rather small scale affair, which further exploited the lias limestone deposits of the lower part of the Vale of Glamorgan. In 1904, Thomas Taylor opened the North Aberthaw Lime Works, just north of St. Mary Church Road Station. This was served by a siding off the loop siding at the station. In November 1907, the TVR accepted an application from Mr Morgan for the use of part of the machine siding at Llantrisant, to serve a small foundry he was establishing on land adjoining the Ely Tinplate Works.

The prospect of a far more important source of traffic was opened up in October 1908, when agreement was reached for the provision of a private siding to serve the Cardiff Hematite Iron Ore Company's new mine at Llanharry. This mine was on the site of the old wharf, which had served the tramway to Bethell's mines, and was connected to the TVR in 1909 by means of a siding, which followed the course of the old 1865 siding. Connection was made to the main line just before the station platform, by means of a junction which was controlled by a new two-lever ground frame, which was unlocked by the train staff for the Llantrisant to Cowbridge section.

The Llanharry mine was to provide the major source of freight traffic for the railway for nearly 70 years. The ore was originally forwarded to Quakers Yard, for transfer to the GWR/Rhymney Railway joint line, but was later routed via the Nelson branch to Ffaldcaiach, for the final journey up to Dowlais. The iron ore company became the Glamorgan Hematite Iron Ore Company in 1921. After the end of steelmaking at Dowlais, in 1930, the iron ore was supplied mainly to the East Moors Steelworks in Cardiff. Owing to the steep gradient up to the mine from the Cowbridge line, the Board of Trade stipulated that the engine should always be at the Cowbridge end of the train, when shunting at the siding. Loaded ore wagons were always propelled from Llanharry to Llantrisant.

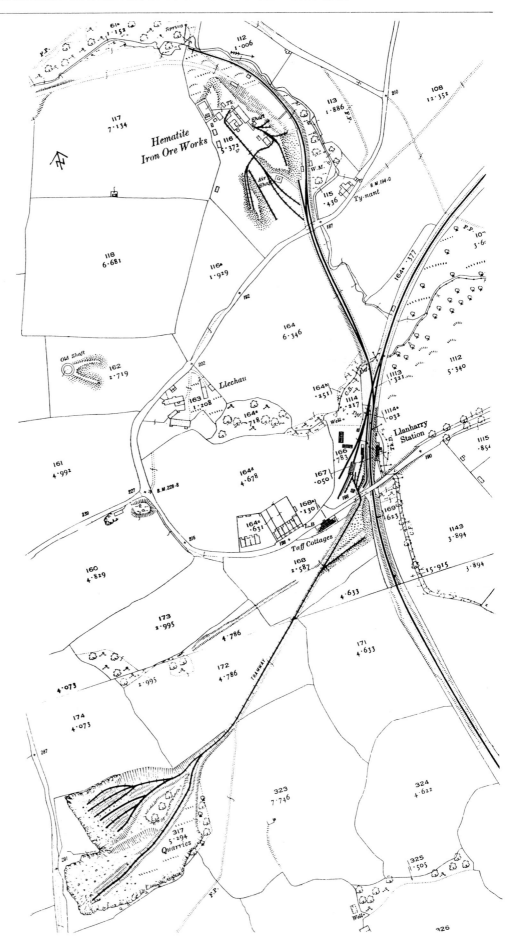

Plan of Llanharry Station : 1919

Aberthaw Cement Works, circa 1916, viewed from the Cowbridge and Aberthaw line.   *C. Chapman*

Another important source of traffic came in 1913, with the opening of a private siding to the Aberthaw & Bristol Channel Portland Cement Company's works. The works was situated to the east of the crossing of the Vale of Glamorgan over the Cowbridge to Aberthaw line. This new works was on a far larger scale than any of the other works which had been established on the lias limestone of the area. Siding connections were made to both the Vale of Glamorgan and the TVR, with the siding forming a continuous line between the two railways, although it was never used for through traffic. The junction with the TVR line was controlled by a two-lever ground frame, and required the widening of two underbridges south of St. Athan Road Station. The cement works generated an inward flow of coal and stone, and an outward traffic of cement, most of which appears to have been via the Vale of Glamorgan. TVR traffic to the works was taken via Aberthaw Station, and shunted off at the siding on the 'up' journey.

However, the cement company does not appear to have been entirely satisfied with the service provided by the railway companies. For in July 1913, it approached the TVR with a request that the TVR provide a siding from its line, to serve a proposed jetty from which small coasters could be loaded with cement. It also wished to work its traffic between its works and the proposed jetty over the TVR, using its own engines. Not unexpectedly, the TVR was not

over-enthusiastic about the prospect of a development which would reduce its own revenue from the cement works traffic, and managed to stall on the issue until the cement company eventually lost interest.

Agreement was reached for another private siding in August 1913, to serve a quarry being developed by Mr Mathias at a point about midway between Llanharry Station and Rhydhalog Bridge. The siding took the form of a loop on the west side of the running line, controlled by 2 two-lever ground frames.

Proceedings at the meeting of the Cowbridge Borough Council, on 4th March 1909, were enlivened when Alderman Jenkins spoke of a rumour that the GWR was contemplating the construction of a loop line. It would run from St. Fagans to Port Talbot via Cowbridge and Porthcawl, to relieve the South Wales main line. The prospect of the town being on the new main line was enthusiastically received, and a committee was formed to watch events and to take any necessary steps. But as there proved to be no substance in the rumour, no action was required.

Shunting operations at Llantrisant Station were eased early in 1912, when the dead end at the end of the line was lengthened, and a new disc signal was provided to control trains from the platform line to the machine siding. An interesting feature of passenger operation at the station at this time was the use that was made of the machine siding,

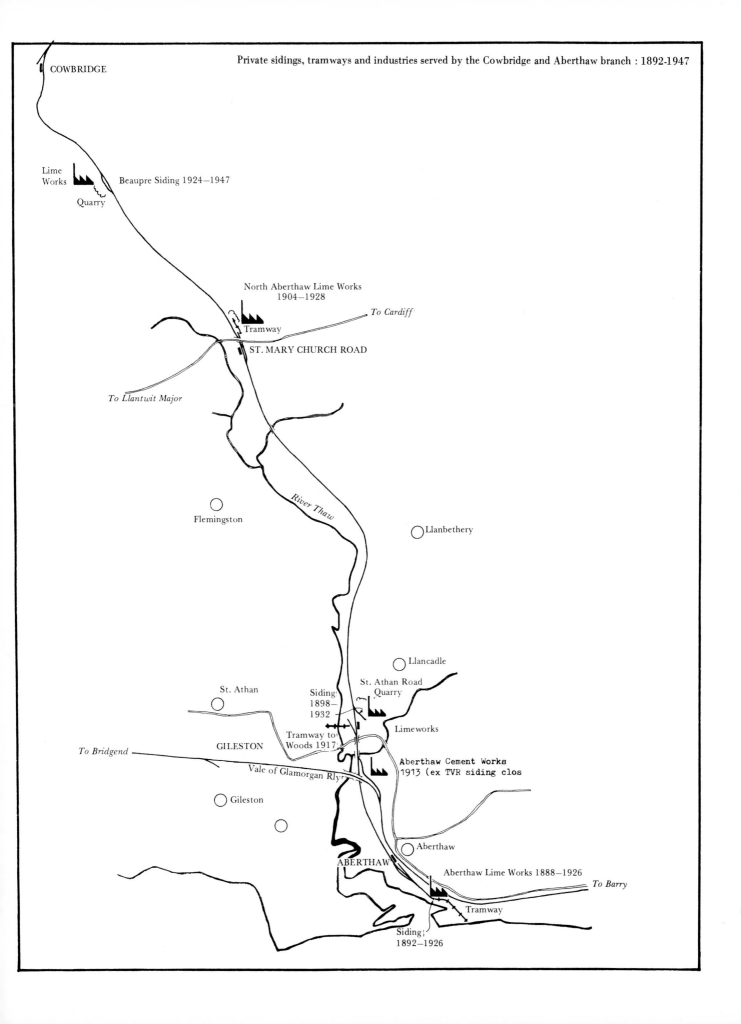

Private sidings, tramways and industries served by the Cowbridge and Aberthaw branch : 1892-1947

COWBRIDGE

Lime
Works

Quarry

Beaupre Siding 1924—1947

North Aberthaw Lime Works
1904—1928

Tramway   *To Cardiff*

ST. MARY CHURCH ROAD

To Llantwit Major

River Thaw

Flemingston

Llanbethery

Llancadle

St. Athan

Siding
1898—
1932

St. Athan Road
Quarry

Limeworks

GILESTON

To Bridgend

Tramway to
Woods 1917

Aberthaw Cement Works
1913 (ex TVR siding clos

Vale of Glamorgan Rly

Gileston

Aberthaw

ABERTHAW

Aberthaw Lime Works 1888—1926

To Barry

Tramway

Siding
1892—1926

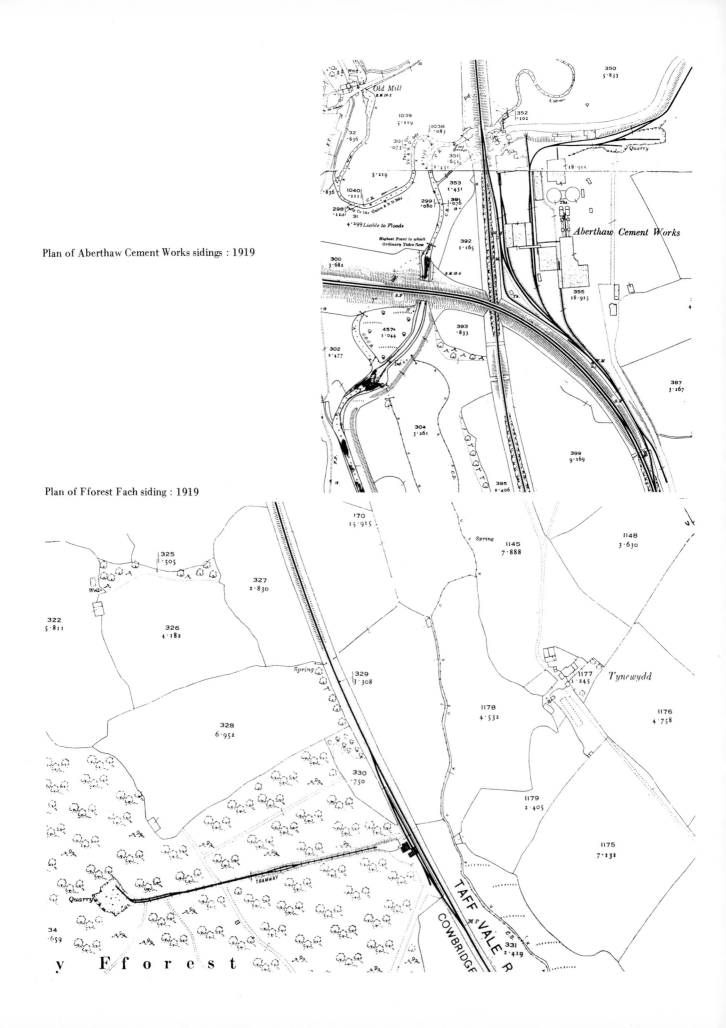

Plan of Aberthaw Cement Works sidings : 1919

Plan of Fforest Fach siding : 1919

A quiet interlude at Llantrisant Station in 1949, with a Pontypridd auto-train on the left and the Cowbridge auto-train on the right. With the decline of through working between Cowbridge and Pontypridd, in the 1920s, Pontypridd to Llantrisant trains began using the Pen-y-graig bay on the 'up' side of the station. The end of through working also enabled improved connections to be made with main line stopping trains at Llantrisant.

L G R P (Courtesy of David & Charles)

The first volunteers for World War I pose for the camera before entraining at Cowbridge in 1914. The branch auto-car is just visible in the background.

C. Chapman (Courtesy of G. Punter)

for passing trains. An 'up' train could be shunted clear on to the machine siding, so that a 'down' train could cross its path, after which it would set back into the platform road before continuing its journey. It was during such a manoeuvre, on 23rd March 1915, that the 12.00 noon Cowbridge to Pontypridd auto-train ran into the tin works siding and collided with a GWR well truck; an accident which resulted from incorrectly set points. However, in most cases, 'up' and 'down' trains crossed on the double track section of the GWR between Llantrisant Station and Mwyndy Junction.

The general increase of traffic on the line in the period up to World War I even extended to the rural somnolence of Ystradowen Station. In December 1911, the TVR accepted an application for the erection of a gate in the fence between the goods yard and a new auction mart, which adjoined the station. The additional cattle traffic which this development generated led to the provision of five cattle pens, in 1913, at the goods station. At the same time, a tramway was constructed from a timber yard next to the station into the goods yard. The goods siding was extended to serve this tramway, which was used to transfer timber to and from the railway.

The years up to World War I were noticeably free of major accidents involving branch trains. The most serious incident occured on 3rd March 1913, when a TVR auto-train collided with a GWR mineral train at Llantrisant, causing the derailment of the leading carriage of the auto set. This accident was due to a misunderstanding between the GWR signalman and the guard of the mineral train, but, fortunately, no injuries resulted.

Following the outbreak of war in August 1914, the railwaymen of the Cowbridge district agreed to contribute 3d in every £1 of their earnings to the war effort, with their War Distress Fund. As the war dragged on beyond the 'over by Christmas' phase, the casualties increased, and two local residences, Ash Hall at Ystradowen and New Beaupre, near St. Hilary, were turned into hospitals for wounded soldiers. This brought a new, and tragic, traffic to the railway.

Cowbridge was designated as a collection point for hay for the cavalry, and also became a depot for the despatch of commandeered horses. The market was used for the grading of fatstock under Government control, with the result that business for the railway increased considerably. Following the weekly market on Tuesdays, railway staff would work into the early hours of the following morning, despatching cattle and sheep. Cowbridge sheep fairs provided a major source of traffic, with up to 100 wagons of sheep to be dealt with. Special cattle trains were run on market days in 1915, but were not found to be justified.

Goods traffic on the branch in 1914 required the running of three trains each way between Llantrisant and Cowbridge, with only one each way from there to Aberthaw. The railway was in use for almost 24 hours a day, with the first goods working leaving Cowbridge at 3.10a.m. and the last 'down' goods arriving at that station at 1.55a.m.

Goods Workings: Cowbridge — Coke Ovens 1914

		Z1	Z3	Z4
Cowbridge	dep.	3.10a.m.	11.00a.m.	4.05p.m.
Coke Ovens	arr.	5.55	2.55p.m.	8.30
Coke Ovens	dep.	6.00a.m.	3.50p.m.	9.05p.m.
Cowbridge	arr.	9.55	6.38	1.55a.m.
		A		

Key: A = to Aberthaw arr. 11.00a.m. returning to Cowbridge at 12.02p.m.

The first 'up' goods always ran non-stop to Llantrisant, and was designated to carry fish and goods from Cowbridge and Llantrisant for TVR stations. In 1914, this train required the assistance of a banking engine between Maesaraul Junction and Llantrisant Junction.

Iron ore empties were brought down by an Abercynon engine from Quakers Yard, arriving at Llanharry at 7.27a.m., the loaded wagons returning to Quakers Yard at

No. 9780 brings some loaded iron-ore wagons out of Llanharry Iron Ore Mine siding on 15th July 1959.   *H. C. Casserley*

7.45 a.m. At this stage, the output of the iron mine had not built up to the level it reached in later years, as the 'up' train also conveyed goods from Llantrisant and served Duffryn Llantwit Colliery between Cross Inn and Llantwit stations.

An interesting working at this time was the conditional goods from Waterhall Junction to Llantrisant via the Railway No. 1 and Common Branch Junction, conveying mineral traffic for the Ely Tinplate Works. The return working was via Llantrisant Junction.

In addition to ore traffic between Llanharry and Llantrisant, the practice of propelling goods wagons was also employed from Llantrisant to the Llanharry Lime Works, with wagons for the works attached to the front of 'down' goods trains. Goods train loads between Cowbridge and Llantrisant were restricted to 10 loaded coal wagons, 20 loaded goods and empties or 30 empty wagons, on account of the severe gradients, and were subject to a speed limit of 15 m.p.h. Wagons could be shunted by means of a tow-rope at Llantrisant Warehouse siding and at Aberthaw, but only when it was not possible for engines to make use of the loops at those places.

Cowbridge was a depot for the cleansing of cattle wagons returned from the GWR at Llantrisant. Wagons not required at Llantrisant (which had to retain two wagons for its own use) were sent to Cowbridge for cleaning, before being worked back to the main TVR cattle wagon storage depot at Llantrisant Junction. However, six wagons had to be retained at Cowbridge for its own use.

Timber traffic during the war brought additional business to the railway. In January 1917, Mr Roberts, the owner of the Ystradowen timber yard, was given permission to lay a tramway into St. Athan Road goods yard, in order to load timber. This tramway ran from a wood on the west bank of the River Thaw, and crossed the river by means of a temporary trestle bridge. Mr Roberts was also allowed to load timber directly from the lineside near Beaupre House, about a mile south of Cowbridge.

As the war progressed, it became necessary to make economies in the costs of working the nation's railways, and in 1917 the passenger service to Cowbridge was reduced to seven trains each way. Only two round trips ran on the Aberthaw line, making it impossible for scholars from the area served by that line to use the train to get to school in Cowbridge. Fortunately, the goods traffic on the Aberthaw line was sufficient to prevent the complete closure, which was the fate of other sparsely trafficked branch lines at that time.

This cut-back in the passenger service was not, however, the end of the wartime economies. On 1st May 1918, the timetable was curtailed further, with only five trains each way between Cowbridge and Pontypridd. Trains from Aberthaw terminated at Cowbridge, so that any through passengers had to wait for well over an hour at Cowbridge, before they could continue their journeys.

The end of hostilities in 1918 did not bring with it the immediate restoration of the service to its former level. It was not until May 1920 that the Cowbridge branch recovered its pre-war glory, with nine trains each way between Cowbridge and Pontypridd. In addition, an early morning train to and from Aberthaw reappeared, and in July 1920, an evening round trip was added to the timetable. However, these improvements on the Aberthaw line proved short-lived, as the extra trains were taken off at the end of the summer timetable, although the evening working reappeared the following July. The pattern of only two trains each way on the Aberthaw line, with an evening round trip between July and September, continued, until the end of the passenger service on this section.

The motor car platforms at Aberthin, St. Hilary and Llanbethery were closed to passengers on 12th July 1920, leaving, of the four platforms opened on the branch in 1905, only Trerhyngyll & Maendy open. Trerhyngyll & Maendy, together with Tonteg Platform and Beddau Platform, which opened in 1910, had been lengthened to accommodate two coach trains. Although the TVR rejected a call in 1910 for the provision of a shelter at Trerhyngyll & Maendy, passenger amenities were later improved by the GWR, in the form of a corrugated iron 'pagoda' style waiting shelter. The GWR also replaced the designation 'platform' with the more usual 'halt'.

The remains of Aberthin Platform on 26th May 1959. It is in remarkably good condition considering the platform had been closed for nearly thirty years. The signal is the 'down' distant for Cowbridge, consisting of a TVR wooden post, complete with ornate cast-iron finial and GWR pressed steel-enamelled arm.

M. Hale

Taff Vale Railway.

YSTRADOWEN

TO

Merthyr

Taff Vale Railway.

Ystradowen

TO

MOUNTAIN ASH

Taff Vale Railway.

COWBRIDGE

TO

Dinas

Taff Vale Railway.

Cowbridge

TO

Radyr.

Taff Vale Railway.

Ystradowen

TO

Treherbert.

Taff Vale Railway.

YSTRADOWEN

TO

Llantrissant

Taff Vale Railway.

Cowbridge

TO

Tylor's Town

Taff Vale Railway.

Ystradowen

TO

MERTHYR VALE.

Taff Vale Railway.

COWBRIDGE

TO

St. Mary Church Road

Taff Vale Railway.

COWBRIDGE

TO

Aberystwith,

(OAM.)

Via Merthyr, B. & M. Rly. Talyllyn and Llanidloes.

Taff Vale Railway.

COWBRIDGE

TO

LLANWRTYD

L. & N. W.

VIa MERTHYR JUNCTION.

A selection of parcel labels
C. Chapman (Courtesy Ian L. Wright)

A new private siding was opened in 1921 at Beaupre, about a mile south of Cowbridge, to serve a quarry and limeworks being developed by Messrs Roberts & Lewis. This siding joined the Aberthaw line by means of a connection which was trailing for 'down' trains.

At the end of World War I, the world was a very different place as far as railways were concerned. Operating costs had increased significantly since 1914 and, in particular, wages were at a much higher level than before the war. Private motoring, although still the preserve of the rich, had increased since the turn of the century, and had already had a noticeable effect on first class rail travel. The war had enabled many men to be taught to drive, and to appreciate the intricacies of the internal combustion engine. It had also released large numbers of surplus lorries, which were bought up by men eager to set themselves up as hauliers. Passenger traffic became increasingly vulnerable to competition from motor buses, serving Cowbridge from 1920 onwards.

The return of peace also forced the Government to give consideration to the future of a national railway network, brought near to exhaustion by the contribution it had made to the war effort. The result was the amalgamation of some 120 companies into the four 'grouped' companies. The T V R became a constituent of the 'Greater' Great Western from 1st January 1922, and so the Cowbridge branch became part of a company which had spurned an opportunity to take it over nearly 60 years earlier.

Chapter Seven
Decline and Fall: 1922-1977

Traffic on the Cowbridge branch at the time of the Grouping was at a relatively high level, with passenger and goods totals reflecting the general recovery after the war. Competition from road transport was yet to make the great inroads into the business of the railway, which were to become a feature of the 1920s and 1930s. In 1923, a total of 66,140 tickets was sold at Cowbridge Station, which amounted to over 220 a day. This was out of a total for the branch, excluding Llantrisant, of 87,800. Passenger traffic on the Aberthaw line remained at a very modest level, with only just over 3,000 tickets being sold at all three stations south of Cowbridge, in 1923. The picture for goods traffic on the Aberthaw line was more encouraging, with over 43,000 tons being dealt with in 1923, mainly from the various private sidings along the line. The most important source of traffic for the entire line continued to be the Llanharry iron ore mine, which in 1923 despatched over 100,000 tons of ore.

This prosperity was not to last, however, as competition was increasing rapidly. It would soon have a devastating effect on the passenger business and, to a lesser extent, on the freight traffic of the railway. The number of cars on the gradually improving roads began to multiply after the hiatus of the war years, being particularly attractive in a rural area which had never enjoyed a lavish public transport system. The first daily bus service to Cowbridge, as opposed to Saturday or other trips, was inaugurated in 1920. In July of that year, the Cowbridge Borough Council welcomed unanimously a proposal of the South Wales Commerical Motor Company to start a bus service, from Cardiff to Cowbridge. A trial run took place, on Monday 27th July 1920, when a South Wales Commercial Motor Company motor-bus ran from Cardiff to Cowbridge, to the welcome of many people along the route. At Cowbridge, the bus was inspected by the Mayor and several members of the Borough Council, who felt that it would admirably serve its purpose. However, this enthusiastic reception was tinged with regret at the news that the Glamorgan County Council had refused to licence the service, on the grounds that the road between Cardiff and Cowbridge was inadequate for use as a bus route. As a result, a motion was passed at the meeting of the Borough Council on 5th August 1920, 'that the establishment of an omnibus service . . . would be of real convenience and benefit to the residents of the Borough.' Faced with these sentiments, the County Council relented and granted the necessary licence, which was for a 35 seat saloon. This vehicle used the side roads by the Town Hall as its terminus in Cowbridge.

The welcome given to the new bus service by the Borough Council and the residents of Cowbridge and district was, in part, a reflection of their dissatisfaction with the service provided by the railway. People were especially disgruntled with connections with the G W R at Llantrisant. Recalling the town in 1919, a former Headmaster of Cowbridge Grammar School, Mr R. Williams said that there was 'no means of getting anywhere except at the cost of long waits at Llantrisant for the infrequent and usually unpunctual trains.' The new buses, although slow and uncomfortable at first, did run direct to Cardiff, the most popular destination for people from Cowbridge. Although certain rail connections at Llantrisant were quite good, giving, in one case, a 45 minute journey from Cowbridge to Cardiff, others were not so well timed. It was possible to spend 1½ hours going by rail, for a journey which was only 13 miles by road. The South Wales Commercial Motor Company bus service was extended to Bridgend in 1921.

In 1921, Albert Maddox, a fried fish shop owner, of Eastgate Street, Cowbridge, obtained a motor-bus and commenced a Cowbridge to Cardiff service under the name of Cowbridge Motors. This service was extended to Bridgend the following year. Complaints arose because Maddox did not keep to his timetable, but ran his bus five minutes in front of the South Wales Commercial Motor Company bus. In return, Maddox complained that the South Wales Commercial Motor Company left their buses at the front of the town hall, and so interfered with the operation of his service. Such conflicts disappeared when Cowbridge Motors was taken over by the South Wales Commercial Motor Company in 1926.

Bus services connecting Cowbridge with a variety of destinations increased during the 1920s and early 1930s, the pattern eventually settling down as a result of amalgamations and the passing of the Road Traffic Act of 1920. This Act aimed to bring greater regulation to the operation of bus services. The following table summarizes the development of bus routes serving Cowbridge after 1922.

Development of bus services to Cowbridge 1922–1937

Date	Company	Service
April 1924	SWCM Company	Commenced Cardiff to Llancarfan to Cowbridge service
August 1925	Rhondda Tramways	Commenced Pontypridd to Cowbridge service
Dec. 1926	SWCM Company	Applied for licence for Cowbridge to Llantwit Major service (extended to Bridgend 1928)
Dec. 1926	Rhondda Tramways	Applied for licence to extend Pontypridd to Cowbridge service to Llantwit Major
1928	Rhondda Tramways	Withdrew Cowbridge to Llantwit Major service
1928	W. H. Wilkinson	Commenced Llantwit Major to Cowbridge service (had previously operated a Saturday only service on route)
Sept. 1929	SWCM Company	Operated a 20 seat one man operated bus on Llantwit Major to Cowbridge route, with some trips extended to and from Cardiff
1929	Western Welsh	Commenced Cardiff to Porthcawl service via Cowbridge
April 1930	Neath & Cardiff Coaches	Commenced Cardiff to Neath service via Cowbridge
1930	Western Welsh	Commenced Cardiff to Swansea service via Cowbridge in competition with N&C, but Traffic Commissioners refused consent for this service and it was withdrawn at the end of 1931
Sept. 1930	Western Welsh	Commenced Cardiff to Neath to Ammanford service via Cowbridge
Nov. 1930	Western Welsh	Commenced Cardiff to Carmarthen service via Cowbridge
Feb. 1937	Western Welsh	Commenced Cowbridge to St. Athan service

Notes:

1. *Gwenllian Edwards, Bridgend: Operated a Llanharry to Cowbridge service via Pentre Meyrick, Penlline and Aberthin and a Llanharran to Green Talbot (Talbot Green) service via Llanharry and Pontyclun in early 1930s, but these ceased in 1933.*

2. *South Wales Commercial Motor Company became part of the Western Welsh Omnibus Company in November 1929.*

Thus by 1930, direct bus services were available between Cowbridge and nearly all the nearby towns. The effect on the railway passenger business was nothing short of catastrophic. The number of tickets sold at Cowbridge fell from over 66,000 in 1923, to a mere 6,000 odd in 1932. Ticket sales at intermediate stations did not suffer to quite this extent, but fall they did, with Ystradowen's total down from 6,394 in 1923 to only 1,975 in 1932. Llanharry was something of an exception in the 1920s, when ticket sales actually increased from 11,923 in 1923 to 13,084 in 1929, mainly as a result of housing development between the village and the station. However, traffic fell away sharply after 1929, with only 3,657 tickets being sold in 1932.

The effect of road competition on the goods traffic of the Cowbridge branch was, however, not so great. Although the high-value general merchandise and livestock business was vulnerable to competition, as were some of the products of certain quarries and works served by the railway, where distribution was often very local, much of the agricultural traffic and domestic coal stayed on the line. The iron ore flow from Llanharry was more or less immune to competition, and more than doubled between 1923 and 1929. At the end of the decade, it amounted to three train loads per day, between Llantrisant and Dowlais. However, many of the concerns served by the railway went into decline from the mid-1920s, and what new industry there was tended, by its nature, to be road orientated. The small lime works served by the Aberthaw line had become obsolete by this time, and the Ely Tinplate Works closed in 1932. Apart from the iron ore, which was worked by separate trains, goods traffic on the Cowbridge line in the 1920s was sufficient only to justify the running of one train each way per day, between Llantrisant and Cowbridge. It also served Aberthaw on an 'as required' basis. The 'down' train left

TVR Class O, 0-6-2T, No. 33. Members of this class appeared at Cowbridge from their introduction into service in 1894, through to closure of Cowbridge Shed in 1924. Sister engine No. 34, was the last TVR 0-6-2T to be shedded at Cowbridge, being transferred to Cardiff Cathays Shed in February 1924.

G. H. W. Clifford (Courtesy of C. C. Green)

Llantrisant at 10.10a.m., and arrived at Aberthaw at 12.59p.m., returning to Cowbridge at 1.36p.m. Having sorted the yard at Cowbridge, it left for Llantrisant at 4.12p.m.

The Grouping allowed the rationalization of a number of previously competitive facilities. The need for two goods stations at Llantrisant disappeared, and the TVR goods shed and cattle pens were closed in June 1922. However, the ex-TVR goods siding, itself was not closed until 21st September 1925.

The engine shed at Cowbridge also became redundant, being closed on 8th March 1924, and demolished during 1927. At the same time, the timetable was altered to reflect this change. All goods and passenger turns were then based at Llantrisant Shed, with the passenger engine working light to and from Cowbridge. It did this at the beginning and end of each day, to collect the carriages which con-

tinued to be stabled at Cowbridge. More workings became short trips between Cowbridge and Llantrisant, with the revised service providing a total of eleven round trips on the branch, but with only two each way between Cowbridge and Aberthaw.

The GWR had inherited two stations at Aberthaw, which had previously been distinguished by their separate company identities. In order to avoid confusion, the stations were renamed on 1st July 1924, with the TVR station becoming 'Low Level' and the Vale of Glamorgan station becoming 'High Level'. Despite its proximity to the ex-Vale of Glamorgan station, the ex-TVR station still retained its own staff, although this had been reduced from two to one in 1923. The ex-TVR goods shed was closed in February 1925, although the siding remained open for what little traffic there was, until the closure of the Aberthaw line in 1932.

The 1920s were not entirely a period of retrenchment, however. A new connection was laid in at Beaupre siding in 1924, turning it into a loop siding. Traffic from the siding was quite heavy in the early 1920s, amounting to about 14,000 tons in 1923, but fell away later to only a nominal amount. In addition to traffic forwarded via Cowbridge, limestone from the quarry was also sent down the branch to Aberthaw Limeworks.

At Llanharry Station, a road approach had existed to a siding adjoining the lime works, but little use had been made of it for general goods traffic. In 1924, the GWR provided a goods shed and improved facilities at the siding, with the result that the annual tonnage of goods handled increased considerably.

With its declining passenger business and limited goods traffic, apart from that produced by certain private sidings, the Cowbridge branch was an obvious candidate for examination, in the report on branch lines of the GWR, prepared in 1926, by the Assistant Superintendent of the line, H. L. Wilkinson. It showed that in 1925, expenses incurred on the branch amounted to £18,423, or 52.9 per cent of traffic receipts. However, this was somewhat misleading, as of the total receipts of £34,378, over £20,000 was accounted for by Llanharry Station, and this was mainly because of the iron ore mine. Taking account of this factor, the financial state of the line was not at all healthy. Passenger revenue on the Aberthaw line could only be described as pathetic, with joint earnings for the three stations amounting to only £133 for the whole of 1925. With regard to goods traffic, the average number of loaded wagons dealt with on the Llantrisant to Aberthaw section was 67 forwarded and 47 received each day, comprising 57 minerals and 10 general goods forwarded, and 25 coal and minerals and 22 general goods received. Wilkinson recommended the withdrawal of the passenger service between Cowbridge and Aberthaw, and the concentration of accounts and supervision at Cowbridge. Also suggested was the reduction of siding accommodation at St. Mary Church Road and St. Athan Road stations, and the discontinuation of the late evening train between Cowbridge and Llantrisant, except on Saturdays. These changes were expected to produce a saving of £4,827. In the wake of this report, the passenger service between Cowbridge and Aberthaw was suspended on 4th May 1926. However, this did not prove to be permanent as the service was reinstated on 11th July 1927, with the summer timetable of three trains each way.

This suspension proved to be a body blow for the already very sickly passenger business of the Aberthaw line. Ticket sales at Aberthaw (Low Level) for 1928 amounted to only 229 compared with 1,187 in 1923, with 451 against 1,232 at St. Athan Road for the same years. Passenger receipts from all three stations on the branch amounted to only

Trerhyngyll & Maendy Halt, looking towards Ystradowen, on 26th May 1959. The pagoda hut was added by the GWR after the grouping.
M. Hale

£60 for the whole of 1928, although passengers from Cowbridge going to the seaside during the summer months probably increased revenue somewhat. Even the very restricted service provided on the line could not continue to be justified for long for such a paltry return, and it came as no surprise when the GWR announced its intention to withdraw the service between Cowbridge and Aberthaw, from Monday 5th May 1930.

Saturday, 3rd May, was the last day of passenger service, and it went largely unnoticed, save by the few who used the train to travel to Cowbridge. It was not attended with the macabre celebration which became a feature of later closures. However, a final excursion was organized by Mr Billy Lewis, the station master at St. Mary Church Road, for Sunday schools and parents, from Cowbridge to Barry Island, changing trains at Aberthaw.

With the end of the passenger service on the Aberthaw line, the two staff, at St. Athan Road and Aberthaw (Low Level), were withdrawn. Their residual duties were covered by staff at Gileston Station on the Vale of Glamorgan line, the staff of nine at Aberthaw (High Level) presumably having better things to do! The Aberthaw line remained open for goods traffic, and a number of track and signalling alterations were carried out at Cowbridge, reflecting this reduced status; a catch point was laid in just beyond the Llantrisant road bridge, protected by a 'down' starting signal of standard GWR design, and a ground disc signal for 'up' trains off the Aberthaw line.

On 5th May 1930, the GWR brought into use a new connection between the former TVR and Barry lines at Tonteg, near Church Village. This involved the construction of a short length of line, from the point at which the Llantrisant branch crossed the former Barry main line, to join that line just before Tonteg Junction. The ex-TVR line, from the point of divergence of the new connection to Llantrisant Junction, was then closed to all traffic, together with Tonteg Halt. A new halt of the same name was opened on 5th May 1930, at the junction of the new line with the Barry line, platforms being provided on both Barry and Llantrisant routes. Llantrisant trains then joined the ex-Barry line at Tonteg Junction, before proceeding via the formerly goods only section between Tonteg Junction and Treforest Barry Junction, where ex-TVR metals were rejoined.

In the autumn of 1930, the GWR reintroduced auto-working on the Cowbridge branch. By this date, through working of Cowbridge trains to and from Pontypridd had ceased, with the service being covered by a single auto-set working between Cowbridge and Llantrisant. At first, the branch carriages continued to be stabled overnight at Cowbridge, with the engine running light to and from Cowbridge at the beginning and end of each day. But from

The crew of the Cowbridge auto-train, hauled by engine No. 6425, pose for the camera on 20th May 1950. Driver Alf Stamp had just given one side of the engine a quick clean for the benefit of the photographer! After the withdrawal of 'Metro' tank No. 3586 in 1949, No. 6425 regularly stood in for diesel railcar No. 18 when the latter was indisposed.

Ian L. Wright

14th September 1931, this practice was discontinued; from then on the carriages were kept at Llantrisant, so the light engine workings were no longer necessary.

An interesting feature of passenger train operation at this time was the practice of running a morning and an afternoon train through to Tonyrefail, on the Ely Valley line, for the benefit of pupils attending school in Cowbridge. The branch train was affectionately known as 'Emma' by this clientele, with segregation of the sexes rigidly enforced, with boys in one carriage and girls in another. In spite of the innovation of through working to and from Tonyrefail (later diverted to Llanharan, on the main line between Llantrisant and Bridgend, following the opening of a new school at Tonyrefail in 1934) increasing use was made of buses for the schools traffic, with use of the train ceasing during World War II.

Staffing levels on the branch were reduced further in 1931, with Cowbridge losing three of its twelve men, the two man staff at Llanharry withdrawn, their duties being covered by Llantrisant Station, and Ystradowen losing one of its two man allocation.

Goods traffic on the Aberthaw line, mainly from the private sidings along the route, had declined markedly by the time the passenger service was withdrawn in 1930. It was only a matter of time before the surviving goods workings eventually followed the passenger trains into oblivion. This decline resulted partly from increased road competition, and partly from the demise of the various small industries served by the railway. Aberthaw Lime Works, by that date the Greldaw (Aberthaw) Lime Works, closed at the end of 1926, after which very little goods traffic was handled at Aberthaw. The Grouping had reduced the need for two rail outlets for the Aberthaw Cement Works, and most of the traffic was dealt with by the ex-Vale of Glamorgan siding. The lime works at St. Athan Road had become the property of the Aberthaw & Rhoose Cement Lime Company in 1917, having previously been acquired from L. Williams & Son by Mr Scull. It remained in use, but sent only a small amount by rail. Thus, by 1932, the Aberthaw line had become little used, apart from a small amount of agricultural traffic. The goods service south of Beaupre siding was withdrawn, and the goods stations at St. Mary Church Road, St. Athan Road and Aberthaw (Low Level) were closed on 1st November 1932. However, the track on this section was not lifted until it fell victim to the wartime drive for scrap in 1940. The Cowbridge to Beaupre siding section continued in use as a long siding, with its limited traffic worked 'as required'.

Following the end of the goods service to Aberthaw, goods workings between Cowbridge and Llantrisant were recast. A 'down' goods train worked from Llantrisant at 7.40 a.m., returning as an engine and brake van from Cowbridge at 8.33 a.m. A second 'down' goods train left Llantrisant at 2.35 p.m., calling at Glamorgan Quarries and Ystradowen, as required. Having sorted the yard at Cowbridge, it returned to Llantrisant at 4.48 p.m. A third working ran as far as Glamorgan Quarries at 11.20 a.m., returning at 11.52 a.m. to form an 'up' iron ore train from Llanharry. In addition, there were two iron ore workings from Llanharry, together with one worked on an 'as required' basis.

The GWR carried out a number of alterations at the Cowbridge yard in addition to the removal of the locomotive depot. The goods shed was altered to make it suitable for side loading, the rail entrance was blocked with corru-

gated iron sheeting and the short siding, which had served the shed, was lifted. An opening was made in the wall of the shed, adjoining the siding to the cattle pens, so that vans could be loaded or unloaded alongside the shed.

During World War II, the Vale of Glamorgan became a place of some military significance, with the opening of a number of airfields and the use of Barry Dock for the importation of war materials. While this led to a great increase in traffic on the Vale of Glamorgan line, the Cowbridge branch benefited little from wartime traffic flows. The major north-south passenger flow, for example, was that of civilian employees travelling from their homes in the valleys to the RAF bases at Llandow and St. Athan. They were conveyed in convoys of buses, which passed through Cowbridge en route. However, with restrictions in petrol consumption, some passenger traffic did return to the railway, but this proved short-lived, and vanished with the coming of peace.

As in World War I, the passenger service was curtailed as a wartime economy measure, with services down to seven trains each way per day, together with a late working on Saturdays. At the end of the war, the number of trains was increased to nine round trips each day.

The last goods train was handled at Beaupre Quarry siding in 1947, after which the 1 mile 3 chains of line south of Cowbridge was lifted, from a point about half-way between the two bridges, just south of Cowbridge Station.

The return of peace saw the railways in an even more run-down condition than had been the case in 1918. Under the Transport Act of 1947, the four grouped companies were dissolved, and were vested in the British Transport Commission, with the running of the railways entrusted to the Railway Executive, and from 1st January 1948, the Cowbridge branch became an outpost of British Railways. However, with the resumption of the growth of road traffic after the interlude provided by the war years, the future for the Cowbridge line looked bleak, particularly as its new owner did not display the same reluctance to branch closures as its predecessor. In addition, the Railway Executive was not encumbered with the lengthy closure procedures which followed the passing of the Transport Act of 1968, and in 1951, the withdrawal of the passenger service between Llantrisant and Cowbridge was announced. There was little opposition to this proposal, and the Borough Council voiced no objection to the proposed closure, which was fixed for Monday, 26th November 1951.

The last day of service, Saturday, 24th November 1951, saw many extra passengers on the branch, including local people anxious to take a last, or first, trip, and numerous railway enthusiasts. At 9.28 p.m., a large crowd cheered as the last 'train', railcar No. 18, pulled out of the station to a fusillade of detonators, which had been placed on the rails between the station and Cowbridge Junction. The railcar was driven by Mr Dick Killick, who had driven on the branch for many years, with Mr Jack Jones of Cowbridge as guard. Mr Jones had been a guard since 1919, and his father before him. On board were about 60 passengers including the Mayor of Cowbridge, Mrs F. C. Hinton, aldermen and councillors of the Borough Council, residents of Cowbridge and district, and many railway enthusiasts. The front of the car was adorned by a large wreath of laurel leaves, with black ribbon and the letters 'RIP'.

The end of the passenger service coincided with the retirement of Mr Billy Lewis, the station master at Ystradowen.

The end of the line at Cowbridge, on 5th May 1951.   *R. C. Riley*

Diesel railcar No. 18 is pictured at Cowbridge in March 1951. The railcar provided excellent visibility and was ideal for appreciating the rolling countryside through which the Cowbridge branch passed.

D. Chaplin

Mr Lewis had been injured whilst employed as a guard, and had been made station master at St. Mary Church Road Station, being transferred to Ystradowen on the closure of the Aberthaw line in 1932.

The signal box at Cowbridge Junction was closed after the withdrawal of the passenger service and the signalling was removed, with the exception of the 'down' distant which took the form of a TVR post fitted with a fixed GWR enamel arm, which managed to outlive the railway by about 10 years. The line from the junction to Cowbridge Passenger Station was lifted, and the former junction altered to form a simple run-round loop for goods trains, from where the engine propelled its train to the goods yard.

The passenger service between Llantrisant and Pontypridd did not long outlive its Cowbridge compatriot, and was withdrawn on 31st March 1952. Looking ahead twelve years, the section between Treforest Junction and Cwm Colliery siding was closed to all traffic on 28th September 1964, the line remaining open, between Cwm Colliery and Llantrisant, for coal traffic.

Apart from the loss of much of the general merchandise and livestock traffic, the general pattern of goods handled at Cowbridge remained much as it always had been, with agricultural produce and supplies and domestic coal predominating. The 1950s saw some new investment at the station, in the form of two new warehouses for the ferti-lizer traffic, which used Cowbridge as the central distribution point for much of the Vale of Glamorgan. One of these warehouses was situated alongside the former machine siding. The original Cowbridge Railway Station building was also converted into a warehouse, its front elevation being badly mutilated in the process. Despite this new business, goods workings were cut back to one trip, which ran down the branch early each morning. Traffic to Glamorgan Quarries was also lost by the railways, even though the entrance to the quarry continued to display a sign boasting of its own rail service, for some years after.

A number of enthusiasts' excursions worked over the line after the withdrawal of the passenger service. Perhaps the most notable was the Midlands Area Stephenson Locomotive Society tour, which ran to Cowbridge on 13th July 1957. This train traversed a number of goods only lines, between Cardiff and Llantrisant, and consisted of a two-coach set hauled by 2-6-2T, No. 5574, which was replaced for the run over the Cowbridge branch by the Llantrisant 0-4-2T, No. 1471. Despite being booked to terminate at Cowbridge Goods Station, the excursion came to a halt at the loop at the site of Cowbridge Junction, and it was only after much protestation that it continued, albeit cautiously, because of the restricted clearances, into the former passenger terminus.

An SLS tour at Cowbridge on 13th July 1957. The train had run into the old passenger station and had then reversed back into the yard for photographic purposes.

J. J. Davies

The last passenger train to work over the Cowbridge Railway was a joint tour by the West Glamorgan Railway Society and the Monmouthshire Railway Society. It is seen unloading its passengers at the site of Cowbridge Junction, on 27th June 1964.

L. Parker

The last enthusiasts' excursion to work over the Cowbridge branch was on Saturday, 27th June 1964. A joint tour, organized by the West Glamorgan Railway Society and the Monmouthshire Railway Society, ran as far as the loop at the erstwhile Cowbridge Junction, there being no doubt about its intended destination on this occasion. The six-coach train was hauled by 0-6-2T, No. 6614, which carried the headboard 'The Leek'.

The goods yard at Ystradowen closed on 9th May 1960, although the sidings remained in place for some years after.

A certain amount of track recovery and sundry demolition took place at Cowbridge, during the summer of 1964. The former carriage shed siding and the adjoining short siding were lifted, and the train shed, cattle pens, water tower and yard crane were removed. By this date, the remaining sidings at Cowbridge were heavily weed-infested, the whole yard having taken on a very derelict appearance.

During the building of the Cowbridge bypass in 1964, a construction depot was established on land to the north of the town hall. Although the Cowbridge branch benefited little from construction traffic, the building of the bypass ironically brought with it the last railway development in Cowbridge. A temporary line was laid from this depot to the line of the viaduct, which was to cross the River Thaw, the railway and the Cowbridge to Llantrisant road. This line was used to transport the concrete beams, which were fabricated at the construction depot, to the site of the viaduct where they were then lifted into place on the piers. This line was not, however, connected in any way to the Cowbridge branch. However, the erection of the pier nearest the railway required the diversion of the Cowbridge branch to the east by a yard, or two, between the yard and the run-round loop.

Having been listed for closure in the Beeching Report of 1963, Llantrisant Station was closed to passengers on 2nd November 1964, the Llantrisant to Pen-y-graig service having been withdrawn on 9th June 1958.

The goods service to Cowbridge was withdrawn on Monday, 1st February 1965, and the branch was closed to all traffic south of Llanharry Iron Ore Mine. The railway to Cowbridge had just managed its centenary, taken from the opening ceremony which had taken place on 30th January 1865, a fact which appears to have gone unrecorded in the locality. The track was dismantled later in 1965, the work taking place from Llanharry southwards.

The former passenger station at Cowbridge had become a British Legion Club on 25th June 1954, the first meeting having been held on 24th November 1954. Early in 1966, British Railways informed the club that the lease of the building would terminate on 30th November 1966, as the Railways Board had decided to dispose of the station site to Messrs Wimpey Limited, for residential development. Wimpey gave notice of their intention to go on site on 12th February 1967, but this was deferred until 28th

February 1967. After this, the British Legion Club retired to a local public house, until their new clubhouse was built on land at the rear of the town hall car-park. The old station site and the goods yard were cleared completely, and a new housing estate erected.

The section between Llantrisant and Llanharry Iron Ore Mine remained in use for another ten years, after the closure of the railway between Llanharry and Cowbridge. The 1½ miles of track to the mine was reduced to the status of a long siding, with the track terminating in the cutting, about 40 yards south of the Llanharry Road bridge. At Llantrisant, the loop on the branch line was removed, together with all traces of the former passenger station.

The end of steel making at East Moors removed the market for the iron ore, with the result that the Llanharry mine ceased production on Friday, 25th July 1975. It was this day that the last iron ore train ran over the line between Llanharry and Llantrisant. The crossover, which connected this line to the 'down' main line at Llantrisant, was taken out on 7th December 1975, and the agreement with the iron ore mine was terminated on 31st December 1975, the line then being closed to all traffic. However, closure was not officially made permanent, as there remained some hope that the iron ore mine might revive. On 29th May 1976, the branch was shortened by 14 chains at the Llanharry end, where it was to be crossed by a new road to Llanharry, which was to bypass the rather tortuous route over the railway bridge. The hopes for a reopening of the iron mine proved illusory, and the closure of the Llantrisant to Llanharry section was made permanent from 10th June 1977. After this date, the track was lifted, and the girders of the bridge over the River Ely at Llantrisant were taken out, with recovery being completed by the end of 1978.

An 0-6-0PT, No. 9780 prepares to couple with a cattle wagon and brake van in Cowbridge yard, on 15th August 1957, before returning to Llantrisant.

Ian L. Wright

Chapter Eight
Locomotives and Rolling Stock

It was clear from the outset that the Cowbridge Railway Company would not have sufficient resources to work its own traffic and, therefore, some kind of working arrangement with the TVR would be required. Although the Cowbridge Railway Act of 1862 contained powers enabling the TVR to work the railway, it was not until 16th September 1864 that the actual mode of operation was determined by the TVR. It was then only on a provisional basis, for a period of twelve months from the opening date, after which it was hoped that both parties would be in possession of the necessary information, with which to consider a more permanent arrangement. This temporary agreement did not constitute the working of the line in the manner usually understood, i.e. with the TVR incurring all working, management, and maintenance expenses in return for a percentage of the gross receipts. Instead, the TVR simply supplied the Cowbridge Company with an engine and rolling stock, together with the services of the train crew, at cost price. In the event, the hoped-for permanent arrangement did not emerge, and the hiring of stock from the TVR continued until the break between the two companies, in 1870.

In spite of the delay in deciding the form of the provisional working arrangements, the TVR had, nevertheless, provided the Cowbridge Company with details of its requirements for locomotive facilities at Cowbridge, the engine shed there being completed in October 1864. It was a two road affair, some 60 ft. in length, probably of stone with a slated gabled roof. Certainly, a section of stone wall about 10 ft. high survived, on the line of the east wall of the old shed, until the very end of the railway's existence. Access to the shed was by means of a 40 ft. turntable, situated on the main approach to the goods sidings. A water tank, fed by a well which had been sunk for the purpose, stood alongside the shed.

The trial run of a TVR engine over the Cowbridge Railway, on 16th January 1865, was reported to have been undertaken by 'one of the largest engines' of the company. With the start of the passenger service in September 1865, only one engine at a time appears to have worked the railway, handling both passenger and goods traffic. Although it is not known which type of engine was used, the above points suggest that 0-6-0 tender engines, possibly of the 'Standard Goods' type introduced from 1859, may have been used. Even these would not have found the line's gradients much to their liking, as shown by the comment made at the Cowbridge shareholders' meeting on 26th February 1869, that the TVR's engines were not powerful enough to work the traffic over the gradients.

With the Cowbridge Company's unilateral declaration of independence, in February 1870, the TVR found it necessary to make new arrangements for working its own traffic between Pontypridd and Llantrisant. On 23rd March 1870, the TVR Directors decided to build a new engine shed at Maesaraul Junction, but at the last minute, the location was changed to Common Branch Junction, which proved to be more convenient for coal traffic from the Common branch, and later from the Ely and Treferig valleys. The passenger service was faced, however, with a run of about two miles for empty stock to and from Llantrisant Station. The new shed was a two road structure, probably of wooden construction in view of its subsequent rapid deterioration.

In spite of the Cowbridge Company's instruction that it should cease to work its railway from 4th April 1870, the TVR appears to have continued to supply an engine for some time after this deadline. For at their meeting on 8th April 1870, the TVR Directors resolved that 'this Company's engine now working the Cowbridge traffic must be withdrawn from 16th inst.'.

In the period of independent working, a variety of odd engines was hired or purchased by the Cowbridge Company from Boulton of Ashton-under-Lyne. This firm specialized in the rebuilding and supply of second-hand engines, to such concerns as the Cowbridge Railway. Quite how the company came into contact with Boulton is not clear, but in February 1869, Dr Nichol-Carne had stated that the contractors, Messrs Griffiths & Thomas, had undertaken to find an engine powerful enough to work the line. As the first engine hired from Boulton subsequently went to Messrs Griffiths & Thomas at Alexandra Dock in Newport, the link with Boulton may well have been provided by these contractors.

Although, at Cowbridge, only one train crew was employed, two engines were usually shedded there. The first to arrive, in 1870, was *Cavendish*, a 2-4-0 tank engine, and an 0-6-0 saddle tank which subsequently acquired the name *Cyclops*. *Cavendish* had started life as a Stephenson 2-4-0 tender engine with 5 ft. coupled wheels, and had been purchased by Boulton in 1870 and converted into a saddle tank. As converted, she worked the Cowbridge passenger service for two years, before going to Messrs Griffiths & Thomas at Newport for a further eight years. After this she returned home to Boulton, being broken up around 1880.

The other engine hired from Boulton, in 1870, was an 0-6-0 saddle tank, with 3 ft. 6 in. wheels, built around 1869, and which had previously been hired to the Newport Pagnell Railway. *Cyclops*, as she was eventually named, stayed at Cowbridge for only a short time, before being hired in succession to the Severn & Wye Railway and Alexandra Docks, Newport. Finally, she was sold to Messrs Cammell Laird & Co., Cyclops Works, Penistone.

The Manager of the Cowbridge Railway, George Howell, does not appear to have been entirely satisfied with the performance of these machines, as in his report of 13th February 1871 he stated that the engines had not worked so satisfactorily as he would have wished.

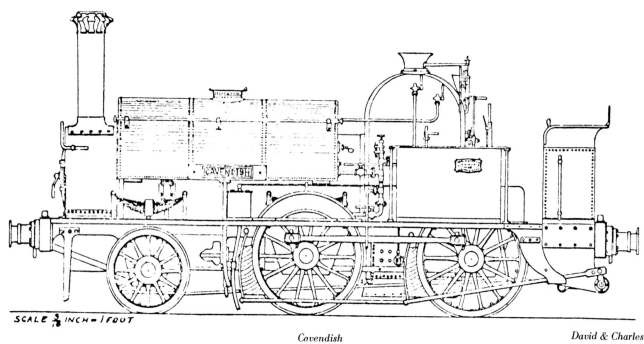

SCALE $\frac{3}{16}$ INCH = 1 FOOT

Cavendish   *David & Charles*

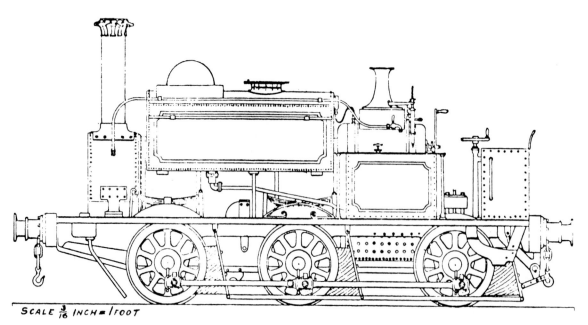

SCALE $\frac{3}{16}$ INCH = 1 FOOT

Cyclops   *David & Charles*

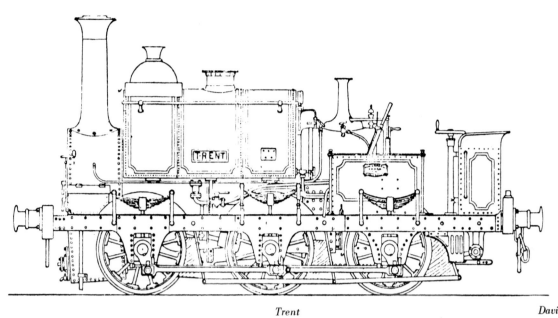

Trent   *David & Charles*

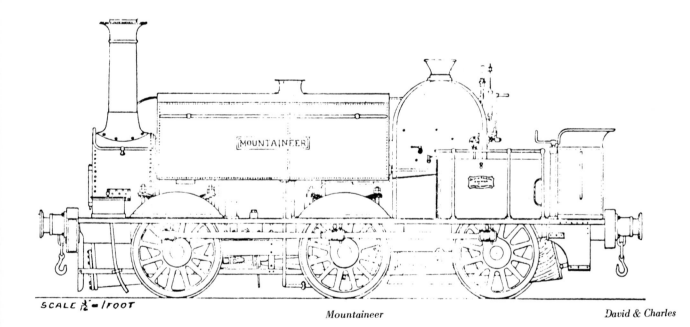

SCALE ⅛"=1 FOOT

Mountaineer   *David & Charles*

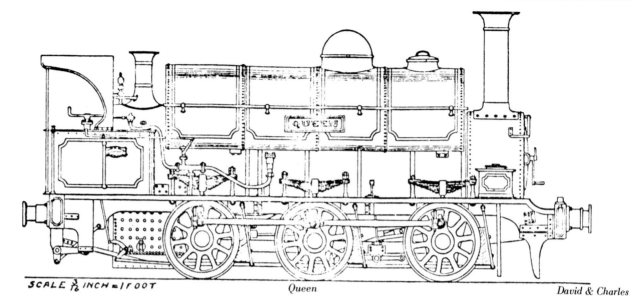

SCALE 3/16 INCH = 1 FOOT
Queen
David & Charles

In 1871, a replacement for *Cyclops* arrived at Cowbridge in the shape of *Trent*, an 0-6-0 saddle tank with outside frames. She had started life as an 0-6-0 tender engine, with 5 ft. 6 in. driving wheels, built by Sharp Roberts & Co., around 1840. In May 1871, Boulton rebuilt her as a saddle tank with 4 ft. wheels, and it was in this form that she was sold to the Cowbridge Railway for £800. However, she did not stay long at Cowbridge, as she was soon repurchased by Boulton, being resold to Chell Ironstone Mines for £850 in August 1873.

On the departure of *Cavendish*, in 1872, the next engine hired from Boulton was an 0-6-0 saddle tank named *Mountaineer*, which Boulton had acquired in 1886. Originally a tender engine, she spent a short period with the Hirwaun Coal Co., before being converted to a saddle tank with 4 ft. 6 in. wheels. Thus altered, she was hired to the Rhymney Railway in November 1871, where she remained until August 1872. Following this, she went to the Cowbridge Railway, where she stayed until the end of independent working.

The final engine to be hired from Boulton was another 0-6-0 saddle tank, one of five ex-LNWR tender engines which he had acquired. Boulton had replaced her 4 ft. 6 in. wheels with a set of 3 ft. 6 in. wheels, and converted her to a saddle tank. In this form, she arrived at Cowbridge in 1873, staying until 1875 when she went to the Severn & Wye Railway.

In addition to these engines, others were hired at various times from the TVR and, after 1872, from the GWR to cover failures and other interludes.

Little is known about the rolling stock hired by the Cowbridge Company during this period, apart from the fact that stock was hired from the Lancaster Wagon Co.

Following its rapprochement with the Cowbridge Railway in 1875, the TVR lost little time in offering to supply the returning prodigal with the services of an engine and rolling stock, albeit at cost price, until it took over the actual working of the railway. On 17th August 1875, the chairman of the Cowbridge Company was instructed by his fellow Directors to take the necessary steps to enable this to take place.

With the restoration of through working of passenger trains between Pontypridd and Cowbridge in 1876, the TVR passenger engines were transferred from Common Branch Junction to Cowbridge. However, Common Branch Junction remained in use for goods engines.

It is not known which types of engines the TVR employed on the passenger services, but it is possible that some of the early TVR 2-4-0 tender engines went to Cowbridge prior to their withdrawal, as E. L. Ahrons states that 'on the appearance of the No. 33 class (the TVR's last 2-4-0 tender engines, built in 1875 and 1878) a few of their diminutive predecessors migrated to some of the branch lines.' Four engines would have comprised these 'diminutive predecessors' in 1876, Nos. 1 and 2 of 1859, both withdrawn in 1880, and Nos. 22 and 24 of 1863 and 1864 respectively, both withdrawn at the end of 1886. Passenger trains were composed of up to five carriages of elderly four-wheeled stock, with only two carriages on certain mixed trains.

Goods trains appear to have been worked by the early 'Standard' type 0-6-0 tender engines, of which 44 were built between 1859 and 1872 with 4 ft. 6 in. driving wheels. Engines of this type probably continued to work the branch goods trains until the arrival, around 1890, of the first 0-6-2 tank engines.

In July 1875, the TVR Locomotive Engineer was authorized to convert an 0-6-0 tender engine of 1861 into an 0-4-4 tank engine, for use on the Ferndale passenger service. Three more 0-6-0s were similarly dealt with between 1878 and 1883. With the advent of more powerful tank engines from 1884, these 0-4-4T engines were relegated mainly to the Cowbridge branch, where most were recorded by Ahrons in 1887. The Class J 0-4-4T finally became redundant, with numbers of mixed traffic 0-6-2 tank engines appearing in the 1890s. Nos. 4 and 5 (which, by then, were transferred to surplus stock and renumbered 260 and 261), were withdrawn in 1893, but No. 59 (277 from December 1905) and No. 66 (278 from 1899) lingered on into the twentieth century, being withdrawn in 1906 and 1902 respectively.

TVR Class J, 0-4-4T, No. 59 in the later black livery, with red, yellow and white lining.

Locomotive Publishing Co.

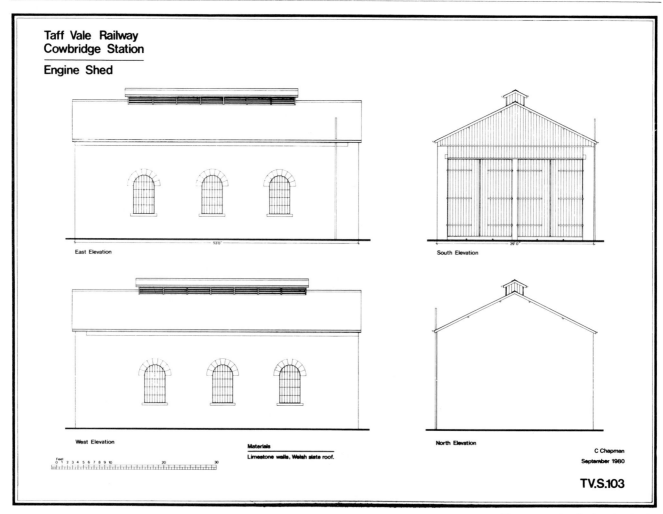

**Taff Vale Railway
Cowbridge Station**

Engine Shed

East Elevation

53'0"

South Elevation

29'0"

West Elevation

Materials
Limestone walls, Welsh slate roof.

North Elevation

Feet
0 1 2 3 4 5 6 7 8 9 10   20   30

C Chapman
September 1980

TV.S.103

The new engine shed at Cowbridge

The alterations to the station layout at Cowbridge in 1886 considerably improved facilities for the locomotive department. The old shed, with its difficult access, was replaced by a new shed, 60 ft. long and of stone construction, situated to the east of the running line. A standard TVR locomotive coal shed of timber construction with a gabled slate roof was provided, which covered a single coal wagon, the engine being coaled alongside the shed. A standard water tank was also erected, but this remained on the site of the old depot, being close to the well. The loss of the turntable at Cowbridge was soon followed by the removal of the one at Llantrisant, with the rebuilding of that station in 1890. Also in 1890, water purifying apparatus was installed at both Cowbridge and Common Branch Junction sheds.

In March 1891, the Traffic Committee of the TVR was informed that the engine shed at Common Branch Junction was in need of rebuilding at an estimated cost of £870. However, a decision on this question was deferred at this meeting, and also on subsequent occasions, with the result that the necessary finance was not made available. The

failure to rebuild Common Branch Junction Shed was followed by the loss of its allocation, although the shed remained open for servicing until 1915, being demolished during World War I.

In 1884, the TVR had introduced the first of a class of three 4-4-0 passenger tank engines, Nos. 67—69. All three were built at the TVR's Cardiff West Yard Works, between July 1884 and September 1885. They were similar in general appearance to the 4-4-0T engines then being used on the North London Railway. They had 5 ft. 3 in. coupled wheels, and were smartly turned out with polished chimney caps and dome covers. For a while they worked the main Cardiff to Merthyr and Treherbert branch services, but with the arrival of more power passenger tank engines in 1888 and 1891, they were displaced to secondary duties, being used extensively on the Cowbridge service, one usually being shedded at Cowbridge.

The first of a type which was to become typical, not just of the TVR, but also of the railways of South Wales, was the 0-6-2 tank engine, introduced by the TVR Locomotive Engineer, Mr Tom Hurry Riches, in 1885. In all, 41 engines

T V R 4-4-0T, No. 67 which was built in 1884, is seen in its original condition without a fully-enclosed cab. It was in this condition that these engines first appeared on the Cowbridge Railway.

Locomotive Publishing Co.

T V R Class O, 0-6-2T engines were employed on passenger and goods workings on the Cowbridge branch from their inception until just after the Grouping. Their 4 ft. 6 in. wheel and high adhesive weight, made them ideal engines for the switchback route between Cowbridge and Pontypridd.

G. H. W. Clifford (Courtesy of C. C. Green)

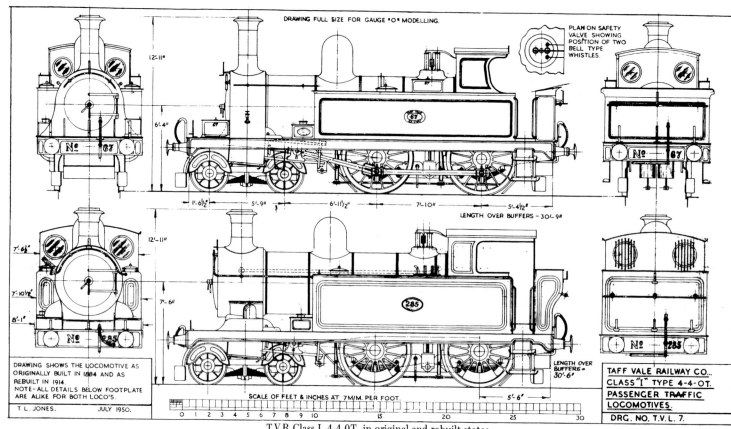

DRAWING FULL SIZE FOR GAUGE "O" MODELLING.

PLAN ON SAFETY
VALVE SHOWING
POSITION OF TWO
BELL TYPE
WHISTLES.

LENGTH OVER BUFFERS - 30'- 9"

DRAWING SHOWS THE LOCOMOTIVE AS
ORIGINALLY BUILT IN 1884 AND AS
REBUILT IN 1914.
NOTE - ALL DETAILS BELOW FOOTPLATE
ARE ALIKE FOR BOTH LOCO'S.

T. L. JONES.   JULY 1950.

SCALE OF FEET & INCHES AT 7M/M. PER FOOT.

LENGTH OVER
BUFFERS =
30'- 6'

TAFF VALE RAILWAY CO.
CLASS "I" TYPE 4-4-0 T.
PASSENGER TRAFFIC
LOCOMOTIVES.

DRG. NO. T.V.L. 7.

TVR Class I, 4-4-0T, in original and rebuilt states

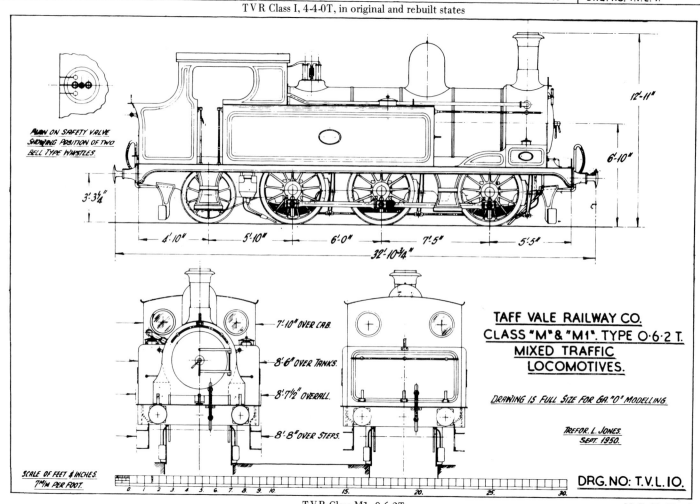

PLAN ON SAFETY VALVE
SHOWING POSITION OF TWO
BELL TYPE WHISTLES.

TAFF VALE RAILWAY CO.
CLASS "M" & "M1". TYPE O·6·2 T.
MIXED TRAFFIC
LOCOMOTIVES.

DRAWING IS FULL SIZE FOR GA. "O" MODELLING.

TREFOR. L. JONES.
SEPT. 1950.

DRG. NO: T.V.L. 10.

7'·10" OVER CAB.

8'·6" OVER TANKS.

8'·7½" OVERALL.

8'·8" OVER STEPS.

SCALE OF FEET & INCHES.
7M/M PER FOOT.

TVR Class M1, 0-6-2T

M. E. M. Lloyd

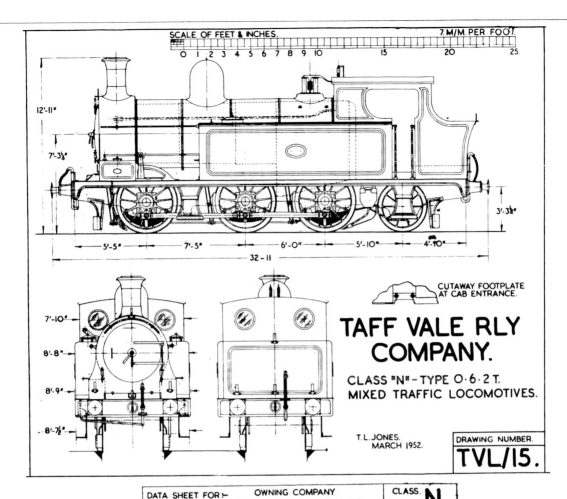

12'-11"

7'-3½"

3'-3½"

5'-5" 7'-5" 6'-0" 5'-10" 4'-10"

32-11

7'-10"

8'-8"

8'-9"

8'-7½"

CUTAWAY FOOTPLATE
AT CAB ENTRANCE.

TAFF VALE RLY COMPANY.

CLASS "N" - TYPE O·6·2 T.
MIXED TRAFFIC LOCOMOTIVES.

T. L. JONES.
MARCH 1952.

DRAWING NUMBER.
TVL/15.

DATA SHEET FOR :-	OWNING COMPANY TAFF VALE RAILWAY CO.	CLASS. **N.**

TYPE. O·6·2 T. MIXED TRAFFIC LOCOMOTIVES.

DIMENSIONAL DATA.

CYLINDERS - 2 INSIDE. 17½" DIA. X 26" STROKE.
   STEAM PORTS - 15" X 1¼"
   EXHAUST " 15" X 2¼"
   INCLINATION OF MOTION 1. IN 9·667

BOILER - FRONT RING - 4'-3¾" O. DIA.
   MIDDLE " 4'-5" O. DIA.┐TOTAL LENGTH. 10'-6"
   BACK " 4'-6¼" O. DIA.┘

FIREBOX - 5'-4½" LONG X 3'-5" WIDE AT FOUNDATION RING
   HEIGHT TO BOTTOM OF PLATE- 5'-10½" FRONT : 4'-2" BACK:
   OUTSIDE DIMS. 6'-0" LONG X 4'-0½" WIDE.

HEATING SURFACE - FIREBOX 92·7 SQ. FT.
   TUBES 1055·8 SQ. FT: 212 AT 1¾" O. DIA. X 11'-1¼" LONG.
   TOTAL 1148·5 SQ. FT.

GRATE AREA - 19·14 SQ. FT.

BOILER PRESSURE - 150 LBS. PER SQ. INCH.

WHEELS: COUPLED 4'-6½" DIA. RADIAL 3'-8¼" DIA.

TRACTIVE EFFORT AT 85% B.P. - 18620 LBS.

WATER CAPACITY OF TANKS - 1400 GALS.

COAL " BUNKER- 40 CWTS.

WEIGHT IN WORKING ORDER -
   LEADING AXLE - 14 T. 8 C.
   DRIVING " 14 T. 9 C.┐
   TRAILING " 14 T. 8 C.├TOTAL. 54 T .4 C.
   RADIAL " 10 T. 19 C.┘

TVR NO.	BUILDERS	WORKS NO.	DATE	GWR NO.	
106	KITSON	3391	1891	485	
107	"	3392	"	486	
182	"	3383	"	494	
183	"	3384	"	495	STOCK- EFFECTIVE - 10 LOCOS.
184	"	3385	"	496	SURPLUS - NIL.
185	"	3386	"	498	
186	"	3387	"	499	
187	"	3388	"	500	
188	"	3389	"	501	
189	"	3390	"	502	

T V R Class N, 0-6-2T

M. E. M. Lloyd

of Class M were built between 1885 and 1892. Their date of arrival at Cowbridge is unclear, but the first record is in August 1894, when No. 54 failed at Church Village with a Cowbridge passenger train. By the mid-1890s, this class and later 0-6-2Ts dominated both the passenger and goods workings on the branch.

The opening of the Aberthaw line, in October 1892, did not significantly increase the demands placed on the locomotive department at Cowbridge. However, in 1894, an engine drop pit was provided at Aberthaw, enabling minor running repairs and maintenance to be carried out at the new terminus.

The Class M 0-6-2Ts were joined by engines of Classes O and O1, from about 1894. The O class comprised six engines with 4ft. 6½in. driving wheels, built at Cardiff West Yard in 1894 and 1895, whilst the O1 class consisted of 14 broadly similar engines, eight of which had been built by Kitsons and the remainder by the TVR in 1894 and 1897 respectively. Generally used on coal traffic, but later relegated to ordinary goods and yard shunting duties throughout the TVR system, they were, nevertheless, mixed traffic engines. They shared this role with the M class (later M1) in the working of the Cowbridge branch until the Grouping. An exception, as far as the passenger service was concerned, was the period of full steam motor car/auto-train operations between 1908 and 1920.

Other classes of 0-6-2T also made appearances at Cowbridge, including engines of the N class of which ten engines had been built by Kitson & Co. in 1891, and the O2 class, of which nine engines were built by Neilson Reid & Co. in 1899.

Although the passenger engines were based at Cowbridge after 1876, for many years at least one goods turn was covered by a Common Branch Junction engine, and later by engines from Coke Ovens. However, by the turn of the century, all such workings were covered by Cowbridge engines. An interesting feature of passenger train working at that time, was the use of a Coke Ovens engine on the first round trip of the day from Pontypridd, the first 'up' train from Cowbridge having continued beyond Pontypridd to Aberdare, returning to Cowbridge later in the morning.

Until the introduction of the steam motor cars in 1905, Cowbridge was always at the tail end as far as the allocation of passenger rolling stock was concerned, with its coaches being 'cascaded' to use the modern term, from more important services. Four wheel stock of the 1870s and 1880s was used well into the present century, trains being formed of five vehicles with a brake van at each end, and on market days and Saturdays they were strengthened to seven vehicles. The quality of the stock used gave rise to a number of complaints, and in March 1895 Cowbridge Borough Council petitioned against the use of draughty open 3rd class carriages, with compartment partitions that did not extend above the backs of the seats. The TVR was unmoved by this plea, and refused a later one for cushions to ease the rigours of 3rd class travel. Six wheel stock constructed in the 1890s began to appear on the branch in the early years of this century.

In 1902, the TVR gave serious thought to a proposal for the experimental working of the Cowbridge to Aberthaw section by means of electric traction. The motivating force behind this idea was partly commercial, with Ammon Beasley, the General Manager, keen to exploit the passenger generating potential of a small self-powered railcar, particularly in view of the threatened competition from street tramways elsewhere on the system. It was also partly technical, with Tom Hurry Riches, the Locomotive Engineer, anxious to explore the frontiers of the new technology. The Aberthaw line was chosen for the trial because of its very limited traffic which could be worked in a self-contained fashion from Cowbridge. In the words of Ammon Beasley, 'it would allow an experiment on the smallest possible scale, to be undertaken with the minimum of pecuniary risk'.

Initially, thoughts were directed to all forms of electric traction, but those involving third rail or overhead sources of power supply were soon rejected, because of their high costs of installation. A specification was drawn up for a battery electric railcar, with seating for six 1st class, ten 2nd class and forty 3rd class passengers, together with a large brake/guards compartment, through which access to the seating accommodation would be gained, under the supervision of the guard, thereby enabling the station staff to be dispensed with. The car was to be capable of a maximum speed of 30m.p.h. Only three round trips per day between Cowbridge and Aberthaw were envisaged, with the car spending long periods at Cowbridge recharging its batteries from either the mains supply, or a purpose-built generating station, whichever was the cheaper.

Tenders were invited for the supply of a battery electric railcar in October 1902, but those received were not found to be satisfactory. In spite of extra time being allowed for revised tenders, Mr Riches remained unhappy on both technical and cost grounds. On 26th April 1903, he appeared before the Locomotive Committee with a photograph and description of the steam railcar which had been designed by Dugald Drummond, for the London & South Western Railway the previous year. At the time, it was loaned to the GWR for trials between Stonehouse and Chalford. With the doubts about the prospects of an electric railcar, and with the tangible evidence of the practicality of the steam version before the committee, Mr Riches was instructed to prepare a further report on the subject of an experimental steam railcar. After presenting a favourable report to the Locomotive Committee on 9th June 1903, he was instructed to 'proceed with all dispatch', with the construction of such a car.

Mr Riches certainly proceeded with 'all dispatch', for in October 1903, steam motor car No. 1 emerged from Cardiff West Yard Works, the last 'locomotive' to be built by the TVR. Trials were undertaken throughout the TVR system before the car entered service on the Penarth branch on 21st December 1903. At the same time, the TVR tried to persuade the Board of Trade to permit the use of a two man crew on the motor cars, with the driver remaining at the locomotive end at all times, whilst the conductor directed operations from the opposite end, when that was leading. However, the Board of Trade insisted that a three man crew be employed, with the driver being at the leading end at all times.

The success of Car No. 1 led to the ordering of five more cars in 1904. Locomotive units came from Avonside, and the Bristol Wagon & Carriage Company supplied the coach units. These cars, numbered 2 to 7, had an enlarged luggage compartment making them suitable for handling the entire traffic on certain branch lines. However, they did not work on the Cowbridge service until after the arrival of a further batch of cars, the locomotive units being built by Kerr Stuart and Bristol Wagon & Carriage Company supplying coach units, in spring 1905.

No. 183 was of the TVR N class of 0-6-2T locomotives which were built by Kitson & Company in 1891. Although less common on the Cowbridge branch than engines of the M1 and O1 classes, the N class was a useful mixed traffic engine well suited to the needs of the branch.
Locomotive Publishing Co.

Coach No. 165 was built for the TVR by the Metropolitan Carriage & Wagon Company in 1874. These vehicles were often criticized as being draughty, uncomfortable and lacking in heating.
Real Photographs

With the introduction of the motor car service between Pontypridd and Aberthaw on 1st May 1905, two cars were based at Cowbridge, sharing the passenger service with a locomotive and coaches set, composed of four and six wheeled carriages.

Motor cars Nos. 1—7 provided both 1st and 3rd class accommodation, whereas Nos. 8 to 13 were 3rd class only, so in theory only cars Nos. 1—7 could be used on the Cowbridge service. However, in practice, the coach units were exchanged quite freely between cars, so that Kerr Stuart units were often seen at Cowbridge.

A number of minor alterations were carried out at Cowbridge, to cater for the cars. In 1906 the locomotive drop pit, situated in front of the engine shed, was lengthened to make it suitable for the cars, and later that year the water tank was raised in height. This enabled the removal of the small water tank at the Llantrisant end of the station platform, which had been necessary because of the height of the passenger station in relation to the old station. It was replaced by two water columns, one on the site of the old tank and the other opposite the station building, in a convenient position for watering the motor cars.

In 1906, a further three motor cars, together with two spare engine units, were introduced, having been built by Manning Wardle, specializing in engine units, and Brush,

who built coach units. These were somewhat larger than the earlier cars, and differed in appearance in a number of respects, but were basically similar in concept. Their increased accommodation made these cars especially suitable for the Cowbridge service.

Two motor car trailers had been built by the Bristol Wagon & Carriage Company in 1905, but as they were not auto-fitted, it was necessary for the car to run-round its trailer at termini. In addition, four six wheel 3rd class carriages were converted into motor car trailers, with auto-gear, in 1909 and 1910. Although the Board of Trade had refused to sanction the use of trailer cars at the short motor car platforms in February 1905, the TVR authorized their use between Llantrisant and Aberthaw. Similarly, the later use of two coach auto-trains at the platforms was in contradiction to the Board of Trade's ruling on the matter.

The motor cars were not entirely suited to the Pontypridd to Aberthaw section, with its long run and severe gradients, and were also prone to failure, usually from hot axle boxes. They also proved rather too successful for their own good, in terms of generating additional traffic, leading to over-crowding at certain times.

Towards the end of 1907, the three Class I 4-4-0T engines which had been built in 1884 and 1885 and had been transferred to the duplicate list and renumbered 285—287 in

TVR Class I, 4-4-0T, No. 285 (formerly No. 67) as auto-fitted in 1907. The unsightly profusion of wires and pulleys is evidence of the Taff Vale Railway's system of auto-working. The engine was fitted with a double-handle regulator, to which two wires were attached. These wires passed through the cab roof and over two pulleys, before passing along the roof of the auto-car. At the driving end of the car they passed round another set of pulleys and into the driving compartment. Here they passed round a large wheel. The driver, by a slight turn of this wheel, was able to open or close the regulator in the engine, as required. He also had control of the vacuum brake and the engine whistle and was in connection with the fireman by means of an electric bell. In spite of its primitive appearance, the system is reported to have worked with reasonable efficiency for nearly twenty years.

Locomotive Publishing Co.

1905, were fitted with the TVR's decidedly Heath Robinson version of auto-gear, with its rather unsightly profusion of elevated wires and pulleys. At the same time, four auto-coaches, two 1st/3rd composites and two all 3rds, were supplied by the Bristol Wagon & Carriage Company, being formed into two auto-trains, thus:

Driving trailer composite+engine+driving trailer 3rd

The third engine was kept as spare. One auto-train worked the Penarth branch, whilst the other went to Cowbridge, replacing one of the motor cars. However, it was not until May 1908 that the branch timetable was modified, to reflect this development, with the withdrawal of the engine and coaches workings. These had persisted since the introduction of the motor cars, in 1905. The auto-set then handled the busy morning shopping and school trips.

The surviving motor car at Cowbridge was usually one of the larger units of 1906. Indeed, a TVR notice, dated 27th November 1909, specifying the use of this type of car on the Cowbridge service, also stated that the small cars were then only considered suitable for use on the Ferndale, Nelson and Ynysybwl branches. However, in spite of this direction, the smaller units continued to make appearances at Cowbridge.

The success of the first auto-trains led to the fitting of auto-gear to six of the M1 class 0-6-2 tank engines, with Nos. 5, 14, 164, 179, 180 and 181 being modified between 1910 and 1912. In December 1910, two bogie 3rds dating from 1903, Nos. 331 and 332, were converted into trailer brakes, for use with the auto-trains. In 1912, two more

auto-trailers, a 1st/3rd composite and an all 3rd, were completed by the Gloucester Railway Carriage & Wagon Company, to a design similar to the original auto-cars. With the introduction of these trailers, the auto-sets were reformed into four sets, as follows:

> 1907 Driving trailer composite + 1910 trailer 3rd
> 1907 Driving trailer 3rd + 1910 trailer composite
> 1907 Driving trailer composite + 1912 trailer 3rd
> 1907 Driving trailer 3rd + 1912 trailer composite

As the reformed sets were equipped with corridor connections, the engine worked at one end of a pair of cars, instead of between the cars, as it had previously. With four sets available, the surviving motor car was taken off the Cowbridge service in 1912, two auto-sets then being allocated to Cowbridge, bringing the total number of engines shedded there up to six. The auto-set allocation, in September 1914 was:

1907 Driving trailer 3rd No. 353 + 1912 trailer composite No. 80
1907 Driving trailer composite No. 79 + 1910 trailer 3rd No. 331

In 1913, the Class I 4-4-0T engines were all transferred to the Penarth branch, their place at Cowbridge being taken by auto-fitted Class M1 0-6-2Ts. These were more suited to the Cowbridge branch, with its severe gradients, and being mixed traffic engines, were equally at home on both goods and passenger work.

As a wartime economy measure, from October 1917, only one auto-set was based at Cowbridge, sharing the passenger service with a Coke Ovens set. Class C 4-4-2Ts, auto-fitted from 1914, and shedded at Coke Ovens, made their first

Locomotive Incidents on Llantrisant to Aberthaw Section 1894-1917

Date	Engine	Class	Type	Incident	Location
6.8.1894	54	M	0-6-2T	Failed	Church Village en route to Cowbridge
26.4.1895	37	01	0-6-2T	Derailed	Cowbridge
15.1.1896	152	M	0-6-2T	Derailed	Llantrisant
10.2.1896	51	M	0-6-2T	Failed	Cowbridge
27.10.1898	15	M	0-6-2T	Derailed	Llantrisant
27.8.1898	186	N	0-6-2T	Failed	Cowbridge
29.3.1901	70	01	0-6-2T	Derailed	Aberthaw Lime Works Siding
22.4.1901	164	M	0-6-2T	Derailed	Cowbridge
9.9.1901	21	0	0-6-2T	Failed	Cowbridge
29.6.1904	83	02	0-6-2T	Derailed	Cowbridge
17.2.1905	26	0	0-6-2T	Derailed	Cowbridge
6.4.1907	34	0	0-6-2T	Collision	With level crossing gate at Aberthaw
13.11.1907	287	I*	4-4-0T	Failed	Llantrisant
26.11.1907	285	I*	4-4-0T	Failed	St. Athan Road
4.5.1908	286	I*	4-4-0T	Failed	Cowbridge
20.3.1909	41	01	0-6-2T	Failed	Llantrisant
17.6.1909	21	0	0-6-2T	Derailed	Llantrisant
19.7.1909	287	I*	4-4-0T	Failed	Cowbridge
26.7.1909	287	I*	4-4-0T	Failed	Cowbridge
25.4.1910	152	M1	0-6-2T	Failed	Aberthaw
12.9.1910	41	01	0-6-2T	Derailed	Llanharry Iron Ore Mine Siding
13.8.1911	286	I*	4-4-0T	Collision	With carriages, Cowbridge Yard
9.8.1911	21	0	0-6-2T	Failed	Cowbridge
3.3.1913	287	I*	4-4-0T	Collision	Llantrisant
11.9.1913	14	M1*	0-6-2T	Failed	Llantrisant
29.9.1914	179	M1*	0-6-2T	Failed	Between Pontypridd and Cowbridge
14.2.1916	26	0	0-6-2T	Derailed	Llantrisant
15.6.1916	29	01	0-6-2T	Derailed	Llantrisant
19.12.1916	179	M1*	0-6-2T	Failed	Llantrisant
27.1.1917	164	M1*	0-6-2T	Failed	Llantrisant
28.2.1917	179	M1*	0-6-2T	Derailed	Llanharry Iron Ore Mine Siding
5.5.1917	173	C*	4-4-2T	Failed	Between Pontypridd and Cowbridge

*= Auto-fitted
Source: TVR Locomotive Committee Minutes 1894-1917

appearances on the Cowbridge branch during this period. The Class I engines, rebuilt in 1914/15 with larger boilers, drum smokeboxes and new cabs, were also shedded at Coke Ovens, and made appearances on the Cowbridge service alongside the more usual Class M1 0-6-2Ts. The practice of basing two auto-sets at Cowbridge was reinstated in May 1920.

With the end of auto-working on the Pontypridd to Aberthaw service, just prior to the Grouping, non auto-fitted M1 engines, together with engines from Classes O and O1, handled both passenger and goods working, although a Class U or U1 0-6-2T was also recorded at Cowbridge at this time. The converted auto-trailers of 1910 continued to be used on the branch, but with their auto-gear out of use. Apart from these two coaches, earlier four and six wheel stock predominated.

The allocation at Cowbridge Shed at the time of the Grouping in 1922 comprised four engines from the M1 and O1 classes. However, the need for a shed at Cowbridge, so close to the G W R shed at Llantrisant, was soon questioned, and in July 1923 the allocation at Cowbridge was reduced to only two engines. This resulted in some of the locomotive men being transferred to Llantrisant.

A number of interesting developments took place at Cowbridge during the last few months of the shed's life. In July 1923, an ex-TVR Class C 4-4-2T engine, No. 1304 (late TVR No. 175) was transferred to Cowbridge. Although this particular engine stayed only a few weeks, a sister engine, No. 1306 (later TVR No. 174) arrived at Cowbridge from Cardiff West Yard Shed, on 30th November 1923, staying until the closure of the shed at Cowbridge. In February 1924, the first and only GWR engine to be shedded at Cowbridge arrived, in the form of 0-6-0 pannier tank No. 1886 of the '1854' class. This replaced the last ex-TVR 0-6-2T at the shed, No. 453 (TVR No. 34) of Class O. Nos. 1306 and 1886 were transferred to Llantrisant Shed on the closure of Cowbridge Shed on 8th March 1924.

GREAT WESTERN RAILWAY

Cowbridge Engine Shed : Allocation 1923/4

4 weeks ending	Class	TVR No.	GWR No.	Transferred from	Transferred to
28/1/23	0	26		West Yard 7/11/22	
	01	29			
	01	41			
	01	70			
25/2/23	0	26			
	01	29			
	01	41			Cathays
	01	70			
25/3/23	0	26			
	01	29			Cathays
	01	41		Cathays	
	01	70			
22/4/23	0	26	448		
	01	41			
	01	70			
20/5/23	0	26	448		
	01	41			
	01	70			Cathays
	01	29		Cathays	
17/6/23	0	26	448		
	01	41			
	01	29			
15/7/23	0	26	448		
	01	41			Cathays
	01	29			Cathays
	C	175	1304		
12/8/23	0	26	448		
	C	175	1304		Coke Ovens
9/9/23	0	26	448		
7/10/23	0	26	448		Cathays
	0	34	453	19/9/23	
4/11/23	0	34	453		
2/12/23	C	174	1306	West Yard 30/11/23	
	0	34	453		
29/12/23	C	174	1306		
	0	34	453		
27/1/24	C	174	1306		
	0	34	453		
24/2/24	C	174	1306		
	0	34	453		Cathays
		—	1886	Llantrisant	
23/3/24	C	174	1306		Llantrisant 8/3/24*
		—	1886		Llantrisant 8/3/24*

*Cowbridge Engine Shed closed 8th March 1924

A TVR auto-train at Cardiff Riverside Station on 11th August 1913. The auto-set consists of a 1907 driving trailer, probably No. 78, and a 1912 trailer, probably No. 355. A set of similar appearance, No. 353 and No. 80, was, at this time, allocated to Cowbridge.

Ken Nunn Collection (Courtesy of the LCGB)

TVR Class M1, 0-6-2T, No. 14 stands at Penarth Town Station in 1920. No. 14 was one of six members of this class which were converted for auto-working between 1910 and 1912, and was shedded at Cowbridge at various times between 1913 and 1920.

H. T. Hobbs

All the ex-TVR engines transferred from Cowbridge in 1923 and 1924, with the exception of No. 1306, went to ex-TVR sheds. No. 1306 was the only ex-TVR engine to be shedded at Llantrisant, where she remained, probably working the Cowbridge passenger service, until March 1925, when she was sent to Swindon, and remained there until her withdrawal on 8th July 1925.

The GWR replaced the ex-TVR engines with its own types, usually of the outside framed '1076' or 'Buffalo' class 0-6-0PT, built as saddle tanks at Swindon between 1870 and 1881. By the time they arrived at Cowbridge, all had been converted to pannier tanks, and being exceptionally free running, they were equally at home on passenger as well as goods workings. Engines of the '1854' class of inside framed engines, originally built as saddle tanks between 1890 and 1895, and later the '1813' class of 0-6-0PT inside framed engines, built as saddle tanks between 1882 and 1884, also appeared.

TVR carriages were replaced by GWR four wheeled stock, dating from the 1890s, forming four coach sets with a brake 3rd at each end.

In 1929, the Llantrisant to Cowbridge section was upgraded to 'blue' status in the GWR's system of route classification. However, as the Aberthaw branch was restricted to 'yellow' types, heavier engines could not be used on trains running beyond Cowbridge. The upgrading of the branch brought with it the use of engines of the '2721' 0-6-0PT class, built at saddle tanks between 1897 and 1901, and the, then, new 57XX class 0-6-0PT, the first to arrive at Llantrisant, on 14th April 1929, being No. 5740. Over the years, earlier 0-6-0PTs gradually gave way to the 57XX class engines, and the modernized '8750' version after 1934.

In the autumn of 1930, 'Metro' class 2-4-0T, No. 3584, built in 1899 and auto-fitted during October 1929, and '1076' class 0-6-0PT, No. 1247, built in 1877 and auto-fitted during May 1930, arrived at Llantrisant in advance of the reintroduction of auto-working on the Cowbridge branch. Although No. 1247 stayed for only two years, No. 3584 remained at Llantrisant, until her withdrawal in 1945.

The first auto-fitted engine of the '517' class 0-4-2T to arrive at Llantrisant, was No. 1485 of 1885, in 1932. From then on, 0-4-2T engines provided the mainstay of Cowbridge branch motive power, until the outbreak of World War II, together with 'Metro' class 2-4-0Ts, and occasionally the, then, new 64XX class 0-6-0PTs.

With the introduction of auto-working on the Pen-y-graig and Llantrisant to Pontypridd services in the early 1930s, more auto-fitted engines were shedded at Llantrisant, resulting in a greater variety appearing at Cowbridge. Apart from No. 1485, '517' class No. 1161 was also at Llantrisant from 1933 to 1937. 'Metro' tanks included No. 617 from 1932 to 1934, No. 3586 from 1936 to 1938 and 1943 to 1949 and No. 3594 which, after a brief visit to Llantrisant in 1935, was at the shed from 1937 until 1947.

In 1936, new Collett 0-4-2T No. 4871 arrived at Llantrisant, and regularly worked the Cowbridge service. Renumbered 1471 in 1946, she remained at Llantrisant until the withdrawal of the Pen-y-graig service in 1958.

For many years the Cowbridge auto-train was formed of two clerestory coaches, one each side of the engine, which the GWR had converted from corridor 3rds in 1905. However, outside school terms, the more typical auto-trailers, in this case converted from the original GWR steam railcars, with vertical matchboarded sides, appeared on the branch.

After the demise of the old clerestory stock, the ex-railcars continued to be used, albeit deputizing for the diesel railcar in later years.

In May 1942, perhaps the most significant motive power development on the branch since the arrival of the steam motor cars in 1905 occurred, when diesel railcar No. 22 arrived at Llantrisant for use on the Cowbridge branch. Railcar No. 22 was one of the 15 cars which the GWR had ordered for branch line work in 1938, and had been built at Swindon in 1940 with AEC engines. On her departure in July 1945, the steam auto-train, with either 4871 or one of the 'Metro' tanks in charge, again reigned supreme. However, this proved to be short lived, as in December 1945, diesel railcar No. 31, sister to No. 22, arrived at Llantrisant. No. 31 stayed only until December 1946, being replaced by car No. 18, which had arrived at Llantrisant the previous month.

Railcar No. 18 was the sole example of an experimental type built, in 1937, by the Gloucester Railway Carriage & Wagon Company with AEC engines. She came to Llantrisant from Reading Shed, where she had worked the Lambourn branch since her introduction. She continued to work the Cowbridge service until the withdrawal of the passenger service in 1951.

During the periods when No. 18 was unavailable for any reason, the service reverted to steam operation, usually with 'Metro' tank No. 3586, sister engines Nos. 3584 and 3594 having been withdrawn in November 1945 and May 1947 respectively. At this stage, No. 1471 made only occasional appearances at Cowbridge, being the regular engine on the Pen-y-graig passenger service. After the demise of No. 3586, in November 1949, auto-fitted 0-6-0PT No. 6425 acted as substitute for the diesel railcar.

With the end of the passenger service in November 1951, the branch goods continued to be handled by engines of the 57XX class, a typical engine being No. 9780. Iron ore trains, from Llantrisant to Cardiff, were handled by 57XX 0-6-0PTs or 42XX 2-8-0Ts, depending on the load available. Although the 56XX class 0-6-2Ts were authorized to work over the Cowbridge branch, the only known instance was in June 1964, when No. 6614 worked through to Cowbridge on an enthusiasts' special.

Diesel engines of the English Electric Type 3 Co-Co class first appeared on the Llantrisant to Cardiff ore trains in August 1964, and for a number of years also worked over the branch to Llanharry Iron Ore Mine. However, they were later displaced on this duty by the Llantrisant yard pilot engine, a Class 08 diesel shunter, which was diagrammed to work the Llanharry branch ore traffic with travelling shunters, in between other shunting duties.

The last Llanharry iron ore working, on 25th July 1975, was performed by Llantrisant pilot Class 08 shunter, No. 08196, driven by Mr Harold Adams of Llantrisant. At 1.30p.m., No. 08196 and a brake van left Llantrisant for the short trip over the truncated remains of the Cowbridge Railway. At Llanharry the brake van was left on the running line, whilst the engine set back into the mine sidings to collect the last loaded ore wagons, which were then positioned against the brake van in readiness for the return trip. At 2.00p.m., the last iron ore train left Llanharry, the engine propelling its train in the time-honoured fashion, for Llantrisant, where arrival was at 2.15p.m. The whole operation had taken only 45 minutes, and with it passed over 110 years of railway service.

TVR Class I, 4-4-0T, No. 286, as rebuilt in June 1914. A larger boiler was fitted, together with a drum smokebox, large diameter chimney and redesigned cab. The original side tanks were also enlarged. The resulting metamorphosis produced something which must be regarded as the reverse of the usual 'Ugly Duckling' story! Engines of this type appeared on the Cowbridge branch between 1917 and 1920, when one auto-set was provided by Pontypridd Coke Ovens Engine Shed.

Locomotive Publishing Co.

Engines of the 4-4-2T C class, appeared on the Cowbridge branch after 1917. Their graceful lines were marred somewhat by the Taff Vale Railway's auto-gear, often referred to as 'aerials'.

Locomotive Publishing Co.

Engines of the 517 class appeared on the Cowbridge branch in early days of auto-working, in the GWR period. No. 1433 of this class is pictured here.

Lens of Sutton

No. 9780 was, for many years, the regular engine on the Cowbridge branch goods. It was first shedded at Llantrisant in December 1939, and is seen here, in August 1957, in Cowbridge yard.

D. Chaplin

BR (WR) Appendix to Working Timetable 1951

Level crossing, Llantrisant to Cowbridge Branch
When shunting over the level crossing leading to the tin works on the Cowbridge Branch, guards must precede the wagons and see that no person is allowed to use the crossing whilst wagons are being moved over it.

Propelling of freight trains, Cowbridge Branch
When a train is being propelled from the direction of Llanharry towards Llantrisant, it must be brought to a stand on the Llanharry side of the level crossing near Llantrisant Station. After it has done so, one of the guards must proceed to the level crossing and remain there, to warn any persons desiring to cross until the train has passed clear.

Llanharry Lime Works siding
The connection for this siding faces in the direction of Llantrisant, and is worked by a key on the Electric Train Staff.
There are no means of running around wagons at Llanharry Station and vehicles for this siding from the direction of Llantrisant must be propelled in front of freight trains from Llantrisant to Llanharry. The number of vehicles so propelled must not exceed 10. When vehicles are propelled the train must be worked by two guards, one of whom must ride in the leading wagon, which must be one suitable for him to do so and he must keep a good look out and be prepared to warn any man working on the line and give any necessary hand signals to the driver.

Glamorgan Hematite Iron Ore Co. siding, Llanharry
The points are worked by a ground frame attached to the ETS.
All traffic for the sidings must be worked from Llantrisant on trains in the usual way. Traffic from the sidings for the direction of Llantrisant must be propelled from Llanharry to Llantrisant with the brake van leading and the guard must ride in the brakevan and keep a sharp lookout and be prepared to exhibit any necessary signal to the driver to warn men working on the line. The maximum number of vehicles to be propelled is 25 wagons plus a brake van. The brake van must be of the 20T type and the guard before starting from Llanharry should apply sufficient brakes on the wagons next to the brake van — according to the weight of the train — to control its passage over the line to Llantrisant, the brake van always to be kept in reserve for any emergency which may arise.
During shunting operations at the sidings the engine must always be at the lower end of the vehicles. The guard will be responsible for seeing that wagons left in the sidings are properly secured and the safety points are padlocked in the open position after work is finished. Engines of all types are prohibited from passing over the weighbridge.

Ystradowen Goods Siding Wheel Stop
A wheel stop is fixed on the above siding near the warehouse door to prevent wagons being pushed against the door. Guards will be responsible for removing this wheel stop before commencing and replacing it after completing any shunting into or out of the warehouse.

127